Samuel M. Smucker

A History of the modern Jews

Or, Annals of the Hebrew Race

Samuel M. Smucker

A History of the modern Jews
Or, Annals of the Hebrew Race

ISBN/EAN: 9783337131111

Printed in Europe, USA, Canada, Australia, Japan

Cover: Foto ©ninafisch / pixelio.de

More available books at **www.hansebooks.com**

A HISTORY

OF

THE MODERN JEWS;

OR,

ANNALS OF THE HEBREW RACE.

FROM THE DESTRUCTION OF JERUSALEM TO
THE PRESENT TIME.

BY

SAMUEL M. SMUCKER, LL.D.,

AUTHOR OF "LIFE, SPEECHES, AND MEMORIALS OF DANIEL WEBSTER," "HISTORY OF ALL RELIGIONS," ETC.

PHILADELPHIA:
PUBLISHED BY DUANE RULISON,
33 SOUTH THIRD STREET.
1860.

Entered according to Act of Congress, in the year 1860, by

DUANE RULISON,

In the Clerk's Office of the District Court of the United States, in and for the Eastern District of Pennsylvania.

PREFACE.

The following work treats of a subject which is not only important in itself, but possesses attractions for the general reader. The Jewish people are more remarkable in some respects than any other which have ever existed. They are the oldest of the races, so far as a direct line of historical descent is concerned, which now flourish upon the globe; for they may trace their genealogy back by an unbroken line to Abraham. Neither the cultivated Greeks nor the martial Romans, in ancient times, were as venerable as the cotemporary Jews; yet these have passed away, while the Hebrews remain. The various races which are now most potent and prominent in the world,—the British, the French, the German,—have all risen into existence, as distinct communities, many ages after the Israelites had attained a world-wide celebrity.

Nor has the past career of the Jews been insignificant in respect to historical importance. They have endured countless persecutions, under which any other people would have vanished, and become extinct. They still survive, and flourish at this late day, invested with such vitality and energy, that they are a clearly felt and recognized power in the commercial, social, and intellectual life of every community among whom they sojourn. The consideration of the history and vicissitudes of such a people, cannot fail to interest every reader who desires to take a comprehensive survey of the various aspects assumed by humanity, during its past diversified and chequered career.

PREFACE.

The present work is intended to convey to the reader some conception of the extraordinary career of the Hebrew race; nevertheless, within limits so moderate as those comprised in this volume, it was impossible to furnish more than an epitome of the most prominent events connected with their annals. The contents of these pages originally appeared in one of the leading journals of this city; and having been regarded by many readers as worthy of being presented in this more prominent form, such alterations have been introduced as seemed necessary for that purpose.

The history of the Jews may be appropriately divided into three great epochs. The first, comprising the interval which occurred between the calling of Abraham and the completion of the Old Testament Scriptures, may be fitly termed their Ancient history. The second, which includes the Era which intervened between the close of the Canon of the Old Testament and the birth of Christ, may be characterized as their Post-Biblical history. The third, which narrates the events which occurred from the birth of Christ until the present time, may be designated as their *Modern* history; and hence it is that the latter title is applied to this volume, although some of its details refer to events which were comparatively remote.

S. M. S.

Philadelphia, May, 1860.

CONTENTS.

CHAPTER I.
The Roman Army under Titus attacks Jerusalem—Incidents of the Siege—Splendor of the Temple—the Capture of the City—Its Destruction—Dispersion of the Jews—Their situation in Babylonia—In Egypt—Hadrian—Barcochab—Roman Colony planted in Jerusalem.. 9

CHAPTER II.
Condition of the Jews in the East in the Second Century—The Patriarch of Tiberias—The nature of his Jurisdiction—Character of Simon—His son Jehuda—The Preparation of the Mischna—Its contents—The Prince of the Captivity—The Babylonian Talmud—Jews in China—Jews in Arabia................... 19

CHAPTER III.
History of Zenobia, Queen of Palmyra—Her Character and Fate—The Jewish Community in Constantinople—The Emperor Constantine the Great—Miracles of rival Jews and Christians—The Jews in the West—The Arian Controversy in the Church—Julian the Apostate—He favors the Jews—His attempt to rebuild Jerusalem—His Death.. 30

CHAPTER IV.
Events of the Fourth Century—Valentinian and Valens protect the Jews—Hostility between the Jews and Christians—Bigotry of Ambrose of Milan—Events which occurred at Alexandria in Egypt—In the Island of Minorca—Bishop Severus—Orestes—History of Hypatia—Events in Crete................... 42

CHAPTER V.
Division of the Roman Empire—The Jews in the Western Empire—Their Sufferings at Naples—at Genoa—Feud between them and the Samaritans—Julian the Apostate—The condition of the Jews under the Emperor Justinian—Gregory I. Bishop of Rome—His Patronage of the Jews.......................... 53

CHAPTER VI.

Downfall of the Western Empire—Christian slaves held by Jews—Decrees of Councils forbidding it—Supremacy of the Bishop of Rome—Condition of the Jews in the Eastern Empire—Events in Syria—Persia—Mesopotamia—The Prince of the Captivity—Rabbi Chinina—Chosroes conquers Palestine and protects the Hebrew people... 64

CHAPTER VII.

The Jews in Arabia in the sixth Century—Their History and Character—Arian Missionaries—Origin of Mahomet—Incidents of his Life—He subdues the Arabian Jews—Jews in Spain—Councils of Toledo—Their persecution o. the resident Jews.. 76

CHAPTER VIII.

Jews in France in the Sixth Century—Scenes in Clermont—Events at Tours—Relations between the Jews and the Moslem sovereigns—Factions among the Jews—The origin of the Karaites—Their doctrines—The Kingdom of Khozan—Jews in the Byzantine Empire—Leo the Isaurian......................... 88

CHAPTER IX.

Accession of Charlemagne—His treatment of his Jewish subjects—His Embassy to Haroun al Raschid—Zedekiah—Condition of the Jews in France—Bishop Agobard—Reign of Charles the Bald—Moorish dynasty in Spain—The Caliphs of Bagdad—Jewish Seminary at Toledo.. 102

CHAPTER X.

Rabbi Moses Maimonides—His early history—His learning—His productions—He removes to Egypt—His great celebrity—Eben Ezra—His youth—Attainments—His travels and writings—Rabbi Judah Hallevi—His poetical genius—His writings and singular death.. 114

CHAPTER XI.

Condition of the Jews in the twelfth century—Hezekiah, last Prince of the Captivity—Western Europe—The Feudal system—Growing prejudices against the Jews—Reign of Philip Augustus of France—The Crusades—Bishop of Beziers—Scenes at Rouen—David Kimchi—His learning, writings, and celebrity.. 126

CHAPTER XII.

The Jews of Paris—Their condition in the thirteenth century—Louis IX.—Persecution of the Jews by his subjects—Their treatment by his successors—Their temporary prosperity—The Jews in Castile—Their misfortunes—Their condition in Arragon—Public disputes between Jews and Christians... 138

CHAPTER XIII.

Ferdinand and Isabella—Their respective characters—Their purpose to expel the Jews from Spain—Agency of the Inquisition—Proceedings in Toledo—

CONTENTS.

Cruel alternative offered to the Jews—Banishment of the Jews—Events in Portugal—Jews in Germany—Switzerland—The Black Death—Scenes in Brussels.. 151

CHAPTER XIV.

Superiority of the Spanish Jews—The Sephardim—Council of Elvira—Rabbi Solomon Levi of Burgos—His history and writings—Alphonzo—Preaching of Vincent Ferran—Cardinal Juanda Torquemada—Conversos, or converted Jews—Their zeal for Romanism—The Spanish Inquisition........................... 164

CHAPTER XV.

Proceedings of the "New Inquisition"—Jews in Morocco, Fez, and Northern Africa—The Jews in Turkey—Condition of the Jews in Italy—Nicholas III. —Eugenius IV.—Monte-di-Pieta—Condition of the Jews in Leghorn—In Florence—In Naples—In Sicily—In Sienna.. 180

CHAPTER XVI.

Rabbi Isaac Abrabanel—His talents, learning and writings—Jews at Genoa—Hebrew Printing-presses in Italy—Hebrew Literature in the Middle Ages—Solomon Usque—Leo of Modena—Jews in the Papal states—Karaite Jews in Russia... 193

CHAPTER XVII.

Jews in Holland—Their origin and history—Their pursuits and character—Manasseh—His Mission to England—Benedict Spinosa—His history and doctrines—Jews in Bohemia—Jews in England—Their vicissitudes and persecutions in that kingdom.. 207

CHAPTER XVIII.

Richard of the Lion Heart—King John—Henry III.—His treatment of the Jews—Their various calamities—Imposture of Sabbathai Sevi—His extraordinary adventures—Sabbathaism—Jacob Frank—His history and teachings —The sect established by him... 220

CHAPTER XIX.

The sect of the Chasidim—Jews in Poland—Israel Bescht—His history—Sect founded by him—Moses Mendelsohn—Incidents of his life—His writings—Their influence—His literary merits... 233

CHAPTER XX.

Jews in the Austrian Empire—Persecution—Individual wealth—The Oppenheimers—Empress Maria Theresa—Joseph II.—Jews in Prussia—Elector Frederick William—Edicts of Frederick the Great—Revolution of 1789 in France—The National Assembly—Treatment of the Jews by Napoleon—The Great Sanhedrim... 246

CHAPTER XXI.

Statement of Jewish doctrines by the Sanhedrim—Condition of the Jews in

France—Adulation of Napoleon by the Jews—The Jews in the Nertherlands—The new Batavian Republic—Schimmelpenninck—Administration of Louis Napoleon—The House of Orange. 259

CHAPTER XXII.

Jews in Norway and Sweden—Abrogation of ancient laws against them—The poet Wergerland—Jews in Russia—Ukase of Alexandria I.—Policy of Nicholas I.—The Karaites—Jews in Poland—Their peculiar character—The Congress of Vienna—Jewish Radicals—Bruno Baur—Ludwig Borne. 269

CHAPTER XXIII.

Jews in Baden—In the free cities of Germany—Persecutions—More recent History of the Jews in Italy—Enactments of Leo XII.—Papal tyranny—Pius IX.—Charles Albert—Duke of Modena—Recent history of the Jews in Turkey—Sultan Mahmoud—The Karaites in Turkey 283

CHAPTER XXIV.

Recent Persecution of the Jews in Damascus—The Schereef Pacha—History of Tomaso—Oriental Justice—Sympathy with the sufferers in Europe—Meeting of the London Jews—Rabbi Solomon Herschell—Sir Moses Montefiore—Jews in Palestine—Present condition of the Jews in Jerusalem 295

CHAPTER XXV.

Recent state of the Jews in Persia—Scenes at Ispahan—The Ten Lost Tribes—The river Gozan—Jews in India—Jews in Malabar—Interesting Document—Jews in Morocco and Tunis—Singular Persecutions—Example of Heroic Fortitude 309

CHAPTER XXVI.

The Hebrew Race in the United States—Early Settlement of Jews at Newpo.—Their Address to General Washington—His Reply—Peculiarities of American Jews—Eminent Living Israelites—Jewish Theory respecting the Death of Christ—Contrast between the condition of the Jews in the United States and in the Dominions of the Pope. 322

APPENDIX.

An Exposition of the Hebrew Law and Commonwealth 333

A HISTORY OF THE MODERN JEWS.

CHAPTER I.

THE ROMAN ARMY UNDER TITUS ATTACKS JERUSALEM—INCIDENTS OF THE SIEGE—SPLENDOR OF THE TEMPLE—THE CAPTURE OF THE CITY—ITS DESTRUCTION—DISPERSION OF THE JEWS—THEIR SITUATION IN BABYLONIA — IN EGYPT — HADRIAN — BAR-COCHAB — ROMAN COLONY PLANTED IN JERUSALEM.

It was in the month of April, in the year A. D. 70, that Titus, the son of the Roman Emperor Vespasian, took his position, and encamped with a numerous army around the walls of Jerusalem. The defenders of the city within it were divided into three garrisons; but between these the fiercest hostility unfortunately prevailed, so that the energy and fortitude which should have been directed against the common enemy were expended among themselves. Their combined forces amounted to about twenty-five thousand men. The troops of Titus were composed of Roman soldiers and some few from Syria, from Egypt, and other portions of the empire, making an immense armament, amounting probably to a hundred thousand men. The fortifications of the city were so extensive and apparently impregnable, that it seemed impossible that any human power could assail them with success. They consisted of three walls, one within the other, which surrounded the city on all sides, except at such places where the nature of the ground being steep with impassable ravines, there was but a single rampart. These walls were surmounted by lofty fortresses built of solid masonry, ninety on the first wall, fourteen on the second, and sixty on the third. The strongest of these bulwarks was that called Antonia. Its elevation was seventy feet, and it stood on a rock ninety feet high. But higher still than all the other edifices of the city, rose the glittering walls and towers of the Temple, each side of which occupied the eighth of a mile in length. It was a magnificent and stately structure, combining together the appearance of a fortress and a palace. Some of the single stones employed in the foundations were seventy feet square. It had its outer courts and inner courts. The gates were constructed of Corinthian brass, and exhibited the most elaborate workmanship. The most beautiful of these was eighty-seven feet high, and was sheeted with gold and silver. Over another gate a golden vine was suspended, to which bunches were attached as large as a man. The roof of this gorgeous edifice was covered with spikes of the precious metals; its spacious courts were built of marble; all the utensils used within it were of gold and silver; splendor and beauty were combined together in every thing connected with it; and its walls and pinnacles were constructed with materials of such strength and solidity that they seemed to have been built for eternity. In five short months this temple and all the principal buildings of Jerusalem were transformed into smoking and crumbling ruins.

Titus immediately addressed himself to the task of sacking the city, and brought his legions and his various implements and engines of war to bear upon the massive fortifications. On some occasions the Jews fought with great heroism, and routed the besiegers. At other times Roman valor and discipline prevailed over the tumultuous fury of their foes. Had the leaders of the different factions within the city—Simon, John, and Eleazar—been united, the conquest of the Jews might have proved a much more difficult task; but these refused, in general, to act in concert, and by their mutual hostilities assisted the Romans. The first important conquest was the taking of the tower of Antonia, which Titus ordered to be leveled with the ground. Next the Romans effected a breach in the wall which connected that fortress with the temple. Meanwhile famine and pestilence began to rage among the besieged, and they suffered excesses of horror at the very details of which the heart sickens. On the 10th of August the temple was set on fire, and soon its snow-white walls and gilded pinnacles were enveloped in flames. After burning many hours the once gorgeous pile became a total ruin; and the Roman army at length entered within that portion of the city in which the edifice had stood. The upper city still remained in possession of the Jews. A conference was proposed between the belligerents, and Titus agreed to permit the Jewish soldiers and people to withdraw unharmed if they surrendered without further delay. The proposition was rejected; and on the 20th of August the Roman troops and battering rams commenced to operate on the upper walls. At length, on the 19th of September, A. D. 70, the final triumph of Roman arms and valor obtained possession of the whole city, and one of the most memorable sieges on record terminated. During its progress the almost incredible number of a million of human beings are supposed to have perished by famine, disease, the sword of the enemy, and the factions and massacres which raged within the walls. Not less than a hundred thousand captives were made among the unfortunate beings who fell into the power of the victors. Many of these were sent to grace the triumph of Titus at the Roman capital, while the vast majority were reserved to labor in the mines of Egypt, or were distributed among the provinces of the empire to be exhibited as gladiators in public shows, or to serve their owners in every menial capacity, till death, more merciful than the conquerors, released them from their miseries.

Thus terminated the long and memorable career of the Jewish state and kingdom. From that hour till the present, during the lapse of nearly eighteen centuries, have the Jewish people continued as exiles on the earth, and strangers to the land of their forefathers. Vespasian, the Roman Emperor, issued an edict putting up all the lands of Judea for sale; and by these means a foreign population became to some extent introduced into those abodes which for so many generations had been occupied by the children of Abraham. A garrison of a thousand Roman soldiers were posted within the ruins to prevent the reconstruction of the walls and the temple; and careful search was made by the imperial order for all those who were in any way related to the royal house of David, that they might be slain, to prevent the possibility of a revival of their claims to the sovereignty of Judea. A portion of the country had in a great measure escaped the horrors of the war; all those cities and districts which lay beyond the Jordan, and had submitted without resistance to the Roman arms, such as Samaria, and the dominions of King Agrippa, were not devastated by fire and sword. There the Jewish people continued to live in comparative security, though their unity as a nation, and their importance and influence as a separate community, had passed away.

During the reigns of Vespasian and Domitian, the Jews in Palestine were subjected to great persecution and cruelty. Previous to the siege, the members of the Sanhedrim had made their escape from the city, and fled to Jammia. Its chief was the celebrated Gamaliel, the Nasi, or Prince. At that town, situated in the tribe of Dan, and near the Mediterranian shore, a rabbinical school of great reputation gradually arose under the influence of the learned men who had located there, and it became a source of authority to the scattered and exiled Jews everywhere, as to the interpretation of their sacred books, and the settling of religious controversies which from time to time arose among them. Other learned rabbis dwelt in different cities, and became the heads of schools, such as R. Joshua in Petrun, R. Eliezer in Lydda, and R. Akaba, in Baar-brak.

After the destruction of their temple, another form of religious service gradually grew up among the Jews, which continues to exist till the present time. This was the worship of the synagogues, where in smaller numbers the Jews convened for public worship, and for instruction in the law. The high priest had perished in the temple at Jerusalem, and no successor was ever appointed; so that gradually the rabbis or teachers began to assume the functions and authority of the Levite's and priests, both at Jerusalem and throughout the dispersed nation. Those increased their authority by the exposition of the *Masora*, or traditions which, as the rabbis asserted, Moses had received on Mount Sinai, and had been handed down by unbroken descent from age to age through the members of the Sanhedrim. Thus it was that gradually the ancient priesthood and the ancient worship among the Jews became to some extent transformed; the officiating priests were no longer the same; the place of worship was no longer at Jerusalem; and the interpretations of the law, which were accredited as authoritative, were to some extent modified.

The most numerous colonies of Jews which were formed after the fall of the capital were in Babylonia, in Egypt, and in Cyrene. In these several places the industry and thrift of the exiles soon put them in possession of wealth, and gave them some degree of importance. After the lapse of a few years, the exactions to which they were subjected induced them to raise the standard of revolt, and to resist and assail the dominant power. The Roman sceptre was then held by Trajan, and the origin of a portion of the rebellion was singular. The birthday of that monarch occurred on the 9th of August, and the anniversary of that event was celebrated by tumultuous joy throughout the empire; while the united Jews commemorated on the same day, with mourning and tears, the sack of their once glorious Temple. The contrast was offensive to both parties, and led to hostilities. So also on another occasion, on the very day that the imperial family were mourning the loss of a daughter, the unfortunate Jews were commemorating their joyful Feast of Lamps. The incensed Empress exclaimed to Trajan, that "before he undertook any other conquest, he should sweep that insolent people from the earth"—a suggestion which he obeyed, to some extent, by a fierce persecution.

Soon afterward, while Trajan was absent with the Roman legions in Parthia, the Jews in Egypt and Cyrene embraced the opportunity to resist their oppressors, and in the outburst of their fury they inflicted on them the most cruel excesses. At Cyprus the Jews massacred two hundred and forty thousand of their enemies. In Alexandria, the whole Jewish community soon suffered a terrible retribution, for they were eventually slain to a man. Martius Turbo, a Roman general, suppressed the revolt in Cyrene with great cruelty, and as many as six hundred thousand Jews are said to have perished by the sword. The succeeding Emperor Adrian promulgated a decree subsequently, that no Jew should ever set foot on the Island of Cyprus, on pain of death; and that even those who were cast upon the shore by shipwreck should suffer the same penalty.

Immediately after the suppression of the Jewish insurrections in Egypt and Cyprus, a smilar rebellion burst forth in Mesopotamia. When the exiled Jews first settled there, they were protected and tolerated under the Parthian rulers who then bore sway over that country. After the conquest of the Parthian dominions by Trajan, the Jews became subject to Roman authority, and soon began to feel the bitterness of Roman persecution. They were compelled, among other exactions, to pay a capitation tax for the support of heathen temples. But their insurrection was suppressed, after various vicissitudes of the contest, by Lucius Quietus, an able Roman general, who was commissioned to expel the Jews from the whole country of Mesopotamia. Before he had entirely completed this task, he was appointed Governor of Judea; and his energies were soon called into active operation in suppressing new disturbances in that ill-fated country.

In A.D. 117 Hadrian succeeded Trajan in the Roman purple. His feelings toward the Jews were hostile, and he issued decrees against them of the severest description. He forbade them to observe anywhere throughout the empire the great distinctive usages of their nation and religion—to circumcise their children, to peruse the Law, or to observe the Sabbath. He announced his determination to establish a Roman colony within the precincts of Jerusalem, and to erect a fane in honor of Jupiter on the very ruins of the Holy Temple. No greater insult could possibly have been offered by the utmost refinement or excess of malice, than this, to the religious feelings of the Israelitish people; and, while they were smarting under the infliction in sullen and gloomy despair, an impostor suddenly appeared, who declared himself to be the promised Messiah, who had come, in the hour of the darkest and deepest degradation of the nation, to rescue it from ignominy, to throw off the yoke of the oppressor, and lay the broad and deep foundations of the future glory, supremacy, and felicity of Israel. His name was Bar-Cochab, the *Son of the Star;* and he was originally an Egyptian juggler, who, among his other tricks, had learned the art of keeping lighted tow in his mouth, and thus, apparently, of breathing flames. After he had obtained numerous followers, amounting in a few weeks to two hundred thousand, it was said that wonders attended him, among which was the fact that flames of fire issued from his mouth, by which he threatened to destroy the oppressors of the people of God.

The first effort of this remarkable impostor was to gain possession of Jerusalem. By celerity of movement he readily accomplished that purpose. He unfurled his banner amid the surrounding ruins, and soon a vast multitude of adherents gathered together, influenced by religious zeal and bigotry. He assumed the title and functions of king as well as of Messiah. When the Roman general, Julius Severus, reached the scene, he found Bar-Cochab in possession of fifty fortresses and nearly a thousand unwalled towns in Judea. Severus immediately commenced to reconquer the land, and at length, after many vicissitudes, the impostor and his adherents were driven to Bithec, the last city and fortress which they possessed. These were stormed, and Bar-Cochab slain. His remaining followers were either killed or sent into captivity, and thus this last and most formidable rebellion against the power of imperial Rome in Judea was effectually crushed.

The triumphant Hadrian now determined to execute his threats in reference to the establishment of a Roman colony in Jerusalem, in order more effectually to destroy all hope on the part of the Jews that their state and kingdom might ever again arise from their ashes. He planted a Roman colony in the irregular town which had arisen within the dilapidated walls; decreed the perpetual banishment of the Jews from the soil of Palestine; founded a new city on the former site of Jerusalem, which he termed Ælia Capitolina; and issued a decree prohibiting any Jew from entering the new city under pain of death, or to approach nearer to its confines than three miles, which would prevent them from even contemplating the former scene of the nation's glory from a distance.

CHAPTER II.

CONDITION OF THE JEWS IN THE EAST IN THE SECOND CENTURY—THE PATRIARCH OF TIBERIAS—THE NATURE OF HIS JURISDICTION—CHARACTER OF SIMON—HIS SON JEHUDA—THE PREPARATION OF THE MISCHNA—ITS CONTENTS—THE PRINCE OF THE CAPTIVITY—THE BABYLONIAN TALMUD—JEWS IN CHINA—JEWS IN ARABIA.

TOWARD the conclusion of the second century of the Christian era, the Jewish nation, though scattered throughout various portions of Europe, Asia and Africa, present themselves to view as arranged under two distinct ecclesiastical authorities. One of these was the Patriarch Simon, whose seat and residence were at Tiberias; the other was the "Prince of the Captivity," who lived at Babylon. Simon was the son and heir of Gamaliel. With him were associated Rabbis Nathan and Meir, as heads of the law. They gave instruction to candidates for the priesthood, and established schools at Tiberias which became celebrated throughout the world for their superior learning. The Jews who dwelt in the western provinces of the Roman empire acknowledged the authority of this school, and admitted the claim of Simon to be regarded as the Patriarch of the church, and the Nasi, or President of the Sanhedrim. His orders were obeyed, and his opinions and decisions in reference to

(19)

the teachings of the law were respected, among the Jews even as far as Spain and Africa. They also contributed to his support and that of his associates without reluctance. Wherever the Jews resided they usually erected a synagogue, proportioned in size and splendor to their numbers and ability. The Patriarch of Tiberias annually sent forth his Legates, who traveled through all those countries, possessing authority to determine disputes, to regulate the religious affairs of the Jews, and to collect the tribute of the Patriarch. On the return of the Legates they informed that dignitary of the condition of the synagogues, of the prospects of their brethren, and advised with him as to the interests of those who acknowledged his supremacy.

At this early period extreme bitterness already existed between the Jews and the Christians; and the latter, though themselves often a persecuted sect, made continual efforts to convert the former. Nor were these exertions always futile; for among the converts whom they succeeded in acquiring, history mentions at least one who was a person of distinction. This was Hegesippus, an ecclesiastical writer of the second century, who was the first author who, previous even to Eusebius, undertook to narrate the history of the early Christian Church; though his works have unfortunately perished. When the Christian martyrs died the Jews generally availed themselves of the opportunity to be present, and indicate their approval of the penalties which they suffered. Thus, when Polycarp expired at the stake, the Jews are represented as having jeered him in his agonies, and to have condemned him with an earnestness equal to that of his heathen persecutors.

At that period the structure of the synagogues subject to the Patriarch of Tiberias generally bore some faint resemblance to the form of the temple at Jerusalem, and the worship which was observed within them was simple. The chief man was he who took the most prominent part in the services, and was termed the angel or bishop. He covered his head with a veil, and ascending the tribune, repeated the prayers. He also scrutinized the reader while he read from the books of the law. The days of public service which were then observed were the Sabbath, or seventh day of the week, Mondays and Thursdays. In the majority of synagogues out of Palestine an officer was used, termed the interpreter, who, understanding both the Hebrew and the vernacular language of the country, translated the prayers and lessons to the congregation. Beside the bishop, there were three elders who assisted him as rulers of the synagogue. The chief penalty which they could inflict was termed the Anathema, or excommunication; and he who became its subject, was not only cut off from the Israel of God, but became an outcast from the whole Jewish community. This punishment was expressed by the most terrible language: the offender was pronounced accursed by the book of the law, by the ninety-three precepts, by the malediction of Joshua against Jericho, by that of Elisha against the children who followed and insulted him, and by every other sort of curse known to the religion and history of the nation;

and when at last the wretch died, the Jews stoned his coffin, and no mourners followed him to the grave.

Simon, the Patriarch of Tiberias, seems to have been an arrogant and ambitious man; and his overbearing temper led to several attempts to expel him from his supremacy. One of these was made by the two Rabbis who were next to him in dignity and authority, Nathan and Meir. They asserted that Simon could not answer every question which might be propounded to him respecting the law; and that therefore he ought to be degraded. Accordingly they conferred together, and devised various questions of extreme subtlety and difficulty wherewith to confound the Patriarch in a public meeting of the Sanhedrim. Fortunately for Simon, a friendly Rabbi overheard the conversation of the conspirators, informed him of their purpose, and repeated to him the questions which they had resolved to ask. He prepared himself with diligence; and when the two rebels assailed him with their knotty enigmas, the Patriarch not only answered them with ease, but also exposed their own ignorance, and put them to confusion.

The influence of the Patriarch of Tiberias was successfully maintained by Jehuda, the son of Simon, who succeeded him, and who was somtimes termed the Holy, in consequence of his superior piety. Though the law of the Emperor Hadrian forbidding the Jews to circumcise their children was still in force, he received the rite on the eighth day after his birth. It was during his supremacy that the celebrated Mischna, containing the authorized interpretation of the Mosaic law was prepared at Tiberias. It was an enormous undertaking, and the sources from which it was derived were the oral law, or explanations of the written law which Moses was supposed to have received from God on Sinai, and which he afterward repeated to Aaron and his sons; the opinions and maxims of the wise men and prophets of the Old Testament; the decisions of distinguished schools and rabbis; and the ancient usages and customs which had prevailed among the nation from time immemorial.

The first part of this celebrated work, which is esteemed and revered by the Jews to the present day, refers to agriculture and the laws relating to it. The second treats of festivals, and the observance of the Sabbath, and other holidays. The third, which is called Nashim, (of women,) expounds the ceremonies of marriage and divorce, and other matters referring to the intercourse of the sexes. The fourth discusses the laws which appertain to men as members of civilized communities, and the punishment to be inflicted for their violation. The fifth treats of holy things and offerings; and the sixth sets forth the mode by which things and persons become unclean, and the ceremonies which should be observed to purify them.

The Mischna soon acquired a supreme authority among the Jews everywhere, and even supplanted the law itself in many places. But in the progress of time, this work also became the subject of numerous interpretations and comments, which soon made its meaning as much the subject of uncertain interpretation as that of the law of Moses. Yet the Mischna retained its authority until it was to some extent superseded afterward by the more voluminous Talmuds of Jerusalem and Babylon.

During the reign of the Emperor Alexander Severus, whose temper was mild and amiable, the Jews throughout the empire enjoyed security and repose. Their credit was raised in consequence of the fact that Zenobia, the celebrated Queen of Palmyra, then flourished, and openly acknowledged her descent from Jewish ancestors. At the same time the proverbial industry and economy of the nation were obtaining for a large portion of them an unusual degree of opulence, which also tended to promote their security. Caracalla, the son and successor of Severus, though cruel to all the world beside, seemed to have entertained a strangely favorable feeling toward the Jews; and Heliogabalus, who subsequently disgraced the imperial throne, went so far as to adopt the custom of circumcision and abstinence from the use of the flesh of swine.

Cotemporary with this period of the supremacy of the Patriarch of Tiberias was the prosperity and influence of the other great source of authority among the Jews, already referred to, the "Prince of the Captivity," who held his Court at Babylon. After the destruction of Jerusalem and the dispersion of the people, that portion of them who fled to Mesopotamia and lived under the jurisdiction of the Parthian monarchs, always flourished, being exempt from exactions and persecutions. Their chief priest, who lived at Babylon, having assumed the rank and title of a spiritual potentate, claimed an absolute religious authority over all the Jews who dwelt in eastern countries, as did the Patriarch of Tiberias over those of the West. At first the Babylonian ruler acknowledged the superior ecclesiastical authority of the western potentate. But that submission was of short duration, and soon the Prince of the Captivity began to surround himself with a degree of dignity and splendor which far outshone those of his rival. He was inaugurated with great pomp, and conducted himself as Oriental sovereigns usually did, by secluding himself in his palace. He patronized also the schools of Hebrew learning at Babylon, and soon the celebrity of those institutions equaled even that of the schools of Tiberias. The Prince was surrounded by Rabbis instead of Satraps; his whole court was modeled after that of the Parthian monarchs; and the Jews throughout the East paid the same tribute to support his display which they would have done for the temple of Jerusalem had it still existed. Many of the nation were then extremely rich; and one of them, it was even said, possessed a thousand ships on the sea and a thousand cities on the land. This prosperity and that of the Jews in general continued till A. D. 226, when a revolution took place, Artaxerxes ascended the throne, and the Magian religion was elevated to supreme authority. All other religions were then forbidden throughout the kingdom, and the Jews were compelled to exercise some reserve and secresy in the practice of their religious rites.

Previous to this period the sacred schools of the "Prince of the Captivity" had attained to great eminence, and those of Nahardea and Susa were regarded as equal in distinction and learning to those of Tiberias. This distinction naturally excited the jealousy of the Patriarch, and he is recorded to have sent a singular embassy to the court of his rival for the purpose of observation and exposure. An open dispute had taken place between the two pontiffs in reference to the proper calculation of the Paschal Feast. The Patriarch sent to the Prince two Legates, to whom three letters were entrusted. One of these, which was first presented, bore the inscription "To his Holiness" —an envied title, which seemed to be equivalent to the acknowledgment of his superiority. Flattered by this mark of respect and deference, the Prince ordered his attendants to admit the visitors to the various schools and to show them every thing. After they had made themselves familiar with all that they desired to see and know, the Legates presented the second letter, which bore a much less complimentary epithet. A long altercation ensued, in which the Legates endeavored to expose the errors of the Prince of the Captivity in reference to the disputed feast. They overpowered him by their arguments; and then, by the production of the third letter at the opportune moment, threatened him with excommunication unless he yielded to the authority of the Patriarch. The Legates are said to have played their part so well that they effectually humbled the pride of the Prince and induced him to acknowledge his inferiority to his ambitious rival.

It was subsequent to these events that the celebrated work termed the Babylonian Talmud was prepared in the schools, and by the most eminent Rabbis, of that city. This work is a commentary on the law of Moses and the Mischna, and was composed by more than a thousand learned men, under the direction of Rabbi Asche. It required the constant labor of thirty years for its completion. Its contents consist of the Mischna and the *Gemara*, or exposition of it. This work is a most extraordinary and unparalleled compound of wisdom and absurdity; containing a confused mixture of wise and foolish observations on religion, ethics, political economy, astronomy, metaphysics, law, allegory and fable. Previous to the preparation of this immense work, another Talmud had been compiled at Jerusalem by Rabbi Johanan; but it is smaller, and less esteemed than the Babylonian Talmud; and its inferiority probably led to the compilation of the latter. These works remain to this day the greatest monuments of the ancient literature of the Jews; and in spite of the vast amount of absurdities which they contain, are inestimable treasures of Hebrew learning, and are frequently consulted even by the more erudite class of Christian theologians and expositors.

During the first two centuries of the Christian era the Jewish people became widely dispersed and settled in various countries, where their descendants still remain, after having maintained a separate and isolated existence in every community by whom they were surrounded. One of the most remarkable instances of this description is to be found in China. Originally there were seventy families who emigrated thither. In the middle of the seventeenth century the Jesuit missionaries found but seven families remaining. They possessed a knowledge of the Hebrew language, and had several valuable ancient manuscripts of the Old Testament Scriptures. They also cultivated learning with success; and some of the men of the community had obtained high favor at court, and been chosen mandarins. These Jews were chiefly employed in agriculture, traffic and commerce. They practiced circumcision; kept the Seventh day as a Sabbath with great strictness; and intermarried only among themselves. They were tolerated and protected by the Chinese because they never attempted to make any proselytes. They worshiped in a synagogue somewhat resembling the temple at Jerusalem in shape, within which they preserved the books of the Law. They had a chief priest or Rabbi, who ministered in the synagogue to the people; and they still entertained strong hopes that the Messiah would at length come to redeem Israel and establish a temporal sovereignty in Palestine. Such were the views and some of the peculiarities of the Chinese Jews at that early period; of their present numbers and characteristics we will speak in a subsequent article.

At the conclusion of the second century many Jews wandered into Arabia. When Mahomet rose in the sixth century, he found members of this race in that country both wealthy and powerful; and a Jewish family had even occupied one of the native thrones, or at least had been the chiefs of one of the nomadic tribes who dwelt in the desert. Throughout Parthia and Persia, and the several countries of Asia Minor, in the East; in Spain, Portugal, Italy, and the northern coast of Africa, in the West, adventurous members of this exiled people traveled and settled, soon acquiring riches by the industry and thrift which always characterized them; often suffering cruel persecutions and impositions, yet always faithful in their attachment to the ancient religion of their forefathers, and never totally extirpated; and sometimes, either through the influence of their wealth, or by their superior intelligence, or from some signal service rendered to the State, and not unfrequently by means of the matchless beauty of some fair daughter of their race, acquiring political eminence, and ruling as ministers of the sovereign in the lands of their sojourn and adoption.

CHAPTER III.

HISTORY OF ZENOBIA, QUEEN OF PALMYRA—HER CHARACTER AND FATE—THE JEWISH COMMUNITY IN CONSTANTINOPLE—THE EMPEROR CONSTANTINE THE GREAT—MIRACLES OF RIVAL JEWS AND CHRISTIANS—THE JEWS IN THE WEST—THE ARIAN CONTROVERSY IN THE CHURCH—JULIAN THE APOSTATE—HE FAVORS THE JEWS—HIS ATTEMPT TO REBUILD JERUSALEM—HIS DEATH.

THE most eminent person connected with the Jewish race during the third century was Zenobia, Queen of Palmyra. She was the wife of Odenatus, the sovereign of a country which bloomed like an oasis in the heart of the Syrian desert, situated about a hundred and fifty miles northeast from Damascus. This is the same city spoken of in the Scriptures as the "Tadmor of the wilderness," and was originally built, as is supposed, by Solomon. During the progress of ages it had become a magnificent and opulent capital, and Odenatus, who was a talented and enterprising prince, added to its splendor. After his premature death, Zenobia ascended the throne, and she administered the government with a degree of ability, and eventually experienced vicissitudes, which have rendered her name immortal. She was the daughter of an Arabian prince and a Jewish mother. Zenobia's father was sovereign or Sheik of the southern portion of Mesopotamia, and the people over whom she ruled, after her husband's death, were tribes of Arabs, some of whom dwelt in the surrounding deserts, and some inhabited the verdant oasis in which Palmyra, the capital of the kingdom, was situated.

Zenobia was a woman of extraordinary talents and of remarkable beauty. She was skilled in all the arts of finance, jurisprudence and government, and was present in the camp at the head of her armies in all the wars in which she was engaged. She is described as having been a brunette in complexion and exhibiting the peculiar features of Jewish female beauty in full perfection. She assumed in person the supreme command of her troops, and appeard on horseback, clad in a helmet, wearing a purple mantle fringed with gold and gems, and clasped with a diamond buckle at the waist, so as to leave one arm bare to the shoulder. She gave her orders with a clear and sonorous voice, and in crises of great danger displayed such extraordinary intrepidity that she was worshiped by her heathen subjects as a divinity. She was pure and virtuous in her conduct, temperate in her habits, and though familiar with the dissolute scenes of courts and camps, she was uncontaminated by either. She was versed in the languages of Syria, Egypt, Greece and Rome, and was herself an author, having written the annals of Alexandria and the East.

No sooner had Aurelian attained the Roman purple than the beauty and fame of Zenobia excited his jealous cupidity, and he marched with a powerful army to invade her provinces and subdue her. Zenobia, undismayed by so formidable an antagonist, made preparations to confront the Roman hero, and at length a general engagement took place between their armies near Antioch. After a desperate struggle Roman discipline and art prevailed over the tumultuous and irregular assaults of the valiant Syrians, and Zenobia was compelled to retire to Euresa. Another conflict took place between the two armies under the walls of that city, and with the same result. Zenobia then fled to Palmyra, and resolved to defend herself and her authority till the last extremity. Aurelian hastened to the attack. His first step was to send the chivalrous queen orders to surrender. She replied in a haughty letter in Greek, penned by her secretary, the celebrated Longinus, defying the invader. The siege was immediately commenced. Zenobia displayed the utmost energy and fortitude in defending her capital and throne, and would probably have succeeded had not the troops, which were marching from the allied kings of Persia and Armenia to her aid, been bought over by Roman gold and induced to desert her cause. When she heard of this reverse of fortune she fled from Palmyra in the night, with the most faithful attendants, on dromedaries; but, being overtaken by the Romans, she was captured while crossing the Euphrates, and brought into the presence of Aurelian loaded with chains. By her eloquence she softened his resentment. She escaped the sentence of death, and was reserved to grace the conqueror's triumph at Rome. As she rode along in the procession behind Aurelian's car, she was almost covered and crushed by the load of gold and jewels with which she was adorned. After having thus contributed without resistance to swell the triumph and glory of the victor she was permitted to reside at Rome; was treated with great humanity by the emperor; a large portion of her wealth, which was immense, was restored to her; and she spent the rest of her life at that city in tranquil security and repose. During her whole career she remained attached to the religion and people of her mother's ancestors, was proud of her Jewish origin, and it is probable that the protection which the Jews enjoyed throughout the Roman empire during her lifetime, was due in a great measure to her kindly influence. She was an admirer of the celebrated Paul, Bishop of Samosata; and at her suggestion, as it is supposed, he made efforts to accomplish a union between the Jews and the Christians. Paul was a Unitarian in sentiment, and might more readily harmonize with the Jews on the subject of the Divine Unity than those Christians could, who entertained a theory on that subject which cannot very easily be distinguished by the unlearned from that of three Gods. But these efforts, like all others made to accomplish that purpose, failed, and few conversions took place on either side.

Yet, as Christianity was gradually becoming more and more powerful throughout the Roman empire, and creeping slowly upward, until at last it seated itself on the throne of the Cæsars in the person of Constantine the Great, continual efforts were made by the Christians to convert the Jews, as well as all other classes of religionists; and many singular scenes took place between them. One of these we may narrate as being indicative of the spirit of the times, which occurred at Rome. A controversy or debate took place in the presence of the Roman Emperor, between the heads of the Jewish and Christiam communities in that city. Sylvester, the Bishop of Rome, was also present, who had acquired considerable fame as thaumaturgist, or worker of miracles. In the debate which ensued, the Christian prelate gained the advantage; and the discomfited Jews, in the excitement of the moment, had recourse to magic, the arts of which were better known at that period than at the present. The Jewish rabbis offered to demonstrate the truth of their doctrine miraculously, by striking dead an ox which was brought forward for the purpose, by the utterance of a single word. The Christians accepted the challenge; the ox was produced; the chief rabbi whispered a word in his ear, and the brute instantly fell dead. The Jews set up a great cry of triumph, and the Christians seemed overwhelmed with mortification. Sylvester answered, that it seemed unaccountable that he who uttered the mysterious and talismanic word was not himself slain by it as well as the beast who heard it. The Jews retorted that so vain a quibble did not invalidate the miracle, or diminish the force of the demonstration produced by it; that acts and not quibbles were the proper tests of truth. "So be it, then," exclaimed the irate Sylvester: "If this ox comes to life again, at the utterance of the name of Christ, will you believe?" The Jews imprudently assented. Sylvester then raised his eyes to heaven, and exclaimed: "If He be the true God whom I preach, I command thee, oh ox, in the name of Christ, to arise, and stand on thy feet." The ox incontinently arose, walked about, and began to eat. The Jews were vanquished: and the Christian version of the story is, that they all acknowledged the force of the argument by becoming converts to the faith of their opponents.

Constantine the Great became sole emperor of the Roman world in A. D. 323. Having become a convert to Christianity, his feelings toward the Jews were hostile. His mother, St. Helena, was an enthusiast in the new faith; and she exerted the influence which she possessed over her son to the injury of the Jews. He decreed that, if persons in that race should in any way molest or injure a Christian convert, they should be burned alive. This law was occasioned by the fact that it had frequently occurred that, when Christian converts either from Judaism or from Paganism happened to fall in their power, they stoned them, sometimes to death. Constantine further decreed that no Christian should become a Jew, under the penalty of very severe punishment; and afterward, he forbade Jews to hold Christian slaves under any circumstances. The Jews were also compelled to perform the functions of certain repulsive public offices, such as the *decurionate;* and the emperor forbade Christians to observe the anniversary of the Passover, because it was a peculiar rite of the Jews, "the most hateful of all people!" As is always the case, the hostility of men in power against any community, induced those whom they governed to follow and imitate their example;

and the prevalent tone of feeling throughout the Roman empire toward the Israelites became greatly imbittered. This feeling was increased when the researches of the Christian priests discovered, that the Mischna actually taught that those Jews who deserted the religion of their forefathers ought to be slain by the faithful.

Constantine also added greatly to the provocations of the Jews by his efforts to adorn and rebuild Jerusalem. This ancient name of the city had been so extirpated and forgotten, and its substitute Ælia had become so universally prevalent, that when one of the Christian martyrs, during the prosecution by Maximin, stated that he was a native of Jerusalem, none who heard him, not even the governor of the province who condemned him, understood the word, or knew what it meant. Constantine restored its ancient appellation to the place. He adorned it with many splendid edifices. St. Helena, his mother, exhibited her Christian zeal by erecting a stately church on Mount Calvary, commemorative of the crucifixion of Christ; and among other pious acts she even discovered the true cross on which Christ had suffered; of which, as Luther satirically yet truly asserted, as many fragments and splinters have been preserved and enshrined throughout the world, as would be sufficient to construct a man-of-war ship.

Soon after the occurrence of these events in the East, the Jews who were dwelling in the western countries of Europe, attracted attention by the fresh persecutions to which they were subjected. A large number of them dwelt in Spain; and the Jews themselves asserted that their residence in that kingdom was dated from a very early period; that they were introduced there by the fleets or Solomon and Nebuchadnezzar; and that subsequently the Emperor Hadrian transported thither forty thousand families of the tribe of Judah and ten thousand of the tribe of Benjamin. During the progress of time their descendants had become numerous and wealthy, and they exhibited a very rare peculiarity with the history of this people, in that they had become, in a great measure, farmers instead of peddlers, and landowners instead of merchants. Constantine, the son and successor of Constantine the Great, decreed that the Jewish and Christian farmers should no longer mingle together to commemorate, by festive entertainments, the gathering in of the harvest. On such occasions the Jews had been accustomed to offer a devout petition to God, that, even in the land of exile, He would permit His rains to descend and His sunshine to ripen the fruits of the earth. This prayer at length gave offense to the Christians; the Jews were thereafter forbidden to utter it, and the Council of Elvira added the solemn sanction of the Church to the prohibition by a decree which furnished a not very amiable exhibition of Christian charity.

Meanwhile the Jews attempted to avenge these injuries by retaliating by similar acts, in those Eastern countries where their greater numbers and superior wealth gave them ample power and efficiency. A favorable opportunity of this kind occurred at Alexandria in Egypt. This city was then disturbed by the fierce commotions and disputes which distracted the Christian community in reference to the doctrines of the Trinity. Athanasius headed the orthodox party, and Gregory of Cappadocia the heterodox. The Jews took side with the latter, and some of them indulged in excesses of the worst description, in burning churches, profaning and insulting sacred things, and violating consecrated virgins. The result of these atrocities was, that Constantine promulgated still more severe decrees against them. They were more heavily taxed than before; they were forbidden under the penalty of death, to hold Christian slaves, or to marry Christian women; and the decree of the Emperor Hadrian, which forbade them to approach Jerusalem, but which had become nearly obsolete and null, was renewed and rigidly enforced. At the same time the mortification of the Jews was increased by the fact, that their ancient capital was gradually becoming more resplendent and renowned as a Christian city, filled with Christian churches, crowded by Christian pilgrims, and consecrated in Christian hearts everywhere by a solemn reverence for those very sites and scenes, such as the Hill of Calvary, the Garden of Gethsemane, the Holy Sepulchre, and the Mount of Olives, which the Jews most heartily detested and despised.

At length, in A. D. 361, Julian the Apostate ascended the imperial throne, and a welcome respite from cruelty and persecution was thus obtained by this people. He carried his protection so far as to send a letter to the Patriarch at Tiberias, terming him his brother, and he proceeded to annul nearly all the vexatious edicts of his predecessors in reference to the Jews. He equalized their taxes, and promised to do great things in their behalf after his return from his expedition against Persia. At the same time he ordered the temple to be rebuilt at Jerusalem, in order that he might demonstrate both to Jews and Gentiles, by the accomplishment of that feat, the falsehood of the prophecy contained in the Christian Scriptures on the subject, which declared that the temple should remain an everlasting waste and desolation. Julian also intended, by these various expedients, to obtain the support of the important and numerous community of Jews who dwelt in Mesopotamia, and were subjects of the King of Persia. In this expectation, however, he was disappointed, for the Jews, being favored by that government and protected in their rights, remained faithful to their legitimate sovereign, and refused to join the ranks of the imperial invader.

While Julian was absent on his Persian expedition, the attempt to rebuild the temple was made. The Jews throughout the world regarded this enterprise with intense interest and approbation; and they contributed largely to the execution of the work. Thousands who could not afford to send money gave materials and labor. Their zeal was shown in a variety of ways. Some sent tools and implements made of gold and silver. Rich and delicate women offered to assist, and might be seen carrying rubbish in their silken robes and mantles. The blind and the aged even offered to assist in the work; and a jubilee of exultation and hope pervaded the whole nation. Scarcely had the operations commenced, under the direction of Alypius, a favorite officer of Julian, than they were suddenly terminated by an extraordinary incident. As the workmen were removing the foundations of the ancient structure, flames of fire, accompanied with loud explosions, burst from the subterranean recesses, and compelled the workmen to desist. This phenomenon was repeated as often as the attempt was made to resume operations, and overcame every effort to continue them.

This remarkable event is recorded by testimony so strong and clear, that it is absurd to deny it. It is asserted by Gregory Nazianzen, Chrysostom, Theodoret, the historians Sozomen and Socrates, by Ammianus Marcellinus, himself a heathen and intimate friend of Julian, and by Zemuch David, a learned Jew. The Christians of course regarded it as a great miracle, which was performed by superhuman power, to assert the truth of the Christian religion and Scriptures. These, indeed, do not depend upon such trivial incidents for the proofs of their divine origin and authority; and the more enlightened or impartial observer will doubtless ascribe this event to the fact, that the inflammable vapors which had been generated in the progress of time in the confined subterranean passages which are known to have existed under the hill, on which the temple was erected, and upon which its crumbling ruins still clustered, were ignited either by the labors of the workmen, or by contact with the external air, and thus produced the dangerous explosions in question. What might have been the ultimate result had the work been continued, it would be difficult to say; but Julian was slain in his Persian expedition, and with him terminated for a time the prosperity of the Jews, and no further efforts to rebuild the doomed edifice were afterward made.

CHAPTER IV.

EVENTS OF THE FOURTH CENTURY—VALENTINIAN AND VALENS PROTECT THE JEWS—HOSTILITY BETWEEN THE JEWS AND CHRISTIANS—BIGOTRY OF AMBROSE OF MILAN—EVENTS WHICH OCCURRED AT ALEXANDRIA IN EGYPT—IN THE ISLAND OF MINORCA—BISHOP SEVERUS—ORESTES—HISTORY OF HYPATIA—EVENTS IN CRETE.

DURING the fourth century the chief incidents which are presented by the history of the Jews are struggles and rivalries between them and the constantly-increasing power of Christianity. As the church became more influential, as the persecutions which she endured became less, her disposition to encroach upon the rights of others became more decided. The Jews generally retorted upon their enemies as far as they had the power, or ventured upon the risk; and in some cases they imitated the example of their opponents, and displayed a spirit of animosity and cruelty equal to their own. For all these excesses they were generally punished very severely in the end; and each conflict of the rival religions resulted in the aggrandizement of the church, at the expense of the security and prosperity of the synagogue.

During the reigns of Valentinian and Valens, the Jews were protected throughout the Roman empire; although they were no longer exempted as before from public and military service. In excuse for this imposition it was urged that the necessities of the State required the services of all its citizens; and as even the clergy of the church were compelled to find substitutes when they devoted themselves to the ecclesiastical life, before they were permitted to enter it, so also the Jews should either perform their duties as citizens whose lives and properties were protected by the civil power, or should procure substitutes in their places.

An illustration of the prevalent spirit of hostility between the Jews and Christians, which existed at this period, will be found in an event which occurred in the town of Callinicum, on the confines of Persia. The Christian Bishop of the place, taking some offense at the Jews, stirred up the populace to burn their synagogue, together with the church of the Valentinian heretics. The deed of violence was done; but the Roman Governor of Callinicum immediately ordered the turbulent prelate either to rebuild the edifices, or to pay the damage which had been occasioned. This demand was appealed from, but the sentence was confirmed by the decree of the Roman Emperor. At this crisis the matter came to the knowledge of the celebrated Ambrose, the Bishop of Milan, who, in consequence of his superior zeal and talents, was at that period regarded as the most distinguished prelate in the Christian Church, and exercised very great influence at the imperial court. He addressed a letter to the then reigning Emperor Theodosius, reproving him for his edict in favor of the Jews; and declaring that had he been in the place of the Bishop of Callinicum, he would have acted precisely as he did. It serves to illustrate both the weakness of the character of Theodosius, and the perverted influence which such an unscrupulous enthusiast as Ambrose had attained, that he succeeded in bending the purpose and the power of the monarch to his will; and the outrage upon the Jews remained unpunished and unatoned for. During the progress of this dispute, Ambrose described a synagogue as being an impious place, the abode of perfidy and insanity, and asserted that, should the demolished structure be rebuilt, it should have inscribed upon it the words: "This is a temple of ungodliness, erected from the plunder of the Christians." Subsequently, however, Theodosius seems to have become ashamed of the tyranny exercised over him by Ambrose; and before his death he decreed that the Christians should not plunder or demolish the synagogues, and expressly ordered the Governors of provinces to see to it that the decree was properly obeyed. At the same time he permitted the Christians to destroy the remaining temples of the Pagans, and the edifices of those Christian sects who were stigmatized as heretics by the majority. Nevertheless the Jews were still forbidden by law to enter the precincts of Jerusalem. In spite of this prohibition, they frequently passed the confines of the city, in disguise, by bribing the guards with immense sums of money; and in defiance of the power and purpose of the Roman Emperor, and his most fanatical prelates, they sat and wept upon the ruins of the temple, and viewed the scene of their forefathers' glory with such emotions as the circumstances would naturally excite.

Alexandria, the capital of Egypt, seemed to be the spot destined to witness the fiercest and bloodiest struggles between the rival races and religions. That city was the chief central seat of the adherents of Arius, and the Jews were also numerous and wealthy. In all the conflicts which took place between the Arians and the Orthodox, the Jews uniformly sided with the former. In that city the Israelites observed the various ceremonies of their religion with greater publicity and boldness than in any other; and on one occasion, about the year A. D. 400, they celebrated the feast of Purim, and their deliverance from the plot of Haman by Esther, in a tumultuous manner, which was calculated both to annoy and to insult the Christians. During the services in the synagogues they beat the benches with stones and mallets as often as the hated name of Haman was repeated; and they also made a public exhibition afterward of the method in which they desired or determined to punish all their enemies who might act the part or display the spirit of Haman. They erected a gibbet, to which was affixed an effigy which represented that unhappy individual; but, in addition to this, it is said that the gibbet bore a strong resemblance to the figure of a cross —a thing which at that period began, for the first time, to be made an object of worship and veneration among the Christians. The latter regarded this display as an effort to throw contempt upon their favorite symbol, and the whole affair they interpreted as a disguised derisive representation of the Crucifixion The consequence was the occurrence of another violent tumult, in which both parties suffered severely, and both gratified their animosity at the expense of their blood. Similar scenes occurred in Macedonia, Illyria and Dacia, where some of the synagogues were even burnt. In the town of Inmester, not far from the city of Antioch, some Jews, who were intoxicated, began to blaspheme and curse the name of Christ in the public streets; and in their frenzy they proceeded to erect a cross, tied a Christian boy to it, whom they seized as he was passing by, and then scourged him to death. This infamous act, which was of course condemned by the better class of Jews, was afterward punished as it deserved; but no atonement could suffice to weaken or remove the intense hatred which it naturally excited against all the Jews in the minds of the Christians. In Antioch a synagogue was soon afterward burnt; and so strong had the current of public sentiment become against the Israelites, that no representations which they could make sufficed to procure an indemnification for the injury.

The island of Minorca also witnessed scenes of violence between the hostile sects. Severus, the Christian Bishop of the place, was prominent in some of these, and his name has been transmitted to posterity in connection with a singular scene, which furnishes an instructive picture of the mingled fanaticism and ignorance of the times. Severus was anxious for the conversion of the Jews, and held many disputations with Theodorus, their most prominent and learned man, to accomplish that purpose. On one occasion the Bishop sent the Jews a defiant letter, inviting them to meet him at the church at Magona, the capital of the island. They complied with the invitation, and during the progress of the dispute Severus charged his opponents with having secreted arms in their neighboring synagogue wherewith to enact some deed of violence. They denied the charge, and offered to prove its falsity by immediately repairing to the synagogue and inspecting it. The Jews and Christians then went in procession thither. After their arrival a tumult occurred between them. No arms were found, but the synagogue was set on fire and burnt. Several days afterwards, while a mingled crowd of Jews and Christians were inspecting the ruins, the dispute recommenced. Theodorus was getting the better of the argument, when the Christians raised a disorderly cry: "Theodorus, believe in Christ!" This exclamation was soon understood or misinterpreted to be, "Theodorus *believes* in Christ!" The Jews, panic-struck at this supposed announcement of the perfidy of their chief, fled from the place. When thus left alone with the Christians, Theodorus could not resist their overwhelming importunities, and finally acknowledged himself a convert to the faith which he had opposed. Both parties seem to have acted throughout like an assemblage of knaves and fools, and neither of them deserves much commendation or respect.

Alexandria, the renowned and opulent capital of Egypt, continued to be the scene, from time to time, of the most important events which occurred in connection with the Jews. About the year 415 another tumult and massacre occurred in that city between them and the Christians, the entire blame of which rests upon the head of St. Cyril, the Archbishop of the place, and one of the most detestable bigots and fanatics who ever lived.

Orestes, a man of probity and respectability, was then the Roman Prefect or Governor of the city. Cyril attempted in various ways to encroach upon his authority and to extend his ecclesiastical jurisdiction—a disposition which naturally excited the just resentment of the Prefect. At that time theatrical entertainments were chiefly given on the Jewish Sunday; and then, as now, both Jew and Christian *connoisseurs* were greatly divided in opinion in reference to the respective merits of grace, agility, and form of their favorite public female dancers. Excitement ran high in the amphitheatre on one occasion; and in the midst of it Hierax, a vulgar schoolmaster and an enthusiastic tool of Cyril, entered by his order for the purpose of examining a proclamation which had recently been made by the Prefect against tumultuous proceedings. The Jews exclaimed that Hierax came for the purpose of making a disturbance, and considered themselves insulted by his presence. Orestes, to deal justly with both parties, ordered Hierax to be scourged, and threatened the Jews with severe punishment unless they ceased their disorderly behavior in future.

Instead of complying with this reasonable demand, the Jews soon afterward raised a cry at midnight that the great church was on fire, and they attacked the Christians as they rushed unarmed from their dwellings to save the edifice. Some were slain, and Cyril determined to take summary vengeance. He attacked the Jews in return with a formidable force of fanatical Christians, slew a large number of them, assailed and destroyed their synagogues, plundered their property, and succeeded in expelling a large portion of them from the city. Orestes, the Governor, was by no means satisfied with these sanguinary proceedings, and was greatly incensed at the triumph of his rival. The feeling of hostility between them increased. Cyril called to his aid some fifteen hundred monks, an ignorant and superstitious herd who lived in the neighboring mountains of Nitria. Thus supported, the Archbishop insulted Orestes, publicly calling him a heathen, an idolater, and various other opprobrious epithets. Orestes defended himself, but in vain, against these charges, by declaring that he had been publicly baptized by Alticus, a bishop of Constantinople. A man named Ammonius, hurled a stone at the head of the Governor at this crisis, which took effect, and inflicted a serious wound. The Alexandrian pupulace rose in defence of their Prefect; the monks were expelled from the city, and Ammonius tried, condemned and executed. Cyril commanded the body of the criminal to be exhumed, invested him with all the honors of a martyr, and dispersed his relics to be honored on the altars of the churches. These acts of mutual animosity finally culminated in the commission of one of the vilest acts of cruelty recorded on the page of history.

At that time there lived at Alexandria a lady of great beauty, intelligence and celebrity, named Hypatia. She was a native of the place and a daughter of Theon, a distinguished mathematician. She devoted herself from an early age to scientific pursuits, and she became a profound adept in the philosophy of Plato, which she preferred to the rival system of Aristotle. Having exhausted all the resources of learning at Alexandria, she resolved to travel. She went first to Athens, and there attended the lectures of the most eminent instructors. After further journeys she returned to her native city, where she was invited by the magistrates to give instruction in Philosophy. She accepted the invitation, and her superior genius and learning soon elevated her to great celebrity. She was an Eclectic; but mathematical science formed the basis of her instructions even in philosophy. Among her pupils there were many persons of distinction, among whom was Synesius, afterward Bishop of Ptolemais, who continued through life to esteem her. Entirely engrossed in philosophical pursuits, Hypatia refused to declare herself a convert to Christianity though she by no means disapproved or condemned it; and though often wooed, she turned a deaf ear to all the tender solicitations of her admirers. She refused to marry because domestic cares, as she thought, would interfere with her intellectual pursuits; while at the same time her conduct was a model of purity and propriety in every respect. She well knew how to restrain the sentimental ardor which her personal charms excited in the minds of her enthusiastic auditors. Orestes, the Prefect of Alexandria, was among the number of these; and this fact was sufficient to excite against the fair philosopher the jealousy of so mean and malignant a fanatic as Cyril. He pretended to regard Hypatia as one of the chief supports of Paganism. He also imagined that her influence dictated the measures of Orestes, which he condemned, and which irritated him. To gratify this mingled spirit of hostility, envy and bigotry, he induced his partisans, headed by a priest named Peter, to stop the chariot of Hypatia as she was proceeding to her school. They forced her to descend, took her to a neighboring church, stripped her of her clothes, put her to death, tore her body in pieces, dragged the still palpitating members through the streets, and at last consigned them to the flames. To render the detestable nature of this crime complete, it should be added, that the bribes and misrepresentations of Cyril and his satellites were so potent in the court of the Christian Emperor at Rome, that no punishment was ever inflicted upon its perpetrators.

About twenty years after these events, a singular excitement occurred among the Jews in the Island of Crete. The Jewish community there was numerous and wealthy. An impostor appeared among them, who assumed the name of Moses, and claimed to be the Messiah. During the period of a year he traveled to and fro, persuading the Jews of the authenticity of his claims, urging them to abandon their possessions, and to follow him toward the Holy Land. At the appointed time he commenced his journey, at the head of many thousand followers. He asserted that the Mediterranian, like the Red Sea of old, would dry up at his command, and enable them to travel through it safely toward Palestine. He then led them to the top of a lofty promontory, from which he commanded the most enthusiastic to throw themselves. Many did so, and were dashed to pieces on the rocks and sands below, and some perished in the waves. At length the deluded fanatics became convinced that their leader was an impostor, and turned to wreak their just vengeance upon him; but, like other knaves, he was not to be fund when justice pursued. He had escaped in the midst of the tumult, with a considerable sum of plundered gold and jewels. It is recorded by the ecclesiastical historian, Socrates, that the Christians asserted that this Moses was the devil in disguise; while the Jews were greatly mortified at the result of the affair, and returned, wiser and less credulous, to their deserted homes.

About this period, A. D. 425, the Patriarchate of Tiberias, which for several centuries had exercised so great an authority in religious matters among the dispersed Israelites, expired in the person of Gamaliel, a descendant of the great Instructor at whose feet Paul had sat. The Emperor Theodosius proclaimed an edict, terminating the jurisdiction and cutting off the revenues of the Patriarchate; so that on Gamaliel's death no successor was appointed. The alleged reason for this arbitrary act was, that the Patriarch, in opposition to express imperial edicts to the contrary, had erected new synagogues, and had used other means to extend the spread of Judaism.

CHAPTER V.

DIVISION OF THE ROMAN EMPIRE—THE JEWS IN THE WESTERN EMPIRE—THEIR SUFFERINGS AT NAPLES—AT GENOA—FEUD BETWEEN THEM AND THE SAMARITANS—JULIAN THE APOSTATE—THE CONDITION OF THE JEWS UNDER THE EMPEROR JUSTINIAN—GREGORY I. BISHOP OF ROME—HIS PATRONAGE OF THE JEWS.

THE division of the Roman Empire in A. D. 395 into two parts, by which one became the Greek or Eastern Empire, with Constantinople for its capital, and the other the Western, with Rome for its centre, produced a marked effect upon the condition and fortunes of the Jews. In the Western Empire they labored under many disadvantages until Odoacer assumed the title of the King of Italy. Fourteen years afterward he was defeated and deposed by Theodoric, the King of the Ostro-Goths, who became the founder of the Gothic sovereignty in Italy. This conqueror, after dividing one-third of the country among his victorious troops as a reward for their services, introduced an equitable government into every part of the administration, and protected the Jews equally with all other religionists. Theodoric was an Arian, and hence his name has been handed down with desecration by a more orthodox posterity; but he exemplified and practiced the Christian virtue of charity in an eminent degree. He ordered the Christians to rebuild, or to make restitution for, the synagogues which they had plundered or burnt at Rome, Milan and Genoa. The consequence of this protection was, that the Jews became greatly attached to his person and government. Being thus encouraged in their legitimate occupation throughout Italy, they increased in wealth and importance, and became a very valuable ingredient in the community; and when Belisarius, the general of Justinian, invaded Italy and besieged Naples, that portion of the city which was next to the sea was intrusted to their defense; and so valiantly did they deport themselves that they would have prevented the capture of the city, had not a secret entrance been discovered in another quarter, by which the hostile troops gained admittance. After the fall of Naples they experienced great cruelties, as a penalty for their patriotic devotion. And when Narses, the successor of Belisarius, overturned the Ostro-Gothic kingdom in 553, twenty-seven years after the death of Theodoric, its founder, a darker era of persecution supervened in the annals of the Jews. Theodoric had decreed that the Christian inhabitants of Genoa, who had deprived the Jews of all their privileges, and had plundered their synagogues, should reinstate them in their rights and repair the injured edifices. He reproved the Senate of Rome—then a pitiful shadow of that powerful and majestic body which, in former ages, had ruled the world, and which had appeared to the ambassadors of Pyrrhus like an assemblage of kings—for their injurious treatment to the Jews; and

Gregory, the Bishop of that city, taking his cue from the imperial pleasure, rebuked those Christians who had insulted the Israelites, by placing the images of the Virgin Mary and of Christ within them. This was the most extraordinary instance of Christian charity, as displayed toward this persecuted people, throughout the whole range of the early history of the church. After the expulsion of the Ostro-Goth kings from Italy by the armies of Justinian, those days of security and toleration for the Jews terminated; and they experienced the rigor of those severe edicts which the Emperor proclaimed and enforced throughout the whole extent of the Roman world. Before narrating these oppressive laws, we must advert to those events which were transpiring in the eastern portion of the empire, and which greatly contributed to their enactment by the Emperor.

In the sixth year of Justin the Elder, a law had been promulgated to the effect that unbelievers, Jews and Samaritans, should thenceforth be excluded from all offices of magistracy, and from every dignity of the State; that none of them should become Judges, Prefects, or guardians of cities, or should hold any military commissions. Whoever violated this law was to be punished by a fine of twenty pounds of gold. This law, which applied to the Samaritans by name, raised an insignificant community to an importance which they did not before enjoy. They still hold possession of Mount Gerizim, which had during many ages been their most sacred spot, and which is referred to as such in the New Testament.

No temple had been erected there, but the Samaritans worshiped constantly on it, and regarded that duty and privilege as the greatest which appertained to their religion. This was enough to excite the pious hostility of the Christians, and they determined that a church of the true faith should be erected on that chosen abode of a false and an abrogated religion. The announcement of this intention drove the Samaritans to frenzy, and they attacked the Christians when assembled in their church on Easter, in Neapolis. They seized the Bishop Terrebinthus while he was celebrating the Eucharist, wounded him by cutting off two of his fingers as he held fast the consecrated emblems in his hand, drove out the congregation, and defaced the sacred edifice in the most shameful manner. The bishop hastened to Constantinople, exhibited his injuries to the Emperor, and demanded the punishment of his assailants. His request was complied with, and a decree was forthwith issued, ordering the offenders to be punished, expelling the Samaritans entirely from Mount Gerizim, and directing that a Christian church should be erected on the summit of the mount, surrounded by a strong wall for its protection.

Some time afterward the Samaritans were induced to engage in a rebellion, and to seek revenge for these indignities, by the efforts of a celebrated impostor named Julian, who represented himself as the Messiah, and assumed the authority and state of a king. He destroyed the property of the Christians around Neapolis, burned their churches, and assailed the priests. He even entered that town, summoned a young man to his presence who had gained a prize in the games which were then being celebrated, asked whether he were a Christian, and being answered affirmatively, immediately struck off his head. Julian desolated the whole of the neighboring country; one bishop was slain, and many priests were imprisoned. These excesses continued until a Roman army reached the scene of hostilities, attacked Julian, defeated and slew him, retaliated on the Samaritans the cruelties which they had perpetrated on the Christians, and reduced the turbulent district to order.

The Samaritans, however, did not submit to these sufferings without employing their exertions by way of intercession with the Emperor, to avert or alleviate them. They sent Arsenius, their principal man, and a person of talent and influence, to Constantinople, to represent their case to the indignant sovereign. The eloquence of Arsenius, which was remarkable, seems for a time to have produced a great effect upon the mind of the Emperor; and he might have succeeded in attaining the object of his mission, by representing that the Samaritans were more sinned against than sinning, had not the Christians dispatched St. Sabas to Constantinople for the purpose of resisting and counteracting his influence. The great age, the venerable character and superior sanctity of Sabas, eventually gained a triumph over the plausible rhetorick of Arsenius; and the Samaritans were condemned. The leaders of the late insurrection were put to death, the people expelled from Neapolis, and a singular law promulgated that Samaritan children should no longer inherit the property of their parents. The result was that Arsenius and many of his co-religionists yielded to this stern necessity which assailed them, and became Christians; and St. Sabas returned home covered with glory and honored with the imperial favor.

This insurrection of the Samaritans caused the most severe edicts to be promulgated by Justinian, not only against them, but against the Jews, as belonging to the same general class of unbelievers. It was enacted that they should thenceforth be deprived of all civil dignities; that all possible burdens of the State should be laid upon them, without the privilege of enjoying any of the advantages or immunities which are generally attached to them; that where marriages had taken place between Jews or Samaritans and Christians, the Christian husband or wife should exercise the entire control in the household. Christian children could exact exorbitant privileges from their unbelieving parents, and might in reality deprive them of the exercise of all paternal authority. In all disputes between Jews and Christians, the testimony of a Jew was made inadmissible; in lawsuits between Jews, their testimony might be received, but the evidence of a Samaritan must be excluded. The Samaritans were deprived of the right of bequeathing their property, or of administering upon the estates of decedents. No Samaritan was allowed to have more than a life estate in his property, unless the children became Christians. Where that event did not occur, his wealth was escheated to the imperial treasury. The children of mixed marriages must become Christian or forfeit their inheritance; and where a part of the children became Christians, they inherited to the exclusion of the rest. The prefects and bishops of the respective districts were ordered to enforce these inhuman decrees by the infliction of the severest penalties; and they remained in full force, until, after a few years, by the quiet submission of the Samaritans—that obedience which despair alone could produce—and in consequence of the benevolent interposition of Sergius, Bishop of Cæsarea, this cruel rigor was to some extent moderated.

During the reign of the pious Justinian, the Jews continued to experience the most unjust impositions throughout the remotest portions of the empire, and his zeal for their conversion induced him to harass them with various restrictions for the purpose of constraining them to adopt the true faith. He ordered the Governor of Africa to prohibit the performance of their worship, and to convert the synagogues into churches. In some places this arbitrary measure produced the desired result; for in Borium—a city on the frontiers of Pentapolis, where there was a splendid temple and a large community of Israelites—the latter abandoned their ancient faith, and became converts to Christianity, and turned their place of worship into a church.

Justinian forbade the Jews to celebrate the Passover on any day except that on which the Christians observed Easter; and they were forbidden under any circumstances to partake of the paschal lamb. He also prohibited them from being received as witnesses in any law-suit between Jews and Christians, or between Christians themselves; and they were allowed to be competent witnesses only in cases where both litigants were Jews. He also decreed that they should not disinherit their children should they abandom Judaism and become Christians; and they were obliged to give such portions to their Christian daughters as seemed fit to the Prefect or the Bishop, who were in effect constituted the guardians of the proselytes. The Christian children of Jews were to receive the same proportion of property by will which they would have inherited had their parents died intestate; and all wills were pronounced invalid which did not allow this proportion. Even in cases where children had been guilty of great improprieties toward their parents, if they professed themselves converts to Christianity, the parents were ordered to treat them with the same consideration in all respects as if they had been exemplary and dutiful.

While the Jews throughout the Roman empire were thus afflicted by the persecutions of those in power, they were also annoyed by disputes among themselves. At this period a difference of opinion arose between some of the Rabbis and the people, in regard to the use of the Hebrew language in the reading of the law in the synagogues, and also in the public expositions which were made of it. The Rabbis wished to retain the ancient tongue; while many of the people, who had been gradually losing their familiarity with it, desired that the Greek language should be substituted.

Very violent disputes occurred between the several parties, until at last it was proposed to adjust the difficulty by an appeal to the Emperor Justinian. He decided in favor of the use of the Greek language, in opposition to the wishes of the Rabbis; and ordered that the well-known Septuagint version of the Old Testament should be employed in place of the original Hebrew. He also excluded the perusal of the Mischna from use in the exercises of the synagogue; stigmatizing it as worthless in itself, and as conducive to the spread of superstition. He likewise threatened a very severe penalty against all those Rabbis who interfered with the free use of the Greek in the synagogues, and piously urged upon the Jews the frequent perusal of the Scriptures as a means of spiritual improvement.

The zeal of Justinian for the conversion of the Jews greatly increased his popularity with the Christian church and priesthood, and they proceeded to assist him in his pious work by performing alleged miracles and exhibiting presumed prodigies. Nothing could be more preposterous than these wonders; but they serve to illustrate the remarkable degree of ignorance and folly which prevailed in those ancient times, which are by some regarded as the halcyon days of Christianity, and the brightest and purest period of its history. We will illustrate this remark by citing one of these phenomena. There lived a person at Emesa, named Simeon, who enjoyed great reputation as a saint, though he much more deserved the epithet of a lunatic. He frequently displayed his zeal by running up and down the streets whipping the pillars and exclaiming to each of them, "This is for dancing!" because the Emesans were fond of that amusement, and because an earthquake had recently occurred in that vicinity, which he regarded as a proof of the Divine displeasure. On one occasion he stopped in his peregrinations before the shop of a Jewish glassblower, who was working at his furnace. The operator was attempting to make a glass, but the material suddenly assumed the form of a cross, and then burst. This incident was curious enough in itself, but to make it still more extraordinary the same thing occurred seven successive times. The Jew was in despair. Simeon informed him that he would never succeed until he made the sign of the cross after the manner in which the Christians were then accustomed to do. The Israelite, whose subsistence wholly depended on his trade, yielded to the injunction, made the sign of the cross, and at the next attempt succeeded admirably with his work. The miracle was so convincing, and the appeals of Simeon were so earnest, that it is said that the astonished Israelite became a Christian and a zealous convert.

Yet it must be acknowledged that while such puerile incidents occurred, and were commended by members of the Church, both among the priesthood and the laity, there were other cases in which pious and enlightened persons interested themselves in the fate of this people, and endeavored to promote their temporal and spiritual interests by such means as were in the highest degree commendable. In that age Gregory the First, the Bishop of Rome, deserved great reverence for his personal virtues. He protected the Jews from persecution and imposition as far as his influence extended. Many instances of this kindly disposition have been recorded, one of which may be here narrated. It generally happened that those Jews who became converts to Christianity were much more zealous than Christians themselves in the persecution and annoyance of their former co-religionists. On a certain occasion an apostate Hebrew gathered together a company of zealots, and on Easter day forced their way into the synagogue, and there set up a cross and an image of the Virgin. The Jews were greatly indignant at this outrage; yet so much in fear were they of imperial vengeance that they dared not remove the obnoxious articles. They applied to the magistrates for relief, and these officials were disposed to grant it. The converted Jew, however, appealed from their decision to that of Gregory. The prelate at once supported the decision of the magistrates, condemned the officious zeal of the convert, severely rebuked him, told him that his zeal was without knowledge, and was highly censurable; and ordered that the cross and the image should be removed, and the Jews in future be allowed to exercise the rites of their religion undisturbed. It would doubtless have been better for the interests of Christianity during many succeeding ages, had the charity and forbearance of Gregory toward these people been more generally imitated.

CHAPTER VI.

DOWNFALL OF THE WESTERN EMPIRE—CHRISTIAN SLAVES HELD BY JEWS—DECREES OF COUNCILS FORBIDDING IT—SUPREMACY OF THE BISHOP OF ROME—CONDITION OF THE JEWS IN THE EASTERN EMPIRE—EVENTS IN SYRIA—PERSIA—MESOPOTAMIA—THE PRINCE OF THE CAPTIVITY—RABBI CHININA—CHOSROES CONQUERS PALESTINE AND PROTECTS THE HEBREW PEOPLE.

WHEN the innumerable hordes of barbarians from the north of Europe poured through the defiles of the Alps, and overwhelmed the western empire of Rome, in the latter portion of the fourth, and during the fifth centuries, an important change was thereby effected in the relations which had previously existed between the Jews and the Christians. The former remained unscathed and uninjured by the storms which desolated and ruined the latter; and those who had been the inferiors and dependents, assumed in some respects the attitude of superiors and masters. The victorious barbarians turned their triumphs to good account. They sold the vanquished Christians as slaves, by myriads; and of these unfortunate persons, the Jews, in a majority of cases, became the purchasers. At that time the Israelites were numerous in Belgium, along the Rhine, in France, Italy, and Spain; for they had been quietly spreading and expanding during several centuries, into every portion of the Western Empire, and the circumjacent regions, where civilization had been carried by the arms and conquests of Rome.

Doubtless the Jews experienced a feeling of exultation in thus observing the change of fortune which had overtaken their Christian oppressors; and it is certain that the latter deeply felt the indignity. Nothing could be more infamous in their opinion than that Christians should be the slaves of the detested race of Israel. The Roman Emperors, in the day of their power, had expressly forbidden such a relation by their edicts. Constantine had published a decree forbidding the Jews to hold Christians as slaves, under penalty of death. After the power of the Emperors had failed in the West, the chief bishops and councils of the Church endeavored to remove this evil by the only means remaining within their reach—by appeals, resolutions, and canons. Thus the Council of Orleans, A. D. 540, enacted that if a slave were commanded to perform any service which was forbidden by his religion, and the master undertook to punish him for his disobedience, he might escape to any church and there find an asylum; and the clergy of that church were not to give him up, but to pay a ransom for him, and set him free. Another Council of Orleans decreed in A. D. 541 still further, that if a Christian slave claimed the protection of any other Christian under such circumstances, the latter was bound to redeem him at a fair price; and that if any Jew had bought a Christian slave, or had taken a Christian slave as wife or concubine, and had induced her to become a Jew, he should lose his property in the slave; and any Christian who had obtained his or her liberty on such conditions, should not be recognized by the law as free, but as still being in bondage, as being unworthy of freedom.

Another Council decreed, in A. D. 582, that if a Jew refused to accept a fair and reasonable price for his Christian slaves, he should be compelled to grant them their liberty on the payment of twelve *solidi*, equal in value to about twenty-five dollars; for, said the Council, "it was unjust that those whom Christ has redeemed by his blood, should groan in the fetters of his persecutors." Individual prelates and dignitaries exerted themselves to diminish the evil. Gregory the First, Bishop of Rome, one of the most excellent characters presented by the history of the Church, denounced the traffic in Christian slaves, in his pastorals, with great earnestness. He wrote to the Prefect Fortunatus that "he had been informed that a Jewish miscreant had built an altar and, compelled or bribed his Christian slaves to worship before it." The Prefect was requested to inflict corporeal punishment on the offender, and set all the slaves in question at liberty. He wrote to Vevantius, a bishop in Tuscany, rebuking him for permitting certain captive Christians to be bought by Jewish speculators. He declared that no Jew or heathen, who desired to become a Christian, should be retained in bondage; and he directed that if a slave desired to become a Christian within three months after his servitude began, he should be ransomed at a reasonable price; but if the Jewish owner refused to accept that price, he should afteward obtain his freedom without any ransom.

In all such cases the ransom was to be furnished out of the goods or public property of the Church. Gregory, writing to Candidus, a priest in Gaul, thus speaks on this subject: "Dominic, the bearer of this letter, has made known to me, with great grief, that his four brothers have been purchased by the Jews, and are now their slaves at Narbonne. We direct you to inquire into the matter, and if it be true to redeem them at a proper price, and charge the same in your annual account." The same zealous prelate wrote to Thierry and Theodebert, kings of the Franks, and to Queen Brunehart, urging them to abolish the traffic in Christian slaves in their dominions; and he insisted that certain funds belonging to the churches in Gaul should be appropriated to the purpose of ransoming Christian slaves. Having been informed that the Samaritan merchants in Sicily were accustomed to purchase heathen slaves for the purpose of making proselytes of them, he wrote to Leo, the Bishop of Catana in that island, requesting him to investigate the affair; and if he should find it to be correct, to insist on the enfranchisement of the slaves without ransom. This instruction was in accordance with the existing yet nearly obsolete law of the empire.

By this period the Bishop of Rome had acquired a general supremacy and jurisdiction over the whole Church; and hence his conduct and policy in reference to any particular matter, possessed great importance and authority. Gregory, the then existing Pontiff, in pursuance of his policy against the bondage of Christians, directed his receiver of taxes in Sicily to pay a third of his collections to those Jews who became Christians, or who were disposed to manumit their Christian slaves on reasonable terms. Inferior prelates followed the example of their chief. Peter, Bishop of Tarragona, was one of these, who had even gone so far as to commend the zeal of some Christians who had expelled the Jews from their synagogues during the celebration of one of their chief festivals. Gregory wrote to him, rebuking this disorderly zeal, but urging him to exert himself to win over the Israelites to the true faith by more gentle and reasonable means. He gave similar advice to the Bishop of Marseilles, who had exhibited a like spirit of violence and hostility. Said he: "If a Jew be brought to the baptismal font by compulsion, not by the sweetness of the word, returning to his former heresy, he will die in a worse state than if he had never seemed to be converted. Preach frequently to the Jews, that they may desire to be changed through the love of what they hear. Thus your desire of saving souls will be gratified, and your convert will not return like a dog to his vomit." It does not appear from the history of those times how far the influence and efforts of Christian prelates in resisting the bondage of Christians to Jews succeeded in remedying the evil; but it is certain that, though the Jews took advantage of the supremacy of the barbarian conquerors to make use of the liberty of holding their rival religionists in slavery, they themselves still continued to be a proscribed and persecuted race; for they were still excluded, as before, from admission to the ranks of the nobility; they were forbidden to be governors of provinces; they could not enter either the Senate or the army; they were not admitted to the society of men of rank; and were only permitted to engage in commerce and acquire wealth to prevent them from starvation, or from becoming a burden to the community around them.

From the Jews in the Western Empire we turn to those in the East, where the once formidable power of Imperial Rome still retained some shadow of its former grandeur, and kept the Jews under subjection. The prevalent peace, however, was broken about the year 555 by the Jews and Samaritans in Cæsarea and in Syria. The origin of the tumult which then occurred is unknown; but the Jews arose, attacked the Christians, destroyed several of their churches, slew Stephanus, the Prefect, in his palace, and plundered the edifice. The wife of Stephanus fled to Constantinople, and having stated the facts to the Emperor, Adamantius was sent by him to Cæsarea to suppress the insurrection. He punished the guilty with great cruelty, and compelled the Jews and Samaritans, who seem in this case to have been chiefly in fault, to rebuild the churches which they had destroyed, and to suffer heavy penalties for their violence.

Other scenes of rivalry between the Jews and Christians occurred at various points, one of which may be particularly mentioned, as it throws light upon the singular degree of superstition and ignorance which then prevailed. A very hostile feeling existed between those sects in Borium, a town near Pentapolis, in which it was the custom for the priests to distribute the crumbs of the consecrated bread, which might remain after the celebration of the Eucharist, to the children who were sent from the schools. On one occasion the child of a Jewish glass-blower happened to be included in the number of those who were thus favored. When the father heard what had happened he became enraged, and shut his child within his blazing furnace, intending to destroy him. The mother was distracted at the cruel deed, and after some hours, as soon as an opportunity offered, she opened the furnace to look for the remains of her unfortunate offspring. Her child was then discovered sitting uninjured among the hot ashes; and he informed his mother that a lady clothed in a purple robe had appeared in the furnace and poured water on the coals which surrounded him. This lady could be no other than the Virgin Mary. The circumstances of the case soon became known, and the town was filled with holy horror at the cruelty of the Jew, mingled with pious joy at the miraculous interposition of the Virgin Mary. Everybody believed the story; the father was immediately executed, and the mother and child baptized. This incident serves to illustrate the hostile feelings existing between Jews and Christians, the degree of credulity which then prevailed among all classes of the community, as well as the vindictive nature of the penal laws as they then existed.

In the remoter East, in Persia and Mesopotamia, the fortune and condition of the Jews during the fifth and sixth centuries were of a mixed nature. In those countries the established religion was still the Magian, and its patrons were disposed to persecute both Jews and Christians with equal hostility. In consequence of the emigration of learned Rabbis and students from Palestine to Babylon and Persia, which took place in the fifth century, a revision and enlargement of the Babylonian Talmud, otherwise termed the Gemara, were made, which contributed to increase the value and authority of that work. At this period the spiritual ruler of the Jews in Persia, and the adjacent countries, was the Patriarch of Babylon, otherwise termed *Resh-Glutha*, the Prince of the Captivity. This office, as we have already narrated, arose after the dispersion of the Jews in consequence of the destruction of Jerusalem. The functions of the Prince in the first instance were rather those of a civil governor than an ecclesiastical superior; and his duties required of him to mediate between the chief Rabbis and heads of the synagogue, and the Parthian and Persian monarchs. The office was invested with a considerable degree of pomp and splendor; the Prince was in fact a Viceroy, having under his authority all the Rabbis of the various synagogues. The office continued to exist in the East until the eleventh century, when it expired in the person of Hizkiah, who was slain by the Caliph Beamzillah. Subsequent to this period we read of a "Prince of the Captivity" during the Middle Ages, among the Jews of Spain, who more generally bore the title of the *Rabino-Mayor*.

In the sixth century the chief afflictions of the Oriental Jews arose from the fierce dissensions which took place between the Prince of the Captivity, in Babylon, and the ecclesiastical head of the rabbinical schools. The former attempted to extend his authority over the latter, and the resistance which this encroachment produced led to the fiercest collisions. These difficulties reached their climax on this wise: About A. D. 539 the Prince Huna had married the daughter of Rabbi Chanina, the Master of the Rabbinical schools; yet the ambition of the former overcame all regard for family ties, and encroached on the functions of his father-in-law, undertaking to interpret the Talmud publicly in the schools. Chanina resisted this attempt; and the result of the fierce feud which followed was, that the Prince enticed Chanina into his palace, plucked out his beard, inflicted other indignities upon him, and then cast him forth, forbidding all the Jews to give him any protection, or even the necessary means of subsistence. The Chief Rabbi in his misfortunes wept and prayed, and the consequence was, as the prevalent legend asserts, that the cruel Prince suddenly died, together with every member of his family, except his wife, who was then pregnant. After the death of the Prince his vacant dignity was purchased by a person named Paphra, who held it during fifteen years. He then opportunely expired, and the son of the Prince Zutra, who was born shortly after his father's death, succeeded to the office of his ancestors, and reinstated the worthy Chanina as Chief Rabbi in his legitimate functions.

Such are some of the tragical incidents which occurred at this period among the Oriental Jews. During Zutra's reign of twenty years, a great commotion was produced among the Persian Jews by an impostor named Meir; who, as was usual with such enthusiasts, pretended to be the Messiah; and having gathered around him a body of followers, ravaged the country, and greatly endangered the safety of the whole Jewish community. Meir was executed by Kobad, the Persian monarch; and with him fell both Zutra, the Prince, and Chanina, his instructor and guide. The Jews were severely persecuted; and it was at this period that many of them emigrated to the distant coast of Malabar, where their descendants have existed during many succeeding generations. A son of Zutra fled to Tiberias; and, carrying with him the Babylonian Talmud, was the first to make the Western Jews acquainted with that extraordinary work. After the accession of the renowned Chosroes to the throne of Persia, the persecutions of the Jews continued. He ordered all their Rabbinical schools to be closed. Having made a truce with the Emperor Justinian, which was termed the "Everlasting," but which endured only seven years, Chosroes, during this interval, continued to follow the example of that Christian emperor, in placing heavy burdens and exactions on the Israelites.

Chosroes died, and was succeeded by Hormisdas, who entertained more favorable sentiments toward this proscribed people. Their schools in Babylon were reopened; a new order of rabbinical doctors, termed the *Gaonim*, or Illustrious, was created; and the Prince of the Captivity was again allowed to exercise the authority of his ancestors. After the death of Hormisdas, the succession to the throne was disputed; and the Jews unfortunately took the side of Varanes, a usurper, against that of Chosroes II., the son and rightful heir of Hormisdas. The latter soon obtained possession of the throne, and the Jews paid severely for their disaffection. Nabod, the general of Chosroes, distinguished himself by his cruelty against them. Many were slain, many were tortured, and many more were sold into slavery. But their day of vengeance was approaching. In Antioch, where they had endured the most excessive barbarities, they arose in a tumult, burnt the palaces of their most prominent and bitter enemies, slew many of them, and seizing the Patriarch Anastasius, dragged him through the streets till he expired.

In A. D. 625 an event of rare interest to the whole Jewish nation occurred. The ambitious mind of Chosroes conceived the purpose of wresting Palestine from the possession of the Roman Emperor. Nothing could be more acceptable to the Jews than this design; and they joined his invading army to the number of twenty-four thousand men. The Jews in Tyre, forty thousand in number, sent intelligence of the approaching events to their brethren who were scattered throughout Palestine, in Damascus, in Cyprus, and in Tiberias; directing them to assemble around the walls of Jerusalem on the night of the Christian Easter.

The inhabitants of that city endeavored to deter the assailants from going to extremes, by inflicting the penalty of death on those Jewish captives who happened to be in their power. At length the Persian army attacked and took the city; and with their victorious ranks, the long exiled Jews re-entered the sacred abode of their ancestors. Bloody massacres occurred within the city, and many Christians were slain. The churches were deluged with blood, and then burned to the ground. It is said that ninety thousand Christians were either slain or sold into captivity. The stately building which the Empress Helena had erected over the Holy Sepulchre, became a smouldering mass of shapeless ruins. For a time the triumph and revenge of the Jews, in return for generations of Christian persecution and cruelty, were complete; but they were destined to be of short duration. The Roman Emperor Heraclius was meanwhile preparing to wrest his conquest from the Persian hero; and at length, in A. D. 628, he succeeded in recapturing Jerusalem, in overrunning the whole of Palestine and Egypt, and regained possession of them. He then visited Jerusalem in person, as a pious pilgrim; restored the ruined churches to their former splendor, re-enacted the law of Hadrian, which forbade the Jews to enter the Holy City on pain of death, and punished their late triumph and excesses with signal severity.

CHAPTER VII.

THE JEWS IN ARABIA IN THE SIXTH CENTURY—THEIR HISTORY AND CHARACTER—ARIAN MISSIONARIES—ORIGIN OF MAHOMET—INCIDENTS OF HIS LIFE—HE SUBDUES THE ARABIAN JEWS—JEWS IN SPAIN—COUNCILS OF TOLEDO—THEIR PERSECUTION OF THE RESIDENT JEWS.

IN extending our survey of the Jewish people during the sixth century, we find them and their vicissitudes assuming a degree of importance in Arabia, where they had then already existed for some centuries. The Arabian Jews dated their first establishment in that country from the visit of the Queen of Sheba to Solomon, referred to in the Scriptures. The truth of this supposition may readily be doubted; but it is certain that a Jewish community flourished in Arabia one hundred and fifty years before the coming of Christ; at which period they were governed by a king, named Abu Caab Asaad, who was said to have been the thirty-third king of the Joktanides, called in Yemen the Homentes.

This Jewish community were divided into two branches, the Bedouins, or Nomads of the desert, who claimed to be the direct descendants of Ishmael, the son of Abraham and Hagar; and the inhabitants of the towns and cities, who were stationary and engaged in commerce, exchanging the merchandise brought by caravans from India and Persia to the traders of western Asia and Africa. When Mahomet commenced his career in Arabia about A. D. 610, the inhabitants of that country consisted of Jews, Arian Christians, worshipers of the sun after the Persian manner, and a sect called Ishmaelites, who were a degenerate people, retaining the form of religion supposed to have been observed by the ancient patriarchs. The chief abode of the Arabian Jews was in that portion of the country which boasted the name of "Arabia the Happy," in consequence of the cheering contrast presented by it to the sandy wastes which existed on one side, and the rocky soil and mountainous defiles on the other. It is supposed that it was within this attractive region that the famous Queen of Sheba held her dominion; and that the pleasant valleys of her kingdom which ran down to the shores of the Red Sea, and furnishing a fit outlet for the fragrant odors and aromatic sweetness which the products of the soil produced, and which greeted and cheered the foreign traders as they passed down toward the Arabian sea, that thus formed a convenient port, whence she sailed on her memorable visit to Solomon.

Christianity had first penetrated into Yemen by means of Arian missionaries, and consequently it exhibited the Arian form of that religion. This event probably occurred during the reign of Constantius, the son of Constantine the Great. With these Christians the Arabian Jews lived in amity, simply because they were not persecuted by them. When, however, the orthodox creed was introduced into Arabia, at a later period, from the opporite shores of the Red Sea, and through the agency of the Abyssinian kings, its partisans immediately began its usual policy of cruelty and violence. Eles-Canaan commanded Dunaan, the ruler of the Jewish community, to pay tribute, and to renounce his faith, together with his people; and when this requisition was refused, it was enforced at the point of the sword. Dunaan, though defeated, determined again to resist his oppressor, and he suddenly attacked the Christians in Yemen, slew a vast number of them, and appeared before Nagra, their capital, at the head of an immense army. He summoned the city to surrender; and a singular negotiation ensued. Dunaan demanded that they should remove the cross which surmounted their chief church; that they should acknowledge the unity of the Supreme Being, and should deny the plurality of persons in the Godhead. They refused, and Dunaan ordered all his Christian captives, who were numerous, to be slain in the sight of the besieged. The latter, overcome with terror, agreed at length to capitulate, on condition that they should be allowed the free exercise of their religion. The gates were opened, the Arabian Jews entered the city, but their leader immediately violated his promises. He arrested and finally executed an immense number of priests, monks, and nuns, and firmly established his sovereignty over the city and adjacent country, rigorously refusing all exercsie of Christian usages or worship. But the triumph of the Jews was, as usual, of short duration. In the next year, Eles-baan invaded the kingdom of Dunaan with a force, it is said, of a hundred and twenty thousand men; and after a brave and desperate resistance, Dunaan was defeated and slain, and with him expired the race of Jewish rulers in Arabia.

At length Mahomet, the great Arabian prophet and impostor, appeared. His first pretensions were only those of a reformer and a poet; and in regard to both of these capacities his first relations toward the Jews were friendly. Several of the Jewish tribes, such, for instance, as the Kazrady, the Koraidha, the Al-nadir, who all traced their origin to Aaron the son of Amran, became his open partisans, and were termed by him his auxiliaries. He also altered and modified some of his precepts in order to please the Jews of Medina. But as Mahomet began to develop his system more completely, and to demonstrate its utter irreconcilability with the Jewish religion, they abandoned him. It is probable that they at first may have regarded Mahomet as the promised Messiah; but as soon as his principles and plans became more thoroughly known, they rejected him as an impostor. From that moment he declared a war of extermination against them, and soon commenced the active work of subjugation and desolation. He asserted, as by express revelation from heaven, that the fires of hell should consume them utterly.

The first attack of Mahomet on the Jews was against the tribe of Kainoka, who dwelt in Medina. He summoned them to embrace Islamism, and commanded them to "lend to the Lord on good interest." Phincas, the head of the Jewish community, replied derisively, that the Lord must have become impoverished to stand in need of a loan. Before the deliberations had come to a conclusion, an untoward event precipitated the crisis. A Jewish goldsmith insulted an Arab girl, and the Arabs slew the offender. The Jews flew to the citadel of the town, and defended themselves against the attacks of the prophet for fifteen days. They were then compelled to surrender. At first a general massacre was ordered, but it was afterward changed into confiscation of goods and banishment into the desert. The unfortunate tribe were subsequently driven forth to seek a resting place and find a home on the confines of Syria.

Mahomet next attacked the tribe of Nadir, who had indeed given him some provocation by attempting his life at a banquet. He beseiged them in their chief castle, about three miles distant from Medina, but they resisted his efforts so obstinately, that he was compelled at last to allow them favorable terms, and to withdraw with the honors of war. Still another tribe of Jews were destined to feel his prowess. These were the Koraidha, who, uniting with the Arab tribe of Koreish, presented a formidable front to their common enemy. They united their forces, and besieged Mahomet in his capital, to the number of ten thousand men. He resisted until a furious storm opportunely destroyed the camp and the resources of his assailants, and compelled them to retire. He then attacked the Jewish tribe of Koraidha separately, and defeated them. They were compelled to come forth from their castle, though they expected to receive honorable terms. Mahomet referred their fate to the decision of his venerable friend Saad, whose cruel judgment was, that all the males should be put to death, and all the women and children sold into slavery. Mahomet exclaimed, enthusiastically, that it was a divine and infallible sentence, descended from the highest of the seven heavens. Seven hundred Jews were accordingly dragged forth, their graves dug in the market-place of Medina, they were commanded to descend into them, and then slain and buried as they fell. Mahomet praised this horrid scene by a chapter of special revelation contained in the Koran.

Still another tribe of hostile Jews remained to be subdued by the Arabian impostor, and in his struggles for their extermination the consequences to himself were much more serious. These were the Khaibar, who inhabited a fertile district six days' journey to the south of Medina, and possessed eight strong castles. Their country was rich in palm trees and pastures. The prophet's force consisted of fourteen hundred foot, and two hundred horsemen. As he entered their territory, he urged his troops to advance with redoubled speed, and offered a prayer that the Lord of the heavens, and the earth, and of the demons, and of the winds, would grant him the spoil of his enemies, and preserve him from evil. The first part of this prayer was granted; but the last was refused. The Jews of Khaibar apprehended no attack from any source, and were, therefore, living in repose and security. Their first castle, called Naem, was easily taken. The defenders of the second made a more vigorous resistance, and, during the siege, the prophet and his troops were reduced to very great distress, as all the palm trees and wells in the surrounding country had been destroyed. At length, however, Mahomet prevailed and triumphed, and he passed on to the third fortress, called Alkamas, which was occupied and defended by Marhaba, a colossal and valiant Jew. At this place Ali, the chief military hero of the prophet, distinguished himself by his bravery, and, it is said, clove the skull of Marhaba through his shield, two turbans, and a diamond which he wore in his helmet, until at last his sword stuck in the jaws of his fallen foe. After this achievement, the besieged capitulated, and the most horrid excesses ensued. Kenana, the chief man of the Jews, was cruelly tortured to compel him to disclose the spot where their treasures had been concealed but he expired in agony without opening his lips. The remaining castles of their unfortunate tribe capitulated on condition of surrendering, yearly, one-half of their revenues to the prophet, though he reserved the right to exile them at any subsequent period, should he desire to do so. This right was afterward exercised by the Caliph Omar, who resolved that none but members of the true faith should exist within the confines of Arabia, and the Jews of Khaibar were banished by him to Syria. It was while Mahomet was before the castle of Chiebar, the last which capitulated, that the wrongs which he inflicted on the Jews were avenged by the act of the niece of the unfortunate Marhaba. The fair Zeinah became the captive, and of course the concubine, of Mahomet. She, in return, presented him with a roasted sheep, which she had thoroughly poisoned. Having merely tasted it, Mahomet was warned not to indulge any further; but so violent was the poison, that its fatal effects lurked in his constitution, and became the ultimate cause of his death a few years afterward, in A. D. 632. The descendants of these Arabian Jews have never been entirely exiled from Arabia, but they have existed there in all ages since, and in the mountainous country of Chiebar, to the northeast of Medina, modern travelers relate that there still exist three distinct tribes of Jews, whom the Arabs call *Beni Chieba*, which they regard as a term of reproach. In 1843 the Jews in Aden were visited by Dr. Wilson, the author of the "Lands of the Bible," and he found their number there to amount to one thousand and seventy.

We turn from these details to the scene of the darkest and fiercest persecution which this unfortunate race have ever been compelled to endure during their whole history; for *Spain*, in accordance with the gloominess and malignity of the character of its inhabitants, has ever been the scene of the direst sufferings and the most infamous cruelties to the Hebrew.

As early as the sixth century of the Christian era, the Israelites had become numerous and opulent in Spain, while at the same time Christianity had kept pace with it as the dominant religion. During the reign of Recared, the first Catholic sovereign of the

Gothic race, the long continued and relentless work of persecution began. He issued edicts to the effect that the Jews should not celebrate the Passover according to their usual custom; that they should in no case be permitted to bring suit against a Christian in a court of justice; that they should never be allowed to bear testimony against a Christian; that they should not be allowed to contract marriages according to their own usages, and should abstain from circumcision. During the seventh century a number of Ecclesiastical Councils were held in Spain, especially at Toledo, and the spirit of animosity toward the utterly harmless Jews was infamous and damnable. Thus the Sixth Council of Toledo decreed that every Spanish king, on the occasion of his accession to the throne, should take an oath to enforce against the Jews all the severe edicts which had already been passed. Such terror had been inspired by the display of this hostile spirit that many Israelites were overcome by it, and informed the Council by a deputation, that they were willing to adopt the Christian religion except as to the matter of eating pork; that their aversion to the meat of that unclean beast was unconquerable. Even this accommodation to an innocent and perhaps even a wise prejudice, they could not obtain.

A singular development was made in a decree passed by the Tenth Council of Toledo, by which it appears that some of these persecuting bigots, who could consign their fellow-men to misery and sometimes to death, in consequence of their conscientious scruples, were in reality such infamous hypocrites as to sell

Christian slaves whom they owned to Jewish purchasers, when by so doing they could obtain a higher price! The words of the Council were as follows: "Even many of the *clergy*— a fact monstrous and incredulous—pursue an execrable traffic with the ungodly, and do not scruple to sell to them Christian slaves, and thus give them up to the peril of being converted to Judaism." Even in this decree the zealous Council did not condemn the traffic in human property because *it* was wrong, or contrary to the spirit of Christianity, but only because those who sold Christians as slaves sold them as such *to Jews!*

The Twelfth Council of Toledo, held under the reign of Ervig, about the year A. D. 680, exceeded all its predecessors in cruelty; for while it approved of the persecuting decrees which had been previously passed, it added thereto others which have been unparalleled in the annals of judicial or legislative ferocity. It decreed that any Jew who profaned or ridiculed the name of Christ, or rejected the Lord's Supper, or blasphemed and denied the Trinity; who refused to have his children and servants baptized, but observed the Passover, the New Moon, or the Feast of Tabernacles; who desecrated the Christian Sabbath, or any of the church festivals, by working in the field or in his shop, should be punished with one hundred lashes on the naked body; after which he should be put in chains, banished from the country forever, and all his property confiscated!

This assemblage of sanctimonious demons further enacted, that if a Jewish father circumcised his child, his person should be mutilated, and the consenting mother have her nose cut off, and all her property confiscated! The same penalty was inflicted on any person who was instrumental in converting a Christian to Judaism. Scourging, imprisonment, banishment and confiscation, were inflicted on all who made "any difference in meats;" that is, who did not relish hog's meat as much as roast beef. No marriage could thereafter be celebrated, unless it was expressly stipulated that both parties would become Christians. All the Christian subjects who harbored, assisted, or concealed a Jew who was subject to these penalties, were to be scourged and lose their property. Whoever received a bribe from a a Jew to induce him to connive at the practice of the Jewish religion, was fined thrice the amount of the sum received. The Jew who himself read or permitted his children to read any book against Christianity, received a hundred lashes for the first offense; for the second he was banished and his property confiscated. All those Jews who held slaves were ordered to bring them on a certain day to the churches to be baptized, under very severe penalties. All Jewish slaves, by professing to embrace Christianity at once, were declared to be free. No Jew could receive any office which gave him authority over Christians. No priest or bishop could intrust any church property to a Jew, under a very severe penalty. No Jew could travel from one town to another without permission from a bishop or a judge. Whoever protected a Jew against the tyranny of his overseer, should be excommunicated, and pay a very heavy fine.

A subsequent Council, convened at Toledo, decreed that all the property of the Jews should be confiscated to the use of the Royal treasury; that all their children under seventeen years of age should be taken from them and brought up as Christians, and the whole Jewish community be sold as slaves. The result of such fiendish barbarity was that myriads of Jews instantly fled from Spain and crossed over into Africa, where, under the mild dominion of the Moorish Caliphs, they enjoyed security and repose. Those who were unable to effect their escape learned, by sad experience, the utmost excesses of ecclesiastical bigotry and ferocity, inflicted under the specious disguise of earnest zeal for the supremacy of the true faith.

CHAPTER VIII.

JEWS IN FRANCE IN THE SIXTH CENTURY—SCENES IN CLERMONT—EVENTS AT TOURS—RELATIONS BETWEEN THE JEWS AND THE MOSLEM SOVEREIGNS—FACTIONS AMONG THE JEWS—THE ORIGIN OF THE KARAITES—THEIR DOCTRINES—THE KINGDOM OF KHOZAN—JEWS IN THE BYZANTINE EMPIRE—LEO THE ISAURIAN.

IF the condition of the Jews in Spain, during the sixth century, was one of extreme misery and excessive persecution, they were the victims of nearly equal cruelties in the neighboring kingdom of France. The Merovingian princes, who then ruled over the several provinces of that country, and whose lives were generally divided between their excesses of debauchery and their mutual conflicts of ambition, agreed at least on one point: that it was their duty and their interest to persecute the Jews. In this amiable work they were assisted, and perhaps impelled, by the zealous co-operation of the clergy; and the annals of those times exhibit proofs that some of those who were the most prominent teachers of Christianity, were utterly ignorant or neglectful of its spirit. Examples like the following prove the truth of this observation.

Avitus, the Bishop of Clermont, instigated the people on Ascension Day to surround the Synagogue in that city and destroy it. When the Jews were duly impressed with terror at this display of the popular feeling respecting them, Avitus sent them a message that they must either abjure their religion immediately or leave the city. He added, however, with a mockery of hypocritical charity, that he did not wish to force them to embrace Christianity, but generously gave them the choice of either of those alternatives. The Jews refused both, and hastily assembling in a large building, they shut themselves within it with their wives and children. The infuriated mob surrounded the edifice, and threatened to force the doors and assassinate every one of them. Overwhelmed with terror, the Jews sent word to the Bishop, beseeching deliverance and promising to comply with his demands. The result was, that five hundred Jews, to avoid being massacred, were publicly baptized on the ensuing Whitsunday; but every rational person will readily believe that conversions produced by such detestable means could not be safely regarded as sincere, and as being more disgraceful than honorable to Christianity and to its over-zealous representatives.

Another circumstance, displaying a similar spirit, occurred at Tours. A wealthy Jew named Priscus, residing at that city, was the chief banker of Chilperic, the king; who was grieved at the reflection that his necessities compelled him to be dependent on an Israelite. He accordingly employed Gregory, the Bishop, to exert his utmost efforts to convert Priscus to the true religion; but the latter was not convinced by his arguments, and remained attached to his hereditary faith. He was soon afterward assassinated when on his way to the Synagogue, by a renegade Jew, who was supposed to have been incited to the deed by the discomfited Bishop; and one circumstance which seems to confirm this supposition is the fact, that the murderer fled to the church and was securely protected there by the Bishop against all the agents and processes of the law. After the lapse of some time, however, he deserted his asylum, supposing that the rage of the avengers had subsided. He was mistaken, and was eventually slain privately by the hand of some one who was probably employed by the family of Priscus. About this period the French synods repeatedly forbade, by their decrees, the Jews to marry Christians, excluded them from all offices of trust and emolument, and made as many distinctions of an unfavorable character as they could between the members of this race and all others.

It is a singular circumstance which has been demonstrated by the whole history of the Israelites, that they have generally been treated with more charity and forbearance by Mahomedan communities and sovereigns, than by those which professed to be Christian. After Mahomet had subjugated the various tribes who inhabited Arabia, as already narrated, some of whom were Jews; and thus executed his determination that none but his own followers should exist in that country, very few instances ever afterward occurred in which his successors on the throne treated the Jews with rigor, while, on the contrary, they usually protected and favored them. Thus, even during the reigns of Mahomet's immediate successors, wherever their conquering armies marched, many Jews attended them, who supplied the wants of the commissariat department. Their ships and caravans, loaded with corn and other provisions, followed their path, and the Jews were always protected in the sale of their property. Their superior intelligence and thrift rendered them valuable allies, and no prejudice existed against them to interfere with the advancement of their interests. Accordingly, when the celebrated Colossus of Rhodes, appropriately called one of the Seven Wonders of the world, was displaced from its position over the mouth of the harbor of that city, the prostrate mass was sold to a Jew of Emesa, at such a price as made him wealthy; and nine hundred camels are said to have been requisite to carry away the broken metal.

It was at this period, in the seventh century, that the Jews had generally exchanged their agricultural occupations for the more secure and remunerative labors of traffic; and they were gradually acquiring the character of the money-changers and money-lenders of the world. During the reign of Omar, the second caliph, so important had the Jews become in his dominions, that the financial department of the administration was chiefly in their hands, and the coinage was entrusted to the care of one of them. To avoid the crime of stamping an image on the circulating medium, the monarch was relieved by the adroit proposition that the words, "There is but one God," should be substituted, a doctrine in reference to which both Jews and Moslems agreed. Omar was a secret follower of Ali, the prophet's vicar, whose name was, at that time, publicly cursed in the Mosques; and he formed the purpose of abolishing the custom, and uniting in friendship the secret partisans of that hero with the rest of the Mahomedan community. To accomplish this result, he had recourse to the preconcerted agency of a Jew, as follows: At a full assemblage of the courtiers and officers of the kingdom in the palace, this Jew boldly approached the sovereign, as he sat on the throne, and demanded his daughter in marriage. Omar replied that he could not give his daughter in marriage to a person of another faith. The Jew rejoined that Mahomet had married his daughter to Ali. To this the caliph answered, that the two cases were not parallel, because Ali was a Moslemite, and the Commander of the Faithful. "Why, then," demanded the Jew, "do you curse him in your mosques?" The caliph then turned to his courtiers, and said: "Answer ye the question of the Jew." A long silence ensued, broken by no response. At last, Omar, as if suddenly convinced of the absurdity and iniquity of the practice, commanded it to be thenceforth abolished forever.

Incidents such as these clearly indicate the favorable position occupied by the Israelites under the dominion of the Mahomedan monarchs. During the eighth century they were permitted to have schools for the instruction of their Rabbis, which became celebrated for their learning; and the order of the Gaonim, or Illustrious, flourished as the most eminent of the Rabbinical doctors. As is generally the case with all men under such circumstances, prosperity led to rashness and freedom; and the school or community of Karaites became more numerous than ever. These were the Protestants or Rationalists of Judaism, who opposed the authority, and condemned some of the teachings of the Rabbins. They rejected the authority of tradition, of the Cabala, of the Mischna, of the Gamara, of the whole body of Talmudic learning, and adhered solely to the written law, as contained in the Old Testament. The chief leaders of this sect at this time were Anan and his son Saul. Disappointed ambition seems to have had something to do with their hostility against the orthodox Jewish faith; because, when a successor was to be chosen to fill the shadowy dignity of the "Princedom of the Captivity," which still continued to exist, Anan, who was a candidate, was rejected, and another was appointed. Anan assembled the remains of the Sadducean faction, who might be termed, in some respects, the predecessors of the Karaites, even in the time of Christ; and he induced them to elect him to the vacant post, thus creating a rival office and a rival incumbent. The consequence was that violent tumults arose between the two factions, and Anan was imprisoned by the reigning caliph as the cause of the disturbance. He succeeded, however, in making his escape by the payment of a heavy bribe; and he then retired, together with many of the Karaites, to the vicinity of Jerusalem, where they continued to believe and to practice the simple tenets of their faith, and to condemn the innovations of the Rabbins.

The former consisted of the pure and unadulterated doctrines which they supposed to constitute the original system of the Mosaic dispensation, and were as follows:

1. That the world and all things were created.
2. That they had an uncreated Creator.
3. That God is without any form, and is in every sense one.
4. That he sent Moses on his mission.
5. That God delivered the perfect law to Moses.
6. That the believer must derive his faith from the study of the law as taught in its original language, and from the pure interpretation of it.
7. That God inspired the rest of the prophets.
8. That God will raise the dead at the day of judgment.
9. That God will reward and punish all men according to their deeds.
10. That God has not rejected the Jews, but that he was purifying them by their sufferings, and preparing them to be redeemed by the coming Messiah.

It is said that the sect of the Karaites exist till this day in various countries, under other names; and that they are still hated and condemned by the Rabbins and their partisans, who constitute the majority of the Jewish community.

This remarkable sect derive their name from the word *kara*, which signifies the *text;* and hence their peculiar characteristic of close adhesion to the Old Testament Scriptures. They claim to have existed as early as the time of Daniel and Ezekiel. They also asserted that Christ himself was one of their number. It is probable that they were *not* identical with the Sadducees, because the latter rejected a portion of the Scriptures even in the time of Christ. The Karaites practice circumcision; they refuse to wear fringes in public worship, as other Jews do, except at morning prayer, when they use the *talith*, which is made of cotton, and has four fringes. The Orthodox Jews have eight threads to their fringes, whereas the Karaites have thirty-two. The Rabbinists make their fringes only of white wool, the others of white and blue silk. The feasts of the New Year and of Pentecost continue among the former two days, among the Karaites only one. Among the former, the feast of dedication continues during eight days; the Karaites do not observe it at all. The latter have four feasts during the year, on the 7th and 10th of *Ab*, on the 10th of *Tabeth*, and the Day of Atonement. Some other differences exist between these two sects of minor importance which serve to keep them separate and even hostile. The Karaites exist in different numbers, in the various countries of Europe, and also in the United States. They are regarded by the great body of the Jews as innovators, while they themselves claim the character of Reformers, desiring to divest the Jewish faith and religion of the additions and corruptions made by Rabbinnical writers and teachers, and bring them back to their primitive simplicity and purity.

About the eighth century a singular development occurred in the history of this people, which furnishes a contrast to the dependence and persecution which were their customary fate. At that period a numerous and powerful tribe of Turkomans inhabited the region of country which exists between the rivers Don and Wolga, in which there were many large and opulent towns. These people exchanged the furs, the dried fish, and the slaves of the northeastern countries of Europe, for the precious metals and the luxurious articles of the South; and traders of many nations constantly visited their ports, among whom the Jews greatly predominated.. At length these people, by their superior intelligence, obtained so great an influence over Bulan, the King of the Turkomans, that in A. D. 740, he publicly announced his conversion to their religion, and he invited Jews and Jewish Rabbis to settle in his territories. He also enacted that devotion to the Jewish religion should be an indispensable characteristic in all his successors upon the throne. His kingdom was known as that of *Khozar.*

This Jewish monarchy, for it well deserved the name, continued to flourish during two centuries and a half, and the fame of it gradually spread over Europe. It attracted much attention; and there were peculiarities connected with it, which naturally made it an object of scrutiny. The king was held in mysterious reverence, and seemed to have had something of a sacred and judicial character. His authority was absolute, and when he ordered his high officers to *slay themselves,* in punishment of some offense which he supposed them to have committed, they are recorded to have at once retired to their homes, and invariably obeyed the command. This singular sovereignty was made more particularly known to the communities of Western Europe by means of Rabbi Hasdai ben Isaac, an eminent and learned Spanish Jew, who addressed a letter to the King of Khoraz, desiring more particular information in reference to himself and the people over whom he ruled.

Rabbi Hasdai lived at Cordova, in Spain, and the great respectability of his character rendered his communication worthy of notice; and after the lapse of some time King Joseph, to whom it was addressed, returned an answer. In it he informed Hasdai that he was the twelfth sovereign of his dynasty; that Bulan, the first of the line, had been converted to Judaism by means of a Divine vision; that the people of Khozar were descended from Japhet and Thogarma, and were related to the Jews through their forefathers' blood; and that they obeyed the law of the Rabbis of the Babylonian and Syrian schools. This letter contained other details descriptive of the extent and resources of the country. As the letter sent by Rabbi Hasdai is more authentic, and as it is a curious specimen of antique writing, containing details which are themselves interesting, we here insert it. The author speaks in the third person, as was proper, while addressing a great potentate like the King of Kohzar; and after using a complimentary and respectful introduction, he continued as follows:

"He believes that the great distance between countries is the cause of ignorance which has hitherto prevailed in Spain respecting the kingdom of Khozar, although report said that already a few learned Spaniards, namely, R. Juda bar Meir bar Nathan and R. Joseph, had the fortune to be shipwrecked on the coast of Khozar, and had beheld the magnificence of that land with their own eyes—a fortune which he wished he had experienced for himself, although he served a king who was considered the greatest of all the caliphs, inasmuch as he governed fertile and wealthy Spain, (of which he would add also a brief mathematical and physical description,) and many kings sought to obtain his favor. He, Hasdai, had the office of receiving all the ambassadors and delivering their presents to his king. He had embraced every opportunity to inquire of ambassadors coming from distant countries about the kingdom of Khozar, but received no intelligence. It was true that a few merchants from Chorazin had given reports of it; but their accounts appeared to him incredible, and he had perceived interested motives in their narrations. However, the ambassadors from Constantinople confirmed him in the existence of a real Jewish kingdom in Khozar, and added that there were still other nations by land between the Greek and Khozar kingdoms, whilst by water a close connection existed between both; that the Khozarites sent fish, hides and other merchandise, to Constantinople; and that, generally, the commerce with the Khozarites was very brisk; and, finally, that the name of the present king was Joseph.

"He had sought for a faithful messenger in order to dispatch him with a letter to Khozar, and had bestowed this commission (the acceptance of which was declined by so many) on a certain R. Isaak ben Nathan, and furnished him with money and recommendations to the Court of Constantinople; but he had been obliged, after the lapse of six months, to return without accomplishing his object, because, said he, the sea was navigable only at certain seasons, and also much too stormy, and the people in the country were engaged in war. This had occasioned him much grief. He had subsequently requested some persons from Palestine to send the letter, and they had promised him to forward it by way of Nisibis and Armenia, inasmuch as the ambassadors of the king of Gabal (interpreted by Al Kozolow, both of whom being unknown to us) had arrived, who had brought with them two Jewish Rabbis, M. Saul and M. Joseph, who had taken upon themselves to forward the present document by other ambassadors to its destination.

"The king has promised to answer this letter by his secretary, and to give him intelligence as to the tradition about a primeval emigration of the Jews from the region of Mount Seir (not the one spoken of in the Bible) to a region which was probably the same with the Khozarites; he lamented that a Khozarite, (according to the account of those men,) who had arrived six years before and been well received at the court of Spain, and who, notwithstanding every endeavor to find him, was not to be found.

"Since he had been thus deprived of the prospect of obtaining more particular intelligence of that kingdom, he would request him to send an exact account of the country of Khozar; the constitution; the internal condition; its inhabitants and products; the provinces subjected to him; the customary wars; moreover the history of the nation and every thing which might be of interest."

After the lapse of several centuries the kingdom of Khozar gradually lost its identity with the Jewish race, in consequence of the influx of foreigners and the change of dynasty; so that at the present time no traces of their former existence can be there discovered.

During the eighth century the condition of the Jews in the Byzantine or eastern portion of the Roman empire continued to be favorable. The sovereigns sometimes sat upon an insecure and tottering throne, and their precarious situation rendered them more disposed to conciliate all classes of their subjects than they might otherwise have been. The Jews profited by these propitious influences, and rose to influence and power by means of their wealth. When the iconoclastic or image-breaking spirit took possession of the Emperors, and induced them to destroy the innumerable fabrications of that sort with which the Christian churches had been crowded, the Jews were charged with having instigated the sacrilege. This circumstance clearly shows the importance which they had attained in the Eastern empire. A romantic incident is also narrated in reference to the accession of the Emperor Leo to the purple, which though of doubtful authority, deserves to be narrated. It is said that two Jews while reposing near a fountain in Isauria, saw a young man pass by who was driving an ass laden with merchandise; and they influenced by some sudden and mysterious impulse, saluted him as the future Emperor, at the same time urging him, after his elevation, to the strict fulfillment of the second commandment. The obscure youth afterward became Emperor under the name of Leo the Isuarian; and he signalized his reign by his zeal against images. Constantine Copronymus, Nicephorus, and Michael the Stammerer, who subsequently wore the purple, displayed the same peculiar zeal; and in return they were generally regarded as the patrons and the allies of the Jews. How far this designation was deserved it is difficult to determine; but during their reigns the Israelites were protected in their rights, and shielded from the fires and torments of persecution, throughout the Byzantine empire.

9*

CHAPTER IX.

ACCESSION OF CHARLEMAGNE—HIS TREATMENT OF HIS JEWISH SUBJECTS—HIS EMBASSY TO HAROUN AL RASCHID—ZEDEKIAH—CONDITION OF THE JEWS IN FRANCE—BISHOP AGOBARD—REIGN OF CHARLES THE BALD—MOORISH DYNASTY IN SPAIN—THE CALIPHS OF BAGDAD—JEWISH SEMINARY AT TOLEDO.

WITH the accession of Charlemagne to the imperial throne, the Golden Age of the Jewish people began in France and Germany; and it continued not only during his lifetime, but during that of several of his immediate successors. That enlightened and powerful monarch readily discovered that the Jews were a harmless people; that, if not oppressed and persecuted, they would be excellent and valuable subjects; that they had no equals in the departments of finance and commerce; that all the injuries which they had endured were undeserved, and were the result of bigotry, fanaticism and jealousy; and that the most judicious as well as equitable policy was, to permit them to live in the enjoyment of the same advantages which were possessed by the rest of his subjects.

Accordingly, the prosperity and security of the Jews during the reign of Charlemagne were greater than they had been at any previous period. Though he was a member and patron of the Roman Catholic

Church, he was not the supple tool of the hierarchy, in their efforts to induce him to withdraw from them his protection. He even went so far as to oppose some of the proceedings of those who then held ecclesiastical power; and, among other things, he condemned the use of the worship of images in the churches, which, for the first time, was pronounced an orthodox custom by the second Council of Nice, which convened in A. D. 737. The protection extended by Charlemagne to the Jews was exhibited by many significant facts, such as the following:

In the year 797 he dispatched an embassy to the illustrious Caliph, Haroun al Raschid, which was composed of Counts Sigismund and Lanfred, and a distinguished Jew named Isaac. The last was the most important person of the three; and the success of the mission was due chiefly to his agency, for he alone could speak the Oriental languages, and thus hold direct communication with the Court and Sovereign of Bagdad. Four years were spent by Isaac in the accomplishment of this mission, and he returned to Europe with the most magnificent presents for his imperial master, among which was an enormous elephant, whose subsequent death was considered an event of such importance that it was duly chronicled by the chief historians of the time. The object of this mission to Bagdad has never been ascertained. Some supposed that it was to procure the transfer of the sovereignty of Judea from Mahometan to Christian rule; others thought that it was to obtain possession of Jerusalem;—but whatever may have been its design, the results attained by the skill and influence of Isaac were highly satisfactory; so much so, indeed, that Charlemagne appointed him to perform a similar journey, and to execute the same functions at the Court of Persia.

Other illustrations of Jewish prosperity, at that period, might be adduced. The chief physician of the monarch was a Jew named Zedekiah, who enjoyed his utmost confidence. All the unjust exactions and laws which had previously existed against this people were annulled, and the Emperor bestowed many privileges upon them. He allowed them to refuse the ordeal of fire and water, one of the absurd and cruel monstrosities used in that age to discover the truth or falsehood of accusations. He released them from several oppressive taxes, under which they had long suffered, such as the *Paraverdum*, or tax for exemption from furnishing post-horses for the high roads; the *Mansionaticum*, or tax for exemption from furnishing lodging for soldiers; and the *Telonium*, or tax on imports from foreign countries. Charlemagne confirmed all these privileges to the Jews by a public edict in 830, addressed to two distinguished Israelites, named Rabbi Domat and his son Samuel. As may readily be anticipated, these advantages were so industriously improved by the Jews that they soon attained to unexampled wealth and influence. The entire trade of France and Germany with Venice and the Levant was in their hands. In the south of France they were the most influential portion of the community. At Narbonne, one of the three chief magistrates of the city, during many years, was a Jew; and, to please the people, the fairs, which had always been held on Saturdays, were subsequently held, by imperial decrees, upon another day. Lyons was the centre of their wealth and influence; and they resided in the most splendid portion of the city. The Jews were placed on the same footing, throughout the empire, with the rest of the subjects. If any dispute arose between a Jew and a Christian, it was settled by six arbitrators, three of whom belonged to each of the rival religions; and if they failed in coming to a decision, the matter was referred to the Emperor, who invariably dispensed impartial justice between the litigants. The governors and magistrates of provinces were ordered to permit the Jews to travel from town to town with their merchandise, without exacting any toll from them. Priests were forbidden to baptize the slaves of Jewish masters without their permission.

The effect of such liberal legislation on the part of the Christian inhabitants of France was most favorable; for they lived with the Jews on terms of the utmost familiarity and friendship. It is said, even, that they took part in Jewish festivals, occasionally attended the synagogues, and often preferred the Jewish to the Christian preachers. Frequent marriages took place between the two races, for the beauty of Jewish women was as transcendant then as it has generally been in all lands and ages. We even read of a deacon who, in A. D. 839, became a public convert to the Jewish faith, and received the rite of circumcision. In Lyons and its vicinity, it seemed to be a doubtful question whether the Jewish race were not more opulent, influential and prosperous than the Christian, and whether the synagogue were not more potent than the church.

This state of things excited the malignity of the priesthood to an unparalleled extent; and it was the more intense from the fact that, for a long time, their opposition was perfectly impotent. All their exertions to undermine the influence and injure the prosperity of the Jews, during the reign of Charlemagne, were utterly useless. With his successor, Louis le Debonnaire, they were equally powerless. An attempt was made to ruin Zedekiah, that monarch's physician, who had held the same important office in the Court of Charlemagne. They attributed his long-continued influence to the power of magic; and they narrated stories how he swallowed a whole cartfull of hay, together with the horses, and how he had been seen flying in the air, as was asserted of Simon Magus of old. But all the falsehoods which were fabricated against the Jews failed to accomplish the intended purpose. At length Agobard, the Bishop of Lyons, could endure their prosperity in silence no longer, for he beheld them occupying the choicest and handsomest dwellings of that city; their innumerable vessels crowding its busy port; their bales of merchandise covering the quays; their extensive and elegant importations adorning the shops; their slaves and servants crowding the thoroughfares; their brilliant equipages flashing along the streets; their bankers and money-changers most potent in the halls of finance; their women most applauded and admired in the polished circles of fashion; their Rabbis and doctors most renowned for learning and eloquence among the celebrities of the day. He commenced his operations with the members of his own church, and forbade Christians to have any intercourse whatever with the detested race; but the Jews complained of this insult to the King Louis, and he ordered the irate Agobard to give them no further disturbance. But the animosity of the prelate could not be restrained, and he ordered his people not to do any labor for the Jews on Sunday, or to eat with them during Lent, or to buy any meat which had been prepared by them, or after their custom, or to drink their wine. These annoyances drew forth another indignant protest from the Israelites, and another prohibitory edict from the king, annulling the counsels and orders of the bishop.

Thus provoked and foiled, Agobard fretted and fumed, and drew up a long memorial against the Jews, which, having made a journey to Paris, he presented in person to the king; at the same time using his utmost exertions and authority, and that of his Order, to diminish the influence which they had attained and exercised. He preferred many accusations against them, asserting that they sold unhealthy meat and wine to the Christians; that they cursed the Christians in guttural and unintelligible Hebrew in their synagogues; that they boasted of their favor with the king in the most overbearing and insulting manner; that by the change of the market day from Saturday, the Jewish synagogues were more crowded than the Christian churches; and last, though most important of all, that they stole the children of Christians, and sold them into slavery to the Moors. The bishop concluded his memorial by adding a long theological argument to prove that it was the duty of all Christian monarchs to persecute and punish the Jews; how St. Paul approved it; how eminent prelates in earlier times, such as Hillary and Appollinaris, had set the excellent example of it; and how the Rabbis taught the most blasphemous doctrines, such as that the letters of the Hebrew alphabet were eternal, and that the name of Christ ought to be derided and blasphemed. All these assertions were nothing but a string of sanctimonious and malignant lies, and so the king, Louis, regarded them. Agobard was received very coldly by the monarch; was compelled to wait a long time in the ante-chamber, which he regarded as a great insult; and was ordered at last to return to his diocese without having accomplished any part of his amiable mission. The result was that the Jews were more protected and prosperous than before; and the mortified prelate poured forth his indignation and spite in a long epistle to his friend Nebridius, the Bishop of Narbonne, whose views on the subject sympathized with his own. He charged the Jews with being "clothed with cursing as with a garment." The cursing was, however, all on the side of the exemplary Christian bishop; for in this epistle he proceeded to execrate the objects of his hatred in a most lavish and wholesale manner,—asserting that their cursedness penetrated to their very bones, marrow and entrails; in the city and in the country; at the beginning and the ending of their lives; in their flocks, meats, granaries, cellars, and magazines of every kind. One consequence of the publication of this letter, so perfect a model of Christian charity and love, was, that one of the highest officers in the royal palace at once abjured the Christian faith and joined the synagogue.

During the reign of Charles the Bald, the son of Louis le Debonnaire, the condition of the Jews in France remained equally prosperous; the only difference between their condition and that of the rest of his subjects, being that they paid into the public treasury a tenth of their gains, while the Christians only an eleventh. The chief banker and treasurer of that monarch was an Israelite named Judah, and he was employed by Charles to perform a mission to Barcelona, and convey thither a present of ten pounds of silver intended for the cathedral of that city. Zedekiah still continued to hold the office of royal physician, although it is asserted that he was bribed by an enormous sum to shorten the life of the sovereign by administering poison; on which charge, whether true or false, he was disgraced and broken on the wheel in the succeeding reign.

It was during the reign of Charles the Bald that the prosperity of the Jews in France began to decline. The gradual rise and supremacy of the feudal system, which took place after the invasion of the Normans, were injurious to the interests of the Israelites; and in proportion as the feudal lords, in conjunction and alliance with the ecclesiastical dignitaries, obtained great authority over the people, the prejudice entertained by the latter against the Jews influenced the conduct and feelings of the former; and the combined tyranny and animosity of both sorely pressed upon the obnoxious race. Their persecutions began by efforts to compass their conversion to Christianity. Even in Lyons many converts were made; and so many Jewish children were persuaded away from their parents, that the Jews were compelled to send their offspring to Vienne, Arles, and other cities where less animosity and zeal prevailed against them, in order to continue and complete their education. As soon as the prelates discovered that they could carry on the work with impunity, they assembled in council at Meaux, and passed a decree excluding the Jews in future from all participation in civil offices; and another council, convened soon afterward at Paris, adopted a similar edict. The death of Charles the Bald, which, as we have said, was ascribed to the purchased perfidy of his Jewish physician, was the signal for the commencement of the ancient horrors of unrestrained persecution against them.

Cotemporary with the Golden Age of Judaism in France was the halcyon era of Judaism in Spain. From the period of the conquest of that country by the Moors, in the middle of the ninth century, till the end of the tenth, the Israelites lived on terms of perfect social and political equality with the Moslems. It was in and around the opulent cities of Cordova and Granada that the civilization, arts and commerce of the triumphant Moorish race centred; and there also the Jewish people, nursed and cheered by external advantages, and by propitious influences, attained a degree of distinction, cultivation and splendor, which had been unknown to them since the downfall of Jerusalem.

The dynasty of the Moors in Spain well deserved to be termed magnificent, and it soon became the rival of the Caliphate of Bagdad; and these two kingdoms were the most splendid seats of Mahometan power which existed in that age. In Spain the Jews attained such prosperity that their chief men held high offices at the court of the Moorish sovereigns. They equaled in wealth the most opulent of the Moors. Their commerce extended along the whole northern coast of Africa and crowded the ports of the Mediterranean, and they lived on terms of the greatest intimacy and equality with the Mahometan community. They then began to cultivate literature with much success, so that their learned men became very celebrated in theology, medicine and astronomy. The ancient harp of Judah, which had hung for so many ages in mournful silence on the willows, was then taken down, and its sounding chords swept by masterly hands, which elicited melodies that rivaled those of the olden time; and hymns were then composed in the Hebrew language, which are used to this day in the services of the synagogues of Germany.

About this period the Caliph of Bagdad unwisely persecuted the Jews; and many of those who resided in Babylon fled from their native land toward the more friendly climes of the west. It is recorded that three eminent Rabbis were taken captive at sea by a Spanish pirate, who was ignorant of their character and quality, and sold as slaves in the market of Cordova. One of these, Rabbi Moses, together with his son, were ransomed and set free by a Jew of that city, who was also in ignorance of the rank of the strangers. Both were poor and destitute, having been robbed of all their wealth by their captor. The elder Rabbi soon afterward entered the chief synagogue of Cordova, clad in the mean attire which suited his destitute situation; but in the discussion which ensued he exhibited such profound and varied learning that the congregation were astonished, and Rabai Nathan, who presided over the whole Jewish community, declared that the stranger was his superior, and that he would immediately abdicate his office in his favor. Moses was afterward chosen Chief Rabbi of the Cordovan Jews; and he subsequently became the founder of one of the most celebrated schools of Rabbinical learning which has ever existed.

About this period the great Jewish seminary of Cordova attained its supremacy, and various other schools were established by the Rabbis at Granada, Toledo, and other cities within the domains of the Moors. The Talmud was translated into Arabic under the direction of the famous Rabbi Joseph ben Schatnes, who was a pupil of Rabbi Moses, and the rival of Rabbi Enoch, the son and successor of Moses. The grandson of Moses, named Nathan, was so much esteemed for his learning by the Cordovan community in general, that when he went forth from the gates of the city to enjoy the relaxation and rural pleasures which were afforded by the luxurious gardens and sumptuous retreats which surrounded it, his disciples and friends escorted him in great numbers; and as many as seven hundred chariots are said to have constituted his imposing retinue.

8

CHAPTER X.

RABBI MOSES MAIMONIDES—HIS EARLY HISTORY—HIS LEARNING—HIS PRODUCTIONS—HE REMOVES TO EGYPT—HIS GREAT CELEBRITY—EBEN EZRA—HIS YOUTH—ATTAINMENTS—HIS TRAVELS AND WRITINGS—RABBI JUDAH HALLEVI—HIS POETICAL GENIUS—HIS WRITINGS AND SINGULAR DEATH.

AN important feature of the golden era of the Jews, which was described in our last chapter, was the production of several men of great learning and eminence, of whom the chief was the illustrious Rabbi Moses Maimonides. His name was more accurately called Moses ben Maimon; and he was born at Cordova about the year 1140, while that city was under the dominion of the Emperor of Morocco. His paternal ancestors during several generations had been eminent Jewish Rabbis and Judges, and his father himself held both of those offices with distinction at the time of his birth. The mother of Maimonides expired in childbed; and his father treated him during his youth, perhaps in consequence of that fact, with improper severity. Soon afterward, however, his father married again; and the arts of the second wife gradually prejudiced the mind of his parent against the offspring of the first. He was eventually treated with such partiality and unfairness that he deserted his home, and fled for protection to a neighboring Jew, whom he knew in Cordova.

During his boyhood, Maimonides furnished no indication of the possession of those splendid abilities which he afterward exhibited. He was more than ordinarily stupid; but after his flight from home, he continued his studies in the Talmud at Lucena. There his mind gradually opened, and he devoted himself with great assiduity and success to Rabbinical, philosophical, and medical science during some years. At length he returned to Cordova, about the age of twenty, and, without visiting his father's house, revealed himself to some old acquaintances of the family. Through their influence he obtained permission to speak in the synagogue; and he subsequently did so with such extraordinary learning and ability as at once to excite the astonishment and win the admiration of the congregation. His father also was present; and at length having detected his son's identity, he greeted him with the utmost pride and affection. With his assistance and approval Maimonides continued his studies, both in Rabbinical lore and in astronomy, mathematics and medicine, in the academy of the famous Averroes at Cordova, and became his most accomplished and distinguished pupil. The peculiarity of Averroes was his boldness and freedom in the investigation of philosophical and theological questions; and Maimonides imbibed from him the same spirit which ever afterward characterized him. In all his subsequent compositions he displayed his dislike of Rabbinical restraints; and without designing to weaken or overturn the Jewish system, he wished so to expound it as to render it consonant and harmonious with the principles of the most rational philosophy.

At the age of twenty-three Maimonides commenced to write his celebrated exposition of the Mischna, in the Arabic language, to which he devoted the unremitted labor of seven years. In this work he endeavored to explain the principles which lie at the foundation of particular laws, on the ground of sound reason, without paying any regard to the disputes and quibbles of the Gemara. After the accession of the Moorish prince, Ali Alkumi, to the sovereignty of Cordova, he issued a decree commanding all Jews and Christians within his territories to embrace Mahometanism, or be expelled from the country. Maimonides pretended to choose the former alternative, and fulfilled all the rites and ceremonies of that religion until he had made the necessary arrangements for his flight; after which he abandoned Spain and removed to Cairo, in Egypt. In that city he opened a school for instruction in philosophy. He afterward became chief physician to the Egyptian monarch, Ali Albason, and was held in high honor at court. But his chief attention was devoted to the composition of his great work, a commentary on the Jewish law according to the Talmud, which is known under the names of *Yad Chaza Kah*, and *Mishneh Thorah*, the former meaning the "strong hand," the latter, a "repetition of the law." This work is a manual of the civil, criminal and canon laws of the Jews; is characterized by extraordinary erudition, and has been held for six centuries in the highest esteem, as one of the ablest commentaries on the law which has ever been written. It was the product of eight years of the most untiring labor; and the object of Maimonides, in its preparation, was that by its use every Jew might become familiar with the real spirit and contents of the law of Moses. As soon as the work became known, it elevated its author, in consequence of its transcendant merits, to great reputation; and it became a common phrase to assert that, "from Moses to Moses none arose like to Moses." Since the invention of printing, several editions of this work have been published. The original is written in the Arabic. A few years after the completion of this work, Maimonides composed another in the same language, called "*More Hannevochim*," or "Guide to the Perplexed," in which he wrote more as a philosopher than as a Jew, and endeavored to elevate the contemplation and discussion of the principles of the Jewish faith from the dry and pedantic method which usually characterized the productions of the Rabbins, to a philosophical and enlightened freedom of thought. This work was soon translated into Hebrew, by a learned Jew of Marseilles, named Rabbi Judah ben Solomon; but as the translator used an imperfect copy of the original, his rendering of it is defective; and subsequently the task was performed with more success, under the direction and with the assistance of Maimonides himself, by a Spanish Rabbi named Judah Ebn Tibbon.

The *More Hannevochim* was written by Maimonides

at the age of fifty, and it contains an explanation of all the difficult passages of the Old Testament. It was condemned by Rabbi Solomon ben Abraham, chief of the synagogue at Montpelier, who declared that all the works of Maimonides were heretical, and infected with philosophical infidelity. He forbade the reading of them to the Jews within his jurisdiction, and burnt all the copies which he could procure. On the other hand, Maimonides was defended by the vast majority of the cotemporary Rabbis, prominent among whom were those of Narbonne, Bezieres, and other cities in the south of France, who, in their turn, excommunicated Solomon and his partisans. The dispute soon assumed more imposing proportions, and the whole body of Rabbis were arrayed on one side or the other of the question as to the orthodoxy of Maimonides, until at last an embassy having been sent to Cordova, which still remained the head-quarters of Jewish learning and zeal, to take the opinion of the Chief Rabbis there, and they declaring in favor of Maimonides, the dispute gradually subsided. Among the peculiar opinions entertained by him was that the future resurrection of the dead would be confined to the pious among the Jews, and that all the rest of mankind, whether Jews or Gentiles, would be left in oblivion—an alternative, by the way, decidedly preferable to that of the orthodox Christian faith, which inflicts on the wicked an eternity of hopeless misery.

During the latter years of his life Maimonides was chiefly occupied by his duties as physician to the royal family of Egypt. He wrote at that time to his friend Rabbi Tibbon, as follows:—"I am so perpetually engaged that it will be impossible for you to obtain a single hour's private conversation with me in any portion of the twenty-four. My usual attendance on the king is once every morning; but when his majesty, or his concubines, or any of his family, are the least indisposed, I am not allowed to leave the palace, so that my whole time is almost spent at the Court. I go there every morning early; if all be well there, I return home about noon; but no sooner do I arrive, than my house is surrounded by various kinds of people, Jews and Gentiles, rich and poor, magistrates and mechanics, friends and enemies, who have been waiting impatiently for me. As soon as I have dined, I attend to this crowd, and by the time I am done prescribing for them as their physician, it is night time, and I am so fatigued that I can scarcely speak. And this is my constant way of life."

This wonderful man was eminent in the several sciences of theology, medicine and mathematics, and was familiar with many languages, among which were Arabic, Chaldee, Greek, and those of Western Europe. He died at Cairo, at the age of seventy-five, universally admired and esteemed; and left behind him a name second to none among the many eminent Rabbis who have since flourished in the different countries of Europe. The estimation in which he is held may be inferred from the various complimentary titles which have been applied to him, such as the "Glory of the East," the "Light of the West," the "Great Luminary," the "Eagle of the Doctors," and the "Great Eagle."

The era in which Maimonides lived produced another illustrious Rabbi, who was scarcely less celebrated than himself. This was Abraham ben Ezra, usually called Eben Ezra. He was born at Toledo, about the year A. D. 1100, and was descended from a very distinguished Hebrew family. He was the cousin of the equally famous Rabbi Judah Hallevi, their mothers being sisters; though he must have been much younger than the latter, inasmuch as he subsequently married his daughter. This young lady was remarkable for her beauty and accomplishments; and though many suitors applied for her hand, her father invariably objected to them. At length her mother, becoming impatient or incensed at this conduct, complained in severe terms to her husband of the injustice done to their daughter. The Rabbi became excited, and took an oath that he would give the young lady to the first suitor who asked for her on the succeeding day. It is probable that information of this oath was promptly conveyed by the mother to the family of her sister; and the consequence was that Eben Ezra presented himself the next day, at an early hour, at the house of his cousin, and thus obtained the prize. He, however, played a practical jest upon the family; for he disguised himself so completely in the habiliments of a beggar, that he was not recognized. The parents, at first, were in despair at the luckless accident which they supposed had occurred. The delusion was rendered still more complete by the extreme ignorance which the visitor affected, who seemed to be unacquainted even with the simplest rudiments of knowledge. After some time, however, Eben Ezra revealed himself; the parents of the lady were highly gratified, and the marriage was soon after celebrated.

Subsequent to this event Eben Ezra made a journey through some of the principal countries of Europe, and traveled eastward as far as Palestine. At Tiberias he spent some time with the learned men who still lingered around that once illustrious seat of Jewish literature, and conferred frequently with them in reference to the mysteries of the Masoretical text, or various readings of the Hebrew Scriptures. On his return he spent many years of his life at Rhodes, at which place he died in 1194, in the seventy-fifth year of his age. He was a very voluminous writer; and his chief productions were commentaries on the Old Testament, which covered the whole of the Jewish sacred writings. His attainments in Hebrew and Arabic literature, in astronomy, medicine, philology and natural philosophy, were extraordinary for the age in which he lived. Yet these qualities were inferior to the great natural talents which he possessed; his mind being profoundly sagacious and his faculties extremely vigorous. As an expositor of the Old Testament, he is regarded by competent judges as the most prudent and judicious among the many eminent Jewish critics who have commented upon the sacred writings. Unlike Maimonides, he was partial to the Rabbinical schools, and appropriated whatever good elements might be contained in their productions to the elucidation of the law. Maimonides regarded Eben Ezra as the most intellectual and learned writer whom the Jewish nation had produced, previous to the period at which he himself lived. The cotemporaries of Eben Ezra generally designated him by the epithet of "The Wise." His style of composition is said to approximate very nearly to that which characterizes the Jewish sacred writers. He displayed his superior astronomical knowledge by the invention of the division of the celestial sphere by the Equator. He lived at Mantua in 1145, at Rhodes in 1156, in England in 1159, at Rome in 1167. Previous to his death at Rhodes, he gave directions that his remains should be buried in Palestine, which order was afterward complied with.

The third great light of Hebrew learning in the twelfth century was Rabbi Judah Hallevi. He was born in Spain, although the precise period of his birth is now unknown. He devoted himself from an early age to Rabbinical studies, and his family being wealthy, he was enabled to gratify his literary tastes without any interruption and under the most advantageous circumstances. This Rabbi was remarkable for his poetical talent; and his writings, which were chiefly in Hebrew verse, were intended to convey to the Jews a knowledge of the most important religious and theological truths by means of poetry. His writings are characterized by great beauty, sublimity and intense feeling; and his elegaic poetry would compare favorably, as is asserted by competent judges, with the most admired productions of the chief writers of the countries of Christendom.

The principal work of Rabbi Hallevi was the book called *Cosri*, a poetical composition displaying a rare combination of talent and erudition. The subject of the work is the Jewish kingdom of Chazaz, established by a monarch named Bulan, which had been described in a previous chapter of this work as existing in the eighth century, between the Volga and the Don Rivers, and near the Black Sea. The book consists of five divisions and contains, under the form of a conversation with the king of the Chazars, a defense of the orthodox Jewish religion against the objections of the Christians, Mahometans, Philosophers, and Karaite, or heterodox Jews. The monarch is represented as having had a dream; and in a vision he is told that his intentions are good, but that his knowledge is deficient, and his conduct consequently censurable. He is then represented as applying to an Epicurean philosopher, to a Mahometan, and to a Christian, for instruction in the way of truth. He soon discovers that philosophic religion rests upon arguments which are merely ingenious and plausible, but not certain or convincing; and that Christianity and Mahometanism both recognize the divine origin of the Jewish religion, while they themselves furnish no conclusive proof of an inspired or superhuman authority. The king then concludes that he will espouse that faith which commends itself both by its inspired origin and by the conclusiveness with which it convinces the reason and judgment of those who give it an impartial examination. An Israelite is then introduced to the monarch, who expounds at length all the doctrines, rites and ceremonies of the Jewish faith; giving the most learned proofs of their truthfulness and value. At the same time the writer embraces the opportunity to demonstrate the consistency of these doctrines and usages with the most enlightened philosophical views. He dwells with great eloquence and power upon the existence and attributes of God; the creation of the universe, the value and merits of the Old Testament Scriptures; the decrees of Providence; on free-will, the resurrection and everlasting life; the public exercises of divine worship, the Hebrew language and sacred poetry, the future return of the Jews to the land of their forefathers, the faculties and immortality of the human soul, and the mysteries of prophecy and the Caballa. The work was written in Arabic; and several rival translations of it have since been made into the Hebrew language.

This extraordidary man met with a singular death in his fiftieth year. In accordance with a custom prevalent among the Jews of that age, he made a pilgrimage to the Holy Land, in order to behold the scenes of the glory and the misfortunes of his forefathers. It is recorded that, as he stood near the walls of Jerusalem, and gazed upon the mournful aspect of the fallen city, he was overpowered by his emotions, and rent his garments, and put off his shoes, in a paroxysm of uncontrollable grief. As he walked along he sang an elegy of his own composition on the fall of Jerusalem and the dispersion of the Jewish people;

and his earnestness excited the derision of a brutal Arab, who, mounted on a wild charger, was riding near him. Hallevi paid no attention to his insults; at which circumstance the Arab became incensed, and spurring his horse upon the unfortunate bard, trampled him to death.

CHAPTER XI.

CONDITION OF THE JEWS IN THE TWELFTH CENTURY—HEZEKIAH, LAST PRINCE OF THE CAPTIVITY—WESTERN EUROPE—THE FEUDAL SYSTEM—GROWING PREJUDICES AGAINST THE JEWS—REIGN OF PHILIP AUGUSTUS OF FRANCE—THE CRUSADES—BISHOP OF BEZIERS—SCENES AT ROUEN—DAVID KIMCHI—HIS LEARNING, WRITINGS, AND CELEBRITY.

THE history of the Jews during the twelfth and thirteenth centuries, presents a gloomy and cheerless aspect, which is made up of several equally revolting elements. Cruelty, ignorance and bigotry on the part of those in power, and subjugation and misery on the part of their victims, constitute the most prominent elements of the picture. In the East, Hezekiah, the last representative of the Prince of the Captivity, was deposed and slain by order of the Caliph Kader, the Babylonian ruler; and about the same period the Rabbinical schools of Mesopotamia, which had flourished with great renown during many centuries, were finally suppressed and abolished. In Palestine, the Jews were few in number, and trodden under foot by every species of tyranny and persecution. It is said, that in Constatinople there were but two thousand Israelites then living, who were despised and obscure. It was in the countries of Western Europe that the Jewish race had chiefly congregated during the Middle Ages; and there they experienced the alternate extremes of prosperity and adversity.

But the latter now greatly predominated over the former. Several causes contributed to the permanence of that spirit of hostility and prejudice which existed against this people throughout Western Europe during the Dark Ages. The first was the general supremacy of the *Feudal System*. In that system there was close connection and sympathy between the several orders of persons existing in the State; beginning with the lowest, the serfs, who were dependent upon and protected by the nobles, their real rulers, whose interests were, in some measure, identical with their own; up to the sovereigns, who were dependent upon the support of the feudal lords for the security of their thrones. But in this pyramidal system, the Jews had no recognized place; for the Church was the foundation-stone of the system, from which the Jews, of course, were excluded, unless they became converts. The second cause of their precarious condition was the spirit of *chivalry* which became generally diffused. With the romantic splendor of the knight-errant the Jew had little sympathy. No Christian lady would consider him as her champion; and as the chivalric spirit became more intense and more generally cultivated, the contempt with which the Jew was regarded became greater. It must also be admitted that the influence of the clergy of the Church was hostile to the Jews. This may often have proceeded from an honest conviction of duty; but, in many cases, personal prejudice and hostility were at the bottom of the general war of opposition and sometimes of persecution with which they visited the Israelites. To all these must be added another cause, more potent, perhaps, than the rest. At the period of which we write, the Jews had generally adopted the business of money-lending and usury as their favorite pursuit; and that fact kindled the jealousy and hostility of the rest of the community. The Jews were driven to engage in this occupation by the various disabilities and restrictions with which they were harassed in the various countries of Christendom. As the possessors of ready money, they could defend their property more easily from plunder and exactions; and, after having been compelled to adopt this pursuit by the treatment received from the other portions of the community, they were censured and persecuted for that which the law of self-preservation had absolutely demanded.

Nowhere, in that age, were the effects of these prejudices more clearly evinced than in the kingdom of France. In that country the Jews had become both numerous and wealthy, in consequence of the prosperity which they had enjoyed under the benignant sceptres of the immediate successors of Charlemagne. In the southern provinces they had become extensive landowners. In the northern, they were equally prosperous. In Paris they were a power very perceptibly felt in the community for their wealth and influence. In Troyes they had an academy for Rabbinical instruction, which had attained great celebrity. Their persecutions began in consequence of the prevalence of an absurd prejudice and slander, that they had conveyed intelligence of the intended movements of the Crusaders to the Mahometan rulers of Palestine. Other misrepresentations, equally false, were industriously circulated: that they had decoyed Christian children into their houses, and there crucified them; that they obtained consecrated wafers by theft or bribery, and then subjected them to every possible species of insult; that they had received the sacred vessels of the churches as security for moneys loaned to the priests, and defamed them while in their possession; and that they fabricated wax images of the crucified Christ, and then punctured them derisively with needles.

When Philip Augustus ascended the throne of France, the worst miseries of the Jews began. He immediately proclaimed an edict confiscating all debts owed to the Jews by his subjects, and commanding them to restore all pledges which they held for the payment of loans to their original owners. Among the latter a golden crucifix and a copy of the Gospel adorned with precious stones were found; and this fact was used as a justification for the most rigorous measures against them. While assembled in their synagogue, the building was surrounded by the royal troops, the Jews were dragged to prison, and their houses taken possession of. After several weeks, another edict followed, commanding them to sell all their movable goods and leave the kingdom, and confiscating all their immovable or real estate to the use of the crown. This edict was rigorously executed, and, by its operation, the whole Jewish community in

France were not only exiled, but absolutely ruined; for they could obtain but little money for those articles which they were commanded to sell, when disposed of under such unfavorable circumstances. It is recorded that the clergy were generally zealots in seeing that this decree was carried into rigorous operation; and a monkish historian relates that these results should be regarded as a jubilee, inasmuch as, by their occurrence, the Christians in France had recovered their liberty, of which they had been deprived by the usurious exactions of the Jews. This observation shows to what degree their influence and importance as the financiers of the community had then extended.

The prevalence of the crusading-spirit was one of the greatest evils which the Jews were compelled to endure; for those absurd enthusiasts, who confounded Christianity with a sepulchre, and the deliverance of a city from Infidel sovereignty with the spread of the true faith, carried their stupidity still further, by regarding the then existing Jews as being as much disposed to persecute Christians and Christianity as if they were the same individuals who were living at the time of Christ. This spirit of hostility to the Jews became more intense at certain particular times, especially at the great festival of Easter. Some of the priests thought that they were doing honor to the Founder of their religion, whose sufferings and ascension they were then commemorating, by persecuting the descendants of those who had nailed him to the cross. This spirit is illustrated by incidents like the following. The Bishop of Beziers ascended the pulpit of the cathedral, and addressing the people said: "You have among you, my brethren, the descendants of the impious wretches who crucified the Lord Jesus Christ, whose passion we are commemorating. Show yourselves animated by the spirit of your ancestors. Arm yourselves with stones; assail the Jews with them; and thus, as far as in you lies, revenge the suffering of that Saviour who redeemed you with his own blood!" The ignorant crowd, inflamed by such addresses, rushed forth from the cathedral, attacked the dwellings of the Jews, and a great tumult ensued, in which many persons were killed and wounded. The Jews, indeed, after the first surprise and terror were over, defended themselves; but their efforts availed little against a whole community infuriated against them.

A similar scene occurred at Rouen. Many adventurers had assembled in that city to join a crusade which was about to start to Palestine; and they imagined that they could not signalize their pious zeal to better purpose, before commencing their journey, than by attacking and punishing the Jews residing peacefully there. Said they: "We are going to march toward the East to avenge the cause of God upon his enemies; but we are leaving behind us a race of people as hateful in his sight as any of the Saracens. Let us therefore commence our holy work by putting them to the sword!" Then followed scenes of the utmost barbarity; and the same spirit was exhibited by the Crusaders in other cities; so that, driven to utter despair, it is recorded that some of the Jews com mitted suicide, while others submitted to baptism as the only means of saving their lives. In Franconia and Bavaria such torrents of blood were shed by the Crusaders, under the plea that the Jews in Europe were as execrable as the Moslems in Palestine, that even St. Bernard, enthusiastic as he was in favor of the crusades to the East, felt constrained to interpose his influence and authority, to put an end to the barbarities which were inflicted. Other eminent saints of that period were not equally charitable or enlightened; for Peter of Clugny, termed the venerable, the friend of Abelard, in writing to Louis VII. of France, recommended that the Jews should be despoiled of all the wealth which they had procured by usury and money-lending; and it is worthy of note that, although the king was too just and equitable to carry out the suggestion of the illustrious Abbot, he was condemned for his disobedience by the majority of the ecclesiastics of his time. The Bishop of Spires, who presented a singular exception to his cotemporaries on this point, and used his authority to shield the Jews from extortion and persecution, was severely censured by the public opinion of the time for his lenity; and the monkish annalists, from whom these details are derived—they being the only surviving historians of those ages—condemn the conduct of the prelate; and plainly intimate that it could be accounted for by no explanation, except that he must have been heavily and secretly bribed by the Jews to protect them.

Notwithstanding the gloomy scenes of persecution which surrounded the Jews at this period, several very eminent Rabbis lived and flourished, whose learning and theological labors were celebrated in their own times, and are still held in such high reputation as to deserve a place in the annals of their people. The chief of these was Rabbi David Kimchi, a native of France, and descended from a family which had for several generations been famous in the Jewish academy at Narbonne. They seem to have been of Spanish origin; for it is recorded that some of them had been rulers of the synagogues and teachers of Rabbinnical lore, both in Arragon and Castile. Joseph, the father of David Kimchi, wrote a commentary on a a part of the Old Testament, and compiled a Hebrew grammar, which were highly esteemed. Moses Kimchi also distinguished himself by his writings; but both of these were inferior in ability and learning to David, who has been termed the most learned of all the Hebrew grammarians.

When the controversy took place among the Jews in reference to the orthodoxy of Maimonides, to which allusion has already been made in this work, the French synagogues were also divided on the subject; and the feud proceeded to such extremes that the hostile Rabbis pronounced a ban against whole congregations; when the more prudent Jews thought that it was time to adjust the difficulty by some means or other. David Kimchi was chosen to accomplish this difficult design, and to act as meditator between the contending factions. With this object in view, and furnished with the necessary documents, he journeyed from Narbonne to Toledo, the residence of Rabbi Alfakar, the chief of the synagogue in that place, and eminent from his learning in medicine. This person was extremely hostile to Maimonides, and was his most active persecutor. His purpose of holding personal interviews with this Rabbi on the subject was defeated by an attack of sickness, which overtook him at Avila; but he sent forward his nephew Joseph, who accompanied him, with letters and other recommendations urging him to heal the existing feud for the honor of their common religion.

After some time Alfakar replied to the communication of Kimchi by a letter written in rhyme, in which he spoke very contemptuously of his correspondent, and even abused him and his associates as persons who had apostatized from the true faith. Kimchi responded in an exceedingly mild and conciliating tone, which drew from his Spanish correspondent an answer still mere offensive and malignant than the first. He compared Kimchi, in undertaking his journey, to Satan's "going to and fro in the earth," as spoken of in the book of Job; and speaks of him as walking in darkness and wandering in the wilderness of error. He accused Kimchi of endeavoring to reconcile the religion of the Jews with the philosophy of the Greeks. He concluded his letter with acknowledging the great learning of Maimonides, and the value of some of his earlier works, and urging Kimchi to abandon his novelties and to return to the true faith. The latter again replied in the same friendly spirit, refusing to become incensed, as he might reasonably have been, at the malignant spirit displayed by his correspondent. In the end, however, the forbearance of Kimchi was not without its influence, and the dissensions which had taken place respecting the doctrines of Maimonides were for a time wholly suppressed.

Kimchi was very learned as a grammarian; and in his commentaries on various portions of the Old Testament, he displays his great philological ability. His Hebrew grammar, his lexicon or book of Hebrew roots, and his commentaries, have been translated into several European languages; and, as biblical students are aware, are frequently quoted as authorities by Christian divines in their expositions of the Old Testament. This writer was very charitable in his spirit toward other religionists, and always spoke of Christians courteously. His fame among the Jews is equal to that of their greatest Rabbis. As the Hebrew word which signifies a *meal* was figuratively used for the *law*, and as, by adding the letter *yod* to that word, it becomes the word *Kimchi*, so the admirers of this Rabbi introduced the proverb in his honor, that "there could be no meal without Kimchi."

The Rabbi Solomon Jarchi, whose name is also sometimes written Zarchi and Raschi, was another illustrious Rabbi of this era, scarcely inferior in fame and learning to Kimchi. He was a native of Troyes, and studied at Narbonne under Moses Hadarshan, surnamed the Preacher, from the eloquence of his addresses in the synagogue. He applied himself so industriously to his studies that at the age of thirty, he had written commentaries on the Old Testament and the Talmud, and had become conversant with the several departments of philosophical and mathematical learning. The subsequent events of Jarchi's life are somewhat involved in doubt. Many legends are extant in reference to his adventures while visiting various countries of the East in search of more knowledge and better acquaintance with the condition of the Jewish people. We will narrate as much of these as seems to be founded on authority which is worthy of credence.

In journeying toward the East, Jarchi visited Maimonides in Egypt, who entertained a very exalted opinion of his merits. He extended his travels as far as Persia, after having visited the Holy Land and Greece. On his return westward he arrived at Prague, and was there received by his Jewish brethren with great honor; but scenes of trial and danger awaited him in that city. Uladislaus, the then reigning Duke of Bohemia, was unfriendly to the Jews; and the *éclat* with which they received the stranger induced some of their enemies to proclaim the calumny that Jarchi was another Bar-cochab, or impostor, who claimed to be the promised Messiah. Jarchi was arrested; and the favorite minister of the duke being greatly indebted to the Jews, was disposed to wipe away his obligations by the perpetration of a general massacre. The Bishop of Olmutz was equally sanguinary in his intentions; but it is said that when Jarchi stood before the duke for trial in the presence of the bishop, the latter recognized in him the physician who, while he had traveled in the East, had saved his life by his medical skill. The bishop therefore interposed, and protected Jarchi, who in his turn succeeded in averting the impending storm of persecution from his brethren. The time and place of Jarchi's death are uncertain, though the most generally received opinion is, that he died many years afterward at Treves, at an advanced age.

CHAPTER XII.

THE JEWS OF PARIS—THEIR CONDITION IN THE THIRTEENTH CENTURY—LOUIS IX.—PERSECUTION OF THE JEWS BY HIS SUBJECTS—THEIR TREATMENT BY HIS SUCCESSORS—THEIR TEMPORARY PROSPERITY—THE JEWS IN CASTILE—THEIR MISFORTUNES—THEIR CONDITION IN ARRAGON—PUBLIC DISPUTES BETWEEN JEWS AND CHRISTIANS.

THE further we advance through the gloom of the Dark Ages, the more dreary and miserable does the condition of the Jewish people appear, and the more extreme and execrable the persecutions to which they were subjected. About twenty years after their expulsion from France, as narrated in a former chapter, the French monarch was compelled by his financial necessities to invite the Jews to return to his dominions; and they, forgetting all their previous sufferings, and allured by the favorable offer which he made them, accepted the proposals in great numbers. Certain streets in Paris were assigned them for their exclusive residence; and their proverbial industry and thrift soon made them the possessors of wealth and of that importance which wealth always confers.

The various losses which the Jews had previously suffered in France by extortion and by exile, had induced them, for the most part, to abandon nearly every department of labor and trade except that of money-lending. Nor was this result unnatural, when we remember what absurd objections were made against them, and to what disabilities they were subjected, when engaged in other callings. Thus, it is recorded that, if they sold milk, the Christian public charged them with mingling with it that of their wives. If they were butchers, it was charged that they reserved all the best portions of their meat for their own people, and sold the refuse to the Christians. If they manufactured wine, it was said to be of inferior quality; and the clergy went so far as to forbid the use of that which the Jews had made in the services of the altar and the administration of the Lord's Supper. Being hampered and crushed in this way in almost every avenue of honest industry, the Jews in France, and especially in Paris, became for the most part the pawnbrokers and usurers of the realm; and as such, by the rigor with which they took advantage of their position, and the extreme exactions which they practiced on the public who were compelled to make use of their services, they soon gathered around themselves another storm of persecution.

The king, Philip Augustus, accordingly decreed that no Jew should exact more than forty-five per cent. per year. But they soon evaded this prohibition by compelling their debtors to engage to pay this interest on a greater sum than was actually loaned. To prevent this practice, the king decreed that no creditor should, under any pretext, demand, and that no debtor should promise to pay interest, or a bonus, for any sum higher than that which actually passed from the possession of the lender to the borrower. But other enactments, more rigorous, followed afterward. Louis VIII., the son and successor of Philip, prohibited the Jews from demanding or receiving any interest whatever for moneys loaned; and declared all agreements which had been made between debtor and creditor for more than five years previously to be null and void. This law was evidently intended as a severe blow to their chief means of wealth, and even of subsistence. The Jews were also attached to the soil, according to the then existing and barbarous usages of Feudalism, and were assigned as property to the feudal lords and magnates.

When Louis IX. ascended the throne of France, the Jews fondly expected a respite from their persecutions; but they hoped in vain. Louis—who has received the epithet of *saint*, chiefly because his zeal for the prosecution of crusades to the Holy Land indicated his unusual devotion to the Church and subserviency to the then existing priesthood—Louis was a rare specimen of fanaticism and imbecility. That he was pious, according to the standard of that age, cannot be doubted; and how much his piety deserved to be commended, may be inferred from the statutes which he enacted respecting the Jews. In the year 1234 he promulgated a law cancelling one-third of the debts which were then due to this people; and he further enacted that no bailiff might arrest or annoy a Christian for any debt due to a Jew, nor could any legal process be entertained to compel payment. The excuse which this royal and saintly thief gave for the execution of such measures was that he wished to convert the Jews, at once, from their false religion and from their devotion to the business of money-lending.

When the boasted lights of the age exhibited such a spirit, it will readily be believed that the populace were not slow in following their example. The persecutions of the Court became the signal for the outbreak of the most cruel spirit on the part of the people. In 1239 the inhabitants of Paris invaded the quarter appropriated to the Jews, and committed the most frightful excesses. The example was followed in Orleans, and other cities of the kingdom. In Brittany a law was promulgated to the effect that the Jews should be banished; that all debts due to them should be annulled without payment; that all who held property belonging to the Jews might retain it; that any Christian might kill a Jew without being in any way molested for it. But the saintly Louis went still further, and by another edict displayed the extreme ignorance of himself and his advisers, as well as their malignity. Some of the Jews were learned men; some of them were eminent and successful physicians; and all this proved that they must have intercourse with evil spirits: and this suspicion was confirmed in the sagacious and enlightened mind of Louis, by the fact that the sacred writings of the Jews, especially the Talmuds, which were composed in a mysterious, and unknown, and apparently uncouth tongue, must be filled with blasphemies against Christ, with dangerous and diabolical secrets, with fearful and cabalistic spells. Accordingly the king decreed that all the Hebrew books in the realm should be burned. Twenty-five cart loads of these volumes were destroyed in Paris alone. The object which the monarch professed to have in this work was to aid in the conversion of the Jews by depriving them of their most valuable theological and religious literature. Many of them fled from the kingdom, carrying with them secretly their best books; and by this means some of those learned commentaries on the Old Testament were preserved, to which we have already alluded, and which are esteemed of the highest value by biblical critics of the present day.

The persecutions of St. Louis did not terminate here. He enacted that in future the Israelites in his dominions should all wear a badge upon their clothes to designate them. It was to be used by both sexes, and consisted of a strip of blue cloth fixed on the front and the back part of the outside garment, in order that thereby the Jew might in effect be outlawed and separated from the rest of the community, and thus be made a ready victim of public and popular insult. This law was passed at the suggestion of Pope Innocent III., and with the approval of one of the Councils of Lateran, and was subsequently recommended by other Councils, such as those convened at Rouen and Arles.

As successive sovereigns ascended the throne of France the Jews experienced different vicissitudes, according as those monarchs were friendly or hostile, liberal and enlightened in their views, or bigoted and despotic in their feelings. Philip the Hardy, who began to reign in 1321, favored the Jews by allowing them to remain exempt from persecution and outrage. Philip the Fair, who succeeded, commanded the Israelites to leave the kingdom, and then confiscated their property. Five years afterward he promulgated a still more severe decree against those who may have ventured to return. Louis X., who followed Philip on the throne, gave the Jews permission to return; and he was induced, it is said, so to do, in consequence of the general desire expressed by his subjects, who regarded the Jews as useful in a financial point of view. But although Louis protected the Jews from the exactions and injuries of others, he took care that they should suffer from his own. He appropriated two-thirds of all debts due them to himself, allowing them only the remaining third.

During the subsequent reign of Philip the Long, while the insane fanaticism in favor of the crusades still continued to convulse France, a great multitude of peasants and vagabonds traversed the country, from one extreme to the other, pretending to be about to start for the Holy Land. But they spent their time and energies chiefly in persecuting the Jews. The Pope, who then resided at Avignon, endeavored to protect the Jews from the fury of these wretches, but in vain. They laughed at his ecclesiastical thunders. It is recorded that a hundred and twenty communities of Jews, who lived in various portions of France, were destroyed by them;

and when, a short time afterward, a pestilence broke forth, in consequence of the excesses which had been indulged in, the cause was attributed to the Jews, who were charged with having poisoned the wells and rivers. Several of them were put to the torture, and, unable to endure their agonies, they confessed anything which was demanded of them, and implicated their brethren. A general persecution of Jews followed. Many were burnt alive. At Chinon alone, a hundred and sixty Jews suffered this horrible death; and the property of all those who were in any way punished, was confiscated by the king to his own use.

The Jews enjoyed a short respite from torture and persecution in France, during the reign of John, the unfortunate monarch who was vanquished at Poictiers, in 1356, by the Black Prince. He was detained a captive during several years; and his kingdom was governed during the interval by his son Charles, justly surnamed "the good." That prince made a compact with the Jews, through Manasseh, their leading man—a wealthy banker, who had loaned large sums of money to Charles at a critical moment—by which the Jews were permitted to return to France by paying a small sum on entering the country, and a reasonable yearly tax afterward. They were to be protected from all other exactions, to be allowed to pursue any honest calling they might desire, to be exempted from baronial jurisdiction, and to be under the control only of an officer called the Guardian of the Jews, who was to be appointed by the king himself. They were allowed to charge interest at the rate of eighty per cent. per year; but were not permitted to receive in pledge the sacred utensils of the churches or the tools of the laborer.

Such unusual prosperity soon rendered the Jews opulent, and the general public hostile. They were attacked by a furious mob in Paris, which slew a large number, pillaged the houses of others, and forced many of their children from them, that they might be baptized. During the subsequent reign of Charles the Sixth, in 1394, the Jews were again commanded to leave the kingdom, on the ground that they had abused the privileges which they had enjoyed; nor were they allowed by law to enter the kingdom or reside in it until the outbreak of the Revolution, nearly four centuries afterward. The kingdom of Provence did not then belong to France; and thither many of the exiled Jews repaired. King Rene was favorable to the persecuted race and protected them. Many of them became eminent for wealth, and for theological learning and medical skill. After this period the famous name of Peter Nostrodamus appears, who was appointed physician-in-chief to the king. When, in 1480, Provence became annexed to France, in consequence of the failure of the royal line, Louis XII. commanded the Jews to leave the country. They obeyed, and many of them took refuge at Avignon, where they were protected by the Pontiff, who still resided there. Several Rabbis of eminence arose at this period, at Avignon, one of whom was Mordecai, otherwise named Philip d'Aquin. He afterward became a convert to Christianity, and a Professor of Hebrew at Paris. Another distinguished writer who lived at Avignon was Joseph Mein, who wrote a "History of France," and "Annals of the French Conquests in the East," which were regarded as works of high repute.

In the adjoining kingdom of Spain the fortunes of the Jews were various during the thirteenth and fourteenth centuries. While the Moors remained supreme they were prosperous and protected; but at length that chivalrous race was expelled from the provinces of Castile and Arragon. Their Christian successors on the throne imitated their charitable and liberal policy toward the Israelites during several generations. Alphonzo X., King of Castile, whose superior intelligence won for him the epithet of "the Wise," patronized and protected them. Their head-quarters were at Toledo, where they had celebrated schools, where they were very opulent and influential, and where they had many learned and eminent men. Judah Morea was the royal physician, who was also one of the ablest astronomers of his time, and prepared at the king's command, the famous astronomical tables called the Alphonsine, and also translated several valuable Arabic works into Spanish. It was at this period that the productions of the renowned Averoes and Avicenna were rendered from the original Arabic into the Castillian, and thus made accessible to the readers of Western Europe.

During the reign of Alphonso XI. the prosperity of the Jews still continued. Don Joseph, one of their number, was the royal treasurer; and although various conspiracies were formed against him by the jealous courtiers, in order to effect his disgrace, so superior was he to all his cotemporaries and rivals in financial ability, that the sovereign found himself unable to dispense with his services. The Cortez of Madrid, in 1309, protested against the retention and the power of Joseph, but in vain; and as long as that monarch lived, the Jew retained his confidence, and was able to protect his brethren from the power of bigotry, and the hatred of their enemies. In Spain, as everywhere else the Jews in that age, were money-lenders; and it is recorded that the law at that time allowed them to exact thirty-three per cent. interest on money loaned—an amount which might be supposed to satisfy the most extravagant, while, at the same time, it would increase the jealousy and animosity of the Christian public who were compelled to have recourse to them.

The calamities of the Jews in Castile began in 1350, when Henry of Trestamara aspired to the crown, and attacked the throne and authority of his brother Peter, the legitimate sovereign. Henry invaded the country, and was accompanied by a body of French troops under the command of Bertrand de Guesclin; and a chief part of their exploits consisted in assailing and persecuting the Jews. This was done in order to gain popularity with the Christian inhabitants of the country. In several places all those Jews were massacred who refused to submit to baptism. In some cities, especially in Burgos, the Jews assisted their patron and sovereign Peter, and behaved with great gallantry in resisting the assailants. At length, when Henry triumphed and Peter was slain, his treasurer,

Samuel Levi, was executed, and the Jews suffered a period of general persecution. But after a time, the importance and value of these people as industrious and thrifty citizens, induced Henry's immediate successors to treat them with lenity and justice.

The greatest enemies of the Jews in Castile, as elsewhere throughout Spain, were the clergy of the dominant Church. These bigots could not understand or conceive how the Jews could entertain feelings of *indifference* toward Christianity; they supposed that they must necessarily be intensely hostile to it, and that therefore they deserved, in return, to be vexed and punished. Accordingly, they embraced every opportunity to persecute the Jews, who, so far as the existing annals of those times and of that country throw any light upon the subject, did nothing to justify such animosity and its consequent persecution. In Segovia, a priest preached so violently against the Jews in the cathedral, that he inflamed the whole community against them; and the spirit of persecution spread even to Sardinia and Majorca. Many Jews were slain, and others were compelled to renounce their religion, in order to preserve their lives. In Valladolid laws were passed by the Cortez in 1412, forbidding them to go beyond the particular portion of the city which had been assigned to them; and they were not allowed to mix with the Christian community, or to exercise the trades of farmers of the public revenues, of physicians, and of many other useful and desirable occupations.

In Arragon, the condition of the Jews during the

thirteenth century was one of danger and misfortune. They were hampered with various laws, which prostrated their industry and diminished their prosperity. At Barcelona they were excluded from all participation in trade and commerce, and they were harassed throughout the province of Arragon by the continued and obstinate efforts of the clergy to compel their abandonment of their own religion, and their adoption of Christianity. To aid in the accomplishment of this result, the king was prevailed upon to establish Professorships of Hebrew in the universities, in order that the priesthood might become better prepared to confront and confound the Jews in public and private disputation. Some of the most talented and zealous of the ecclesiastics addressed themselves to this new branch of knowledge, and under the guidance and tuition of converted or apostatized Jews, became proficient in the Hebrew language. Several public debates ensued between the champions of Christianity and Judaism, which were very famous in that day. One of these occurred in 1263, in the presence of James I. of Arragon, at Barcelona. The champion of the Church was Paul Christiani, an eminent priest; that of the Jews was Moses, a learned Rabbi. The court, clergy, and a vast assemblage of people, attended the debate, during which both disputants displayed great abilities; and the result was, as might have been expected, that not a single convert was made by either side. The only consequence was disastrous to the Jews, for the priests prevailed on the monarch to order the Jews to bring all their books to Barcelona, that they might be examined as to whether they contained any passages hostile to Christ and to the true faith. The Jews complied to some extent, and sent many of their Rabbinical and Talmudic writings to the appointed place for inspection; but the result which they feared actually occurred. The priests destroyed or mutilated nearly every book which passed under their scrutiny; and had the prudent Jews not reserved some copies of all their best works, many of the most valuable treasures of Hebrew literature would now be either unknown to the world, or would exist only in an imperfect state.

CHAPTER XIII.

FERDINAND AND ISABELLA—THEIR RESPECTIVE CHARACTERS—THEIR PURPOSE TO EXPEL THE JEWS FROM SPAIN—AGENCY OF THE INQUISITION—PROCEEDINGS IN TOLEDO—CRUEL ALTERNATIVE OFFERED TO THE JEWS—BANISHMENT OF THE JEWS—EVENTS IN PORTUGAL—JEWS IN GERMANY—SWITZERLAND—THE BLACK DEATH—SCENES IN BRUSSELS.

THE reign of Ferdinand and Isabella in Spain, which has been so much glorified by the laborious but common-place talents of Prescott, was the period when the most infamous persecutions were practiced upon the Jews, of which their checkered and calamitous history makes mention. Isabella was a weak-minded and superstitious woman, to whom mankind have generally accorded the praise of great amiability and tenderness of heart. Yet it was at her request, acting under the influence of her bloodthirsty confessor, that Ferdinand made a vow at the commencement of his war of extermination against the Moors, to the effect that, if his arms were crowned with success, he would either banish all the Jews from Spain or compel them to become Christians. Ferdinand was one of the most selfish, unprincipled and crafty despots who ever reigned, and he readily acquiesced in the demand of the queen.

Accordingly, after the Moors had been vanquished

by Christian arms; after myriads of them had been slain in propagating the "true faith;" after the survivors had been deprived of homes, property and friends, and driven as exiles to a foreign shore; the pious and grateful conquerors bethought them of their charitable intentions toward the Jews in their dominions, and prepared to execute their purpose against them. To aid in this good work the Inquisition was either established in Spain, or its powers were greatly enlarged, and the Jews were transferred to the jurisdiction and authority of the most cruel and infamous institution which has ever existed out of Pandemonium. It commenced its operations in March, 1492. The special fury of the "Holy Tribunal" was directed against the "Enussim," that class of Israelites who had professed, in view of the terrors which surrounded them, to abjure their faith and become Christians. Even these converts received no credit for sincerity. If they refused to adopt the Roman Catholic religion, they would be punished. If they did adopt it, their condition was little better; for they then became the objects of suspicion, and were punished for being such. It is recorded that, during the persecutions which followed, ten thousand Jews were burned alive, seventeen thousand were compelled to do penance, and minor penalties were inflicted on many others.

In Toledo a heavy tax was laid upon the citizens by the nobility, and the people took the impression that the Jews were the cause of it. The consequence was, that the popular rage broke out against them to increase the horrors already inflicted by ecclesiastical bigotry; and the houses of the principal Israelites were attacked and plundered, and many persons were murdered. At length Isabella and Ferdinand promulgated a decree, that every Jew who would not abandon his religion and become a convert to the Church, should leave the Spanish dominions within four months; and all Christians were forbidden, after the expiration of that period, to afford food and shelter of any sort to the proscribed. This cruel order was equivalent to an edict of ruin to eight hundred thousand persons; and the scenes which followed in the execution of the law transcend the powers of imagination. The most eminent and opulent Jews endeavored to induce the monarchs to relent and change their purpose. It was in vain, for Ferdinand was urged on by the bigoted queen, whose influence over him was absolute, because she had his own interests in her power; and the infamous law was rigidly enforced.

The terror and dismay which overwhelmed the Spanish Jews in this awful dilemma can scarcely be imagined. Wailing and lamentation pervaded every dwelling, and resounded in every synagogue. Only two resources were left to those who were unwilling to abjure the religion of their forefathers. One was to escape into Portugal; the other, to flee to Morocco and other countries, where the followers of Mahomet, more Christian in feeling than the professed followers of Christ, would afford them an asylum and protection. The scenes which occurred among those who preferred to escape entirely beyond the limits of the

Roman Catholic countries, were horrible, from the disasters and casualties which attended them. It happened that many of the ships which contained the emigrants were too heavily laden, and sank after setting sail. Other ships are recorded to have taken fire, and been lost amid all the indescribable horrors of a conflagration at sea. In many vessels diseases broke out, which carried off immense numbers of the fugitives. Several captains of vessels ordered all their Jewish passengers to be slain as the cause of the misfortunes which overtook their ships. Of those who reached the shores of Fez, many perished by a violent storm which swept the deep and drove their vessels on the rocks. A famine is said to have prevailed in that country at the time the survivors landed, and a vast number perished of hunger; yet of the survivors, it is said that, on the Friday they gathered what herbs and roots the land afforded, that they might keep the ensuing Sabbath according to their law. A large number were sold by the captains of vessels as slaves to the inhabitants of Barbary, because they were unable to comply with their exorbitant demands for the payment of passage-money. It is recorded by Christian writers that as many as thirty thousand Jews perished on this occasion, from the various calamities which overtook them after they had left the soil of Spain, their native land. The extermination of the Moors and the persecution of the Jews cover the characters of Ferdinand and Isabella, so proudly termed "the Catholic," with a mantle of eternal infamy.

The fate of those Jews who took refuge in the neighboring kingdom of Portugal was at first more fortunate. John II. regarded the fugitives as valuable accessions, and enacted laws for their government and protection, which were in a great measure wise and liberal. He allowed them to name their own judges, who decided those law-suits among them which appertained to civil affairs, though in criminal matters they were subject to the authority of the Christian tribunals. These Jewish judges were subject to superior officers of their own people, one of whom resided in each of the capital cities of the seven provinces into which the kingdom was divided. These seven judges were all subject to a chief Rabbi, who resided at Lisbon, and was appointed by the King, and whose decisions the King alone could reverse. Under the influence of the protection which they enjoyed, the Portuguese Jews soon became opulent, and many of their teachers were eminent for their learning. Rabbinical schools were established at Lisbon, which eventually rivaled those of Toledo and Seville, adorned by eminent writers, of whom David Jarchia, Isaac Avuhaf, and Moses ben Thabiba, were the chief. Several celebrated physicians arose among them; and John II. employed two, Joseph and Roderigo, to prepare astronomical tables for the use of vessels engaged in the African trade, according to then improved state of astronomical science.

As long as the reign of this monarch continued, the condition of the Jews in Portugal was tolerable. They were allowed to establish a printing press at Lisbon, at which several very valuable and elaborate works were executed. One of these was the Pentateuch in Hebrew, accompanied by the paraphrase of Onkelos, in Chaldee, and the commentary of Rabbi Solomon Jarchi, whose life and character we have already described. Subsequently the books of Isaiah and Jeremiah, with the commentary of David Kimchi annexed, were issued in a style of superior excellence and beauty. Nor were the Jews unknown or obscure among those bold and adventurous navigators, for whom the Portuguese nation was remarkable in the fourteenth and fifteenth centuries. Several expeditions of discovery were conducted under Jewish commanders; two of whom, Abraham de Beza and Joseph Zapatero, succeeded in discovering several important islands, and in obtaining rich cargoes of treasure, in the East Indies.

The successor of John II. on the Portuguese throne was Manuel, whose disposition toward the strangers at first was friendly; but having subsequently married the daughter of Ferdinand and Isabella, he soon imbibed the same spirit of persecution and bigotry which characterized them. In 1496 he even issued an edict banishing the Jews from his dominions, and, at the same time, ordered that they should be deprived of all their children under fourteen years of age, who were retained to be educated in the Catholic faith. It is recorded, that when the Jews became the victims of this new persecution, they were overwhelmed with despair, and many committed suicide. There were some who abjured their faith, and proclaimed their conversion to the religion of their persecutors.

Others prepared to emigrate to foreign countries; but before they could execute their purpose they were subjected to the utmost cruelties. At Lisbon their houses were plundered by the infuriated populace. The wives and daughters of many were outraged, and others were murdered in cold blood. The majority of those who fled from Portugal on this occasion took refuge in Constantinople, where they enjoyed greater protection and security.

The condition of those converts from Judaism who remained in Portugal soon became extremely miserable. They were suspected of being still Jews in reality, and as practicing in secret the rites and ceremonies of their ancient faith. On one occasion, a popular tumult was excited in Lisbon against them, by one of their number detecting and exposing the pious fraud of a priest, who pretended to exhibit to the people a crucifix from which the light was streaming. The ex-Jew pointed out a lamp adroitly placed in the rear, so as to produce the mysterious effect exhibited. He was immediately torn to pieces by the populace; and the mortified ecclesiastics inflamed their minds so successfully against the brethren of the unfortunate man, that a general massacre of the converts took place, which continued during three days, and as many as two thousand are said to have perished. The "holy Inquisition" was afterward introduced into Portugal, in 1536, with special reference to the examination and punishment of the converted Jews; and so great were the horrors perpetrated by that tribunal, that immense numbers fled into France, and settled chiefly at Bordeaux and Bayonne. These and their descendants became successful in commerce; they obtained the protection of Henry II., who, in 1550, extended to them all the privileges which belonged to French citizens. His successor, Henry III., continued to protect the "converted Jews" in France; and in 1574 he issued an edict forbidding his Christian subjects to annoy the descendants of these Portuguese Jews on the charge or suspicion that they secretly practiced the religious rites and ceremonies of their forefathers.

The history of the Jews in Germany, during the fourteenth century, presents the same chequered scenes of popular prejudice, kingly persecution, priestly animosity, and financial success, which marked the experience of this people in other portions of Europe. They had gradually extended, during several preceding centuries, through the various countries of Austria, Brandenburg, Bavaria, Wurtemburg, Silesia, Bohemia, and Poland. They generally pursued the business of money-lending and usury, as the only safe way of procuring a subsistence, and of avoiding to some extent the exactions to which they were generally subjected. This very fact increased the popular prejudice against them; and of the bloody persecutions which were waged against them, the annals of those times present many heart-sickening details. At Frankfort, a company of insane enthusiasts, called the Flagellants, who publicly scourged their naked bodies as a punishment for their own sins and those of others, imagined that it was their duty to show their zeal for religion, by plundering and murdering the Jews.

The emperor endeavored to control and suppress the enthusiam of these wretches, but his efforts were fruitless; and many hundred Jews were slain and wounded in that city, on that occasion, without the least show of justice or reason on the part of their persecutors.

In Switzerland the experience of the Hebrews, during this dark era, was equally afflictive. At Berne the body of a murdered infant was found, and the Jews of that place were charged with having caused its death Without the slightest evidence to support the allegation, some of them were seized and put to the torture. Unable to endure the agonies inflicted on them, they confessed whatever was required, and implicated their Jewish brethren as the authors of the murder. A terrible persecution broke out against them in consequence. Rudolph of Hapsburg, the founder of the present imperial house of Austria, who then held jurisdiction over that canton, endeavored to protect the Hebrews, but was unable to do so. They were all at last banished from the canton, and compelled to seek homes and safety elsewhere.

The popular fury of those execrable times was often aroused by the most groundless and preposterous rumors; and the people, generally urged on by the priests, as it must be reluctantly confessed, assailed the Jews with intense animosity, without any evidence to justify or sustain the charges which were made against them. Thus at Dissenhofen, on the Rhine, an infamous person was tried and convicted of infanticide. Before suffering the penalty of his crime he asserted that he committed the act because a Jew named Michael had offered him a large sum for the blood of a Christian child. Without the least evidence to corroborate the testimony of this convict—without even entering into any scrutiny or judicial proceeding whatever, to ascertain, not the certainty, but at least the probability of this charge—the Jew was arrested and burnt to death; while the popular frenzy extended to the whole race in that vicinity, and even to the adjoining cantons. The inhabitants of Zurich demanded the entire expulsion of the Jews from the city; nor were they even allowed to depart until they had paid a large sum for their safe exit. At Schaffhausen and Winterthur thirty-eight Jews were burned at the stake, on what charge and for what real offense it is impossible to ascertain, except that the animosity of the brutal multitude demanded their immolation.

When Albert I. became Emperor of Germany, he protected the Jews as far as his power extended; and when tumults arose against them in Bavaria and Swabia, he endeavored to suppress them. He readily discovered that the Hebrews were a harmless people, notwithstanding all the various injurious reports which were industriously propagated against them; and he urged the princes who ruled the several provinces and kingdoms which composed the empire to do them justice. In some instances he succeeded; and while a law generally prevailed prohibiting the Jews from owning landed property or acquiring the right of citizenship, they were at the same time exempted from the heavy taxes to which those who owned the soil were subjected.

In the year 1348 a terrible persecution broke out against the Jews in Germany, in consequence of the prevalence of a fatal disease called the *Black Death*, the existence of which was attributed absurdly to them. This disease resembled the Asiatic cholera of modern times in its effects, and the Israelites were charged with having caused it by poisoning the wells and rivers, and by infecting the atmosphere through magical incantations. It was in vain that those unfortunate people asserted and protested their innocence; in vain they procured the depositions of the most eminent physicians of those times, asserting that the epidemic could not have arisen from such causes; and in vain did they point to the fact that as many Jews died of the pestilence, in proportion to their numbers, as any other part of the community. The populace would hear of no vindication or defense. Albert, as Duke of Austria, endeavored to protect them, but was overborne by the popular clamor, and was compelled to permit three hundred Hebrews to be burnt by the exasperated crowd at Kyburg. Terrible scenes occurred at Strasburg. The authorities of the city were disposed to defend the Jews, well knowing their innocence. They were immediately deposed, and other persons selected to fill their places, who were more obsequious to the popular madness. Several Jews were then arrested and tortured, and confessions of guilt were extorted from them. They were then broken on the wheel, and the signal given for a general license of persecution.

11

The houses of the Jews were entered and plundered, and the inmates dragged to an open space, without regard to sex or age, and an immense funeral pile was erected, composed of their own furniture. On this the trembling wretches were placed, to the number, it is confidently asserted by such eminent writers as Basnage and Depping, of two thousand persons; and actually burnt to death, while the surrounding multitude rent the air with their exultant shouts of joy.

A similar scene of infernal cruelty occurred some years later, at Brussels. A report was circulated throughout Brabant that a Jew named Jonathan had obtained sixteen consecrated wafers, by means of a heavy bribe, from a church in Louvain; and that these had afterward been taken to the synagogue in Brussels, and there pierced with knives, and subjected to every possible species of insult and indignity. The elders of the synagogue were arrested and tortured, to obtain a confession of the alleged offense; and their flesh was torn from their bones by red-hot pincers, without extorting any acknowledgment. All the Jews in Brabant were nevertheless banished from the country, and their property confiscated; although not a particle of evidence which deserved confidence was ever produced to prove the guilt of the accused. It is more probable that the wafers were stolen by some daring thief, who afterward charged the Jews with complicity in the act. It is recorded that eighteen enormous pictures were afterward painted for that church of St. Gudule, at Brussels, and hung up in the edifice, to commemorate the incidents connected with these events; and that, until within a few years, an annual procession publicly took place in the city, to commemorate and glorify the circumstances connected with this display of popular delusion, religious bigotry, and infamous persecution.

CHAPTER XIV.

SUPERIORITY OF THE SPANISH JEWS—THE SEPHARDIM—COUNCIL OF ELVIRA—RABBI SOLOMON LEVI OF BURGOS—HIS HISTORY AND WRITINGS—ALPHONZO—PREACHING OF VINCENT FERRAN—CARDINAL JUAN DE TORQUEMADA—CONVERSOS, OR CONVERTED JEWS—THEIR ZEAL FOR ROMANISM—THE SPANISH INQUISITION.

IT is a singular circumstance, worthy of note, that the Jewish race attained to greater importance and distinction in Spain, during the period of their sojourn there, than they did in any other country to which they have wandered, or in which they have ever dwelt. The epithet by which the Spanish Jews are designated is *Sephardism*, and by that term they are known throughout the world. They may be considered as the *aristocracy* of the dispersed tribes, and they are regarded as such by the various portions of their own race. The reason why the Spanish Jews possess this distinction is, because they are supposed to have attained greater consideration and wealth in that country than in any other; because they generally used the Spanish language both in public worship and in private intercourse, in connection with the Hebrew, at a time when the Spanish language was spoken by one of the most renowned and powerful nations then existing in Europe; and because, since their banishment from Spain, the Jews have retained the use of the Spanish language, in preference to the languages of the several countries to which they have emigrated.

Another ground for the superiority claimed by the Spanish Jews is, their great antiquity in that country; for they contend that the legends of the Catholic Church assert that, when the Apostle St. James, the St. Iago de Compostella, preached the gospel and worked many miracles in that country, he succeeded in converting many Jews to Christianity; and thus formed the first Christian Church which existed in that country. This fact, as the Jews allege, proves their great antiquity in Spain; and they account for the existence of Jews there, anterior to the destruction of Jerusalem, by asserting that King Solomon, the son of David, planted colonies and exercised authority in Spain, which in Scripture was called Tarshish, at the period of his reign. Other Jewish writers contend that the first Jews arrived in Spain at a later date, soon after the destruction of the *first* temple; and that an expedition of them, comprising many noble families connected with the royal line of Judah, then settled in Spain and built cities, and attained to great power and opulence.

Nor is this theory destitute of some very plausible arguments to support it,—among which may be mentioned the fact, that the names of some of the most ancient towns of Spain are evidently of Hebrew origin, such as Toledo, Maqueda, and Escalonia; while the names of other places in Spain resemble some in Palestine so closely that the inference is a reasonable one that the former were originally called after the latter,—such as *Tavora*, from Tabor; *Yepes*, from Joppa; *Avila*, from Abila; *Gaona*, from Gaon; *Zacuto*, from Zachut. Other arguments go to prove the great antiquity of the Jews in Spain, such as the circumstance that the names Philip, Alexander, and Mark, which were in general use among the Jews in all other portions of the world in the early ages of the Christian era, were never employed by the Spanish Jews; and as these names were first introduced into Palestine when that country was under the dominion of the Romans, and thus became diffused after the destruction of the second temple, the inference is that the Spanish Jews had settled in that country previous to the date of that event. St. Paul also speaks of his intention to visit Spain, in his Epistle to the Romans, (xv. 24, 28,) showing that that country was then well known to Eastern nations. Josephus asserts that when Herod Antipas was banished by the Roman emperor, it was to Spain; and when the Emperor Adrian had suppressed the revolt of Bar-Cochab, he allowed the Jews, whom he had made prisoners, to emigrate and settle in Spain.

Other facts of similar import may be adduced. In the council of *Elvira*, which was assembled in A. D. 305, about twenty years before the Christian faith became the established religion of the Roman Empire, decrees were passed defining the relations which were to exist between Jews and Christians in that country. The Christians were forbidden, for example, to allow the Jews to bless the produce of the land; as it was then the custom of the Israelites yearly to bestow a blessing on the first fruits of the ground and of the trees. The same charitable assemblage of ecclesiastics forbade the Christians to eat with the Jews, though it is worthy of remark that the Council condemned usury among their own clergy.

During some centuries the Jews continued to experience alternate prosperity and misfortune in Spain; but while the supremacy of the Moors continued, they were exempt from special persecution. We have already narrated how, after the expulsion of the Moors and the supremacy of the Roman Catholic Church in Spain, the Jews who refused to become converts were compelled to endure exile. About this period commenced that remarkable phenomenon which the history of the Spanish Jews presents, of apostate Jews, who, after abjuring the faith of their forefathers and entering the dominant church, became remarkable for the fury with which they persecuted their former co-religionists. Some of those Inquisitors general, who were remarkable for the ferocity with which they inflicted the horrors of the Inquisition on the Israelites, were either converted Jews or descendants of converted Jews; thus presenting one of the most revolting exhibitions of depravity of which human nature is capable.

A convert of a very different character was made about this period from the Jewish to the Christian religion in the person of *Rabbi Solomon Levi, of Burgos*, afterward celebrated as Paul of Burgos. This man was highly esteemed among the Jews for his learning and piety; but at the age of forty he became acquainted with the productions of Thomas Aquinas, the eminent scholastic theologian. By the perusal of the work of Aquinas, *De Legibus*, he was converted to the Roman Catholic faith and was baptized, together with his four young sons. He devoted himself to the study of theology, and became profoundly versed in that science as then taught. The University of Paris bestowed upon him the degree of Doctor of Divinity —a title which was then really a distinction, as it was not then bestowed, as now, upon every clerical pretender who could make sufficient interest to procure it.

Paul of Burgos was a very eloquent preacher; and was appointed Archdeacon of Burgos, and subsequently Bishop of Carthagena, and last of all, Bishop of Burgos. Henry III., King of Arragon, appointed him to the office of High Chancellor of the kingdom, and tutor to his son and successor, John II. At the time of his death in 1435, Paul was a member of the Council of Regency, and the most influential and important person in the kingdom. Nor was he unworthy of the high eminence which he attained, both as an ecclesiastic and as a statesman. Spanish writers generally speak of him with extravagant praise for his superior talents, his sagacity, learning and eloquence. He seems, in fact, to have belonged to the class of men of whom Richelieu and Mazarin were the most eminent, without the hypocrisy, perfidy and cruelty which deformed their characters. Paul died at the age of eighty-three, after a long career of honor and usefulness.

He was eminent, also, as an author and an expounder of the Scriptures. He wrote "Additions to the Postills of Nicholas de Leira," and a *Scrutinium Scripturarum*, the latter of which is a labored refutation of Judaism and defense of Christianity. He dedicated this work to his son, Alphonso, then Archdeacon of Compostella, who afterward became celebrated as an ecclesiastic, and the spirit of the man may be inferred from the following extract from the dedication:

"What would you most wish, my dearly beloved son, that I should give you whilst I am alive, or leave as a legacy to you at my death? What could be better than to add to the knowledge you already possess of Holy Scripture, which will strengthen your feet in the path of a well-directed zeal for Christian truth? It is this which I bear in my heart, of which I make confession with my lips, and concerning which I 'understand the words of the prophet: 'The father shall teach his children thy truth.'—(Isa. xxxviii. 19.)

"I was not myself thus taught in the days of my youth, but was brought up in Jewish blindness and incredulity; while learning Holy Scripture from unsanctified teachers, I received erroneous opinions from erring men, who cloud the pure letter of Scripture by impure inventions, as such teachers have been wont to do. But when it pleased Him, whose mercies are infinite, to call me from darkness to light, and from the depth of the pit to the open air of Heaven, the scales seemed, as it were, to fall from the eyes of my understanding, and I began to read Holy Scripture with my mind in part released from the bonds of prejudice and unbelief. I began to seek for truth, no longer trusting to the power of my own intellect, but with a humbled spirit, praying to God from the heart to make known to me what might be for the salvation of my soul. Day and night I sought help from Him; and thus it came to pass that my love for the Christian faith so much increased, that at length I was able openly to confess the belief which my heart had already received. Having then attained the age at which you now are, my son, I received the sacrament of baptism, and was sprinkled with the holy water of the Church, receiving, at the same time, the name of Paul. You, my dear son, were then in the innocence of childhood, and received this purification at that tender age, while yet unsullied with the sins of riper years. You were baptized by the name of Alphonzo before you could say your letters!

"Afterward, as time passed on, I devoted myself yet more to the study of Holy Scripture, reading both the Testaments, hearing the words of living teachers, and consulting the writings of holy men, our predecessors. Thus I, who was formerly a teacher of error, have become, by the grace of God, a learner of the truth, and have continued so to the great age I have now attained. I can say in truth that amid the pressure of worldly business, and the cares of my bishopric, which have occupied much of my time, there is no consolation to be compared to that I have found in the contemplation of the Eternal God by the study of his holy and spotless word.

"I have also enjoyed what the world calls prosperity. In my utter unworthiness, God has raised me to high honors in his Church. Called first to the Bishopric of Carthagena, then raised to that of Burgos, I have been, so to speak, gifted with the choicest portions in the Church of God. To these have been also added other temporal advantages. With King Henry III., of glorious memory, and with his illustrious son, our present monarch, I have been on terms of familiar intercourse while holding the office of Chancellor. How the goodness of God has also been manifest in his dealings with you and your elder brother, I need not recall to you. One circumstance, however, I cannot pass over in silence—that to us, the descendants of Levi, have been fulfilled the promises written so many hundred years ago: 'Wherefore there shall not be for the Levite a portion or inheritance among his brethren; the Lord himself is his inheritance, as the Lord thy God hath said to him.' (Deut. x. 9.) Truly God himself is our inheritance! Christ is our portion! who has said of old time, that he would cleanse the sons of Levi and purify them, and they shall be the Lord's, to present an offering in righteousness. He now allows us to present this offering, which he will not only look upon, but accept at our hands. It is not without a purpose that I have thus related to you the experience of my past life. It is useful and necessary you should know all the mercies of my God towards me, and a true and sincere memorial of them cannot be taxed with pride."

Alphonso, the son of Paul, to whom these words were addressed, afterward became celebrated, and resembled his father in his talents, his position, and his influence. He also became Bishop of Burgos; and when the Council of Basle convened in 1431, he was chosen to represent the kingdom of Castile in it. He was treated with great consideration; and Æneas Sylvius, who afterward became Pope as Pious II., spoke of him as "an ornament to the Episcopal dignity." When afterward it became known that Alphonso was about to visit Rome, Pope Eugenius confessed, before a full conclave of Cardinals, that in the presence of such a man he felt ashamed to be seen sitting in the chair of St. Peter. The writings of Alphonso were numerous,—the most important of which were a History of the Kings of Spain, a Treatise on Christian Morals, translations of Seneca and Cicero, and a Commentary on the 26th Psalm. He likewise lived to a great age, and died in the odor of sanctity.

His brother, Don Gonzalo de Santa Maria, was also eminent in the Church. He represented Arragon in the Council of Constance in 1416, and afterward became Bishop of Placentia. The third son of Paul of Burgos, named Alvar, became distinguished in Spanish literature. He was appointed chief secretary to John II., King of Castile; and afterward he held a high place in the court and service of Ferdinand of Arragon. His most important work was a History of the reign of John II. until the year 1420, which was afterward completed by another hand. This remarkable family retained their eminence in Spain during several centuries. The fourth son of Paul of Burgos married, and his descendants ranked with the first nobility of the country. Of these, Pedro de Carthagena became "illustrious" as a soldier; and on several occasions he entertained the King of Arragon at his palace. He also distinguished himself in the wars against the Moors, and behaved with great gallantry at the siege and fall of Granada in 1431. His son, called Alvar, emulated the fame of the father in martial exploits; and his name frequently occurs in the annals of the bloody civil wars which took place and desolated Spain during the turbulent reign of Henry IV.

The efforts made by the Roman Catholic Church in Spain, during the fifteenth century, for the conversion of the Jews, were not always confined to measures of compulsion and royal authority; but occasionally the zeal of some eloquent and enthusiastic preacher interposed to accomplish the same purpose by more commendable means. An example of this kind is presented in the case of Vincent Ferrar, a distinguished Dominican monk, whose piety and ability have been admitted by Protestant as well as by Catholic writers. He traveled through Spain, preached with great earnestness and good feeling to the Jews, and addressed himself to the task of convincing them that Christ was the real and only Messiah, and that it behooved them to accept Him without waiting for any other. It is recorded that his efforts were very successful, and that thirty thousand Jews and also eight thousand Moors professed themselves converts to the Church.

It was of course impossible to determine how great a proportion of these converts were sincere. It is probable that this large number comprised three separate and very different classes;—the first, including those who were real and sincere converts to the faith which they adopted; the second, those who, though Jews by faith, never cared for any religious faith, had never been sincere or conscientious in their profession of Judaism, and who, when they professed to become Christians, merely made the exchange without any real intention of adopting the Christian religion, or practicing Christian morals. They were worthless Jews, and became equally worthless Christians. The third class were those who, having been sincerely attached to the Jewish faith, professed to become Christians to avoid the miseries and persecutions which threatened them; while in reality and in secret they remained attached to the religion of their forefathers.

Among the number of converts included in these several classes, there were not a few who afterward became eminent in the church, beside Paul of Burgos and his sons. Prominent among these were Cardinal Juan de Torquemada, who should be carefully distinguished from Thomas de Torquemada, the celebrated and infamously cruel Inquisitor-General, of whom we will have occasion to speak hereafter; Don Francisco, Bishop of Coria; Don Alonzo de Valladolid, Bishop of Cuidad Rodrigo, and Don Alonzo de Palenzuela, who succeeded him in that dignity; Juan Ortega, afterward Bishop of Coria, and others, who were less distinguished. Of this number, Torquemada was the author of several famous works in theology, and was frequently employed by the Spanish sovereign in embassies of importance. These eminent Jewish converts were always zealous for the conversion of their brethren to the Roman Catholic Church; although they condemned the use of any severe or cruel measures to accomplish that end.

The annals of those times present several very remarkable instances in which converted Jews of superior talents and learning attained to high stations in the Church, and became celebrated as ecclesiastics, while in reality they remained Jews, and secretly practiced the rites and ceremonies of that faith. The most extraordinary case of this description was in the family of Gonsalvo Alonso, who professed to be converted by the eloquent preaching of Vincent Ferrar, and eventually attained high dignity in the church. One of his sons, Don Alonso, became Archbishop of Montreal in Sicily; the other, Don Pedro, became Bishop of Calahorra, and President of the Council of Castile during the reign of Ferdinand and Isabella. The latter was charged, toward the close of his life, with being a concealed Jew; and with having endeavored secretly to extend and advance the Jewish religion in the diocese over which he presided. The Inquisition boldly preferred these charges against the prelate. He appealed to the Pope at Rome; and going thither, he gained over Alexander VI. by his arts and eloquence to his side; who protected him and appointed him his ambassador to the Republic of Venice. Some time afterward Alexander found it necessary to appoint a Committee of Ecclesiastics to examine into Don Pedro's orthodoxy. A hundred witnesses, whom the bishop had himself cited, were examined; and their testimony conclusively proved that he was a concealed Jew, and that he had secretly endeavored to extend the Jewish religion in his diocese. The result was that Don Pedro was condemned to perpetual imprisonment; he was confined in the castle of St. Angelo at Rome, where after some years he died.

The talents and energy of the converted Jews soon gained them great influence and high places in the court of Ferdinand and Isabella; and the consequence was that they were hated and envied not only by the Jews whom they had left, but also by their Christian rivals. Among these *Conversos*, as they were called, and their immediate descendants, were such eminent persons as Gonzalvo Fernandez, the conqueror of the Moors in Spain, the family of the Guzmans, and the Arias of Avila, all of whom had Jewish blood in their veins. One of the most distinguished statesmen of that era was Ferdinand Dias de Toledo, a converted Jew; and his son, Don Pedro de Toledo, afterward became first Bishop of Malaga, after it was taken from the Moors in 1489. Ferdinand del Pulgar, the Secretary to Queen Isabella, Alonzo de Avila, Chief Secretary to King Ferdinand, and Alvarez de Toledo, Prothonotary of Granada, were all converted Jews; as were Philip de Clemente, the Prothonotary of Arragon, Luiz Gonzales, one of the royal secretaries, and Luiz Sanchez, the king's treasurer. The Vice-chancellor of Arragon during Ferdinand's reign was Alonzo de la Cavalleria, who was descended from a Jewish family. His grandson, Don Francisco, was afterward honored with an alliance with the royal family, having married the Countess de Ribagorza, cousin of the Emperor Charles V.

It is a curious circumstance that the prosperity of the converted Jews in Spain was the means of eventually gathering around them the storms and persecutions of the terrible Inquisition. That wonderful tribunal kept a secret record of the genealogies and private history of all the families of the *Conversos*, and of the noble families of Arragon which had intermarried with them, so that it might be used upon a future occasion for their ruin. A tribunal called the Inquisition had existed for some years in Spain previous to the accession of Ferdinand and Isabella. It had been introduced from France, where it was first invented and established by the Dominican Order, for the persecution and murder of the Vaudois. This institution, as it first existed in Spain, was very hostile to, and suspicious of, the *Conversos;* but its powers were limited, and its influence of little importance. The infamy belongs to the much-praised Ferdinand and Isabella, and especially to the latter, of having enlarged and extended the powers of the "Holy Tribunal," till it became one of the most formidable engines of destruction which ever existed. This tribunal was called the "New Inquisition," and it differed from the old in the following particulars: first, the converted and the unconverted Jews were made the special subjects of its scrutiny and jurisdiction; secondly, it was a permanent institution, sitting constantly, whereas the former tribunal only sat when a special requisition of the sovereigns demanded it; and thirdly, its powers were much more absolute and extensive, and its facilities for secret, rapid, and irresponsible injury to its victims, much greater.

To show with what *animus* toward the Jews this institution was established, it may be stated that a decree was made that no bishop or priest, who was in the remotest manner connected with the Jewish race, should be employed in any capacity in the institution. The regular clergy of the Church were designated as the persons from whom all its officials should be selected; and the Dominicans, from the peculiar severity and bloodthirstiness which has ever characterized that Order, were chosen as its special patrons and executive officers. It is recorded that Isabella at first felt great repugnance to the establishment of this formidable institution, and some of the most eminent men about the Spanish Court shared her apprehensions. It is said that Ximines opposed it; and that Cardinal Mendoza and Talavera, Archbishop of Granada, used their utmost influence to resist its establishment. But the Queen had made a vow on the subject of the extermination of heresy from her dominions after the subjugation of the Moors, and her confessor succeeded in convincing her that the fulfillment of this engagement required the use of such an agency as the proposed Inquisition alone could furnish; and thus it was, that she became instrumental in the perpetration of the most horrible cruelties which blacken and deform the history of men

CHAPTER XV.

PROCEEDINGS OF THE "NEW INQUISITION"—JEWS IN MOROCCO, FEZ, AND NORTHERN AFRICA—THE JEWS in TURKEY—CONDITION OF THE JEWS IN ITALY—NICHOLAS III.—EUGINIUS IV.—MONTE-DI-PIETA—CONDITION OF THE JEWS IN LEGHORN—IN FLORENCE—IN NAPLES—IN SICILY—IN SIENNA.

THE papal bull which established the "New Inquisition in Spain," with special reference to the persecution, vexation, and conversion of the Jews, was issued in the year 1478. The results of the operation of that institution on the Jewish people may be inferred from the fact that in Seville alone three hundred *conversos,* or converts, whose sincerity was suspected, were burnt to death in the year 1481; and throughout Spain in the same year, for the same cause, the number of the burnt amounted to two thousand. Torquemada, the Inquisitor-General, having appointed a savage confederate, similar in spirit to himself, named Pedro Arbues d'Avila, as Inquisitor of Arragon, the despair of the unfortunate Jews induced them to assassinate him. At Vespers, on the 13th of December, 1485, while leaning against a pillar in the cathedral, he was attacked and so severely wounded, by several assailants, through the coat of mail which he wore under his garments, that he expired after a few hours. Ferdinand and Isabella erected a statue to the momory of Arbues, and Pope Alexander VII. canonized him in 1664; but the task of punishing his murderers was a more immediate and agreeable one. Two hundred converted Jews, suspected of having been privy to his death, were arrested and suffered various punishments, including death, proportioned according to the supposed degrees of their guilt.

It is curious to observe, that some of the highest personages then living in Spain were involved in this charge, such as Don Jacques, the "Infant" of Navarre, a near relation to King Ferdinand; Don Lopes Ximines, the Count of Aranda, Don Blasco d'Alagon, Lord of Sastago, and others. The sum total of those who were burnt to death during the administration of Torquemada amounted to *ten thousand*, while ninety thousand persons were condemned to suffer other and minor penalties. The amount of material furnished by the Jews and converted Jews in Spain for the suspicious scrutiny and jealous hate of the Inquisition, may be inferred from this fact: that at that period, and even since, scarcely a family of any importance existed in Spain which was not descended on the father or mother's side from Jews who had professed the Roman Catholic religion, either from conviction or from motives of prudence and policy. Hence, among so many it was easy to find large numbers who might be regarded with suspicion, as being still secretly attached to the faith of their forefathers.

When at length the Jews were banished from Spain

and Portugal, as already narrated in a previous article, by the decrees of 1492 and 1496, the fugitives scattered themselves among many different nations, in Africa, Asia and Europe, and even in South America. Not a few fled to Barbary, in northern Africa, others settled in Tripoli, Tunis, Algiers, Oran and Fez, and throughout the empire of Morocco. They were generally protected by the Emperor of the latter country, and by the several Beys and Deys of those minor States; though sometimes they suffered severe exactions, and were compelled to wear a distinctive dress, such as black turbans and boots of a peculiar color, that they might not be confounded with the Mahometan population. As was usual with this people, some of their chief members gradually worked their way to places of importance and distinction about the courts of the respective sovereigns under whose jurisdiction they lived. One of these, Don Samuel Palache, was dispatched by the Emperor of Morocco as his confidential agent to the Hague; where he died in 1616, and his funeral was attended by Prince Maurice, the States-General, and the Councillors of the United Provinces. In 1642 another Jew, Don Joseph Toledano, was selected by Muley Ismael, the Prince of Morocco, to conclude a treaty of alliance with the Republic of the Netherlands. All the important financial affairs of the sovereigns of Morocco seem to have been in the hands of the Jews during several generations. Thus, in 1675, a Jew, named Masahod de la Mar, was sent by the Emperor of Morocco on a financial mission to England, and afterward to Amsterdam, where he resided as the permanent representative of that monarch. Various examples of this nature demonstrate that, as usual, the Jews received more toleration and enlightened treatment from the disciples of Mahomet, among whom their checkered destiny threw them, than they did from some of those who professed the religion of Christ.

A portion of the Jews who fled from Spain took refuge in Turkey. When Constantinople was captured by the Moslems in 1453, a considerable number of Israelites were found residing there, who possessed both wealth and consideration. When the Spanish exiles arrived they found many synagogues and learned Rabbis already existing, both in the Turkish capital and in other cities of the empire, especially in Aleppo, Damascus, Tiberius, Nicopolis and Jerusalem. When the Spanish Jews settled in these several cities, they generally erected new synagogues for themselves, in the progress of time; and retained the liturgy, language and customs which they had employed in Spain. They even continued to designate themselves by the names of the Spanish and Portuguese cities from which they had fled, such as those of Toledo, Lisbon, Lorca and the rest. They also carried with them to Constantinople their Hebrew printing-presses, and soon they were able to distribute throughout the East copies of the Hebrew Scriptures, which, till that period, were very rare and expensive.

During many generations the social and political relations of the Jews in the Ottoman empire remained prosperous; and they were treated by the successive sovereigns who reigned as the representatives of Mahomet with liberality and protection. The Jews gradually acquired the confidence of the Sultans by their superior financial ability; and prominent Israelites often served as royal treasurers, and sometimes as the royal physicians. One of them, named Joseph Miquez, was a favorite of Selim II. This person was a native of Spain, and had emigrated from that country to avoid persecution. He was a man of superior talent and of highly respectable character. He first made application to the Duchess of Parma, who then ruled over the Netherlands, to be permitted to settle in that country with a colony of his brethren. The request was refused, through the influence of the bigoted Philip II. He then made a similar request of the Republic of Venice, and received a refusal for a similar reason. He then transferred his intentions to the Ottoman capital, where his abilities and integrity soon secured for him the confidence of the Sultan. He was appointed Governor of twelve Islands in the Archipelago, and he administered this high trust with such success and ability, that he received the title of "El Nassi" the Prince. In 1566 the Consistory of the Reformed Dutch, or Protestant Church of Antwerp, received a secret communication from Miquez, urging the Protestants of the Netherlands to hold out in their struggles against the tyranny of Philip II., because the Sultan Selim was then preparing an expedition against the Spanish dominions of Philip, which would suspend, for a time at least, his hostile demonstrations against the persecuted Protestants of the Netherlands.

Many of the fugitive Jews from Spain took refuge in Italy. The peculiar condition of that country, divided as it was into many small principalities, was favorable to the interest of the Israelites; because they became of too much importance in each State to endure oppression, and because no single sovereign ruled over one enormous territory, so that, if persecuted in one State, they could escape into another with greater convenience. Occasionally, however, the Jews in Italy experienced symptoms of their hereditary fate, in the outbreaks of popular violence and hostility. An instance of this description occurred at Naples. In that kingdom the Jews were numerous, even before the expulsion of that race from Spain. They had many synagogues and learned Rabbis; enjoyed high influence and favor at court; yet, though protected by the monarch and nobility, they were hated by the populace. On the death of one of the sovereigns, in the thirteenth century, who had been their special patron, the fury of the mob could not be restrained. A great tumult occurred in Naples; many Jews were slain; and such stringent laws were extorted from the succeeding monarch, that all the Jews were compelled to profess to become converts to the Catholic faith to save their lives and property. Another King of Naples had borrowed enormous sums of money from the Jews of his capital, and on his death-bed he enjoined upon his son that the loan should be faithfully repaid. The successor, however, thought the only payment which he could make would be, to compel his creditors to receive the boon of baptism; and thus, by the administration of this rite, he conceived that he had conferred an equivalent for the sums for which his crown was indebted to the unwilling and disgusted proselytes.

It is pleasing to observe that sometimes the Roman pontiffs had intelligence and charity enough to defend these people against the constant and groundless complaints which were preferred against them. Thus in 1247, Innocent IV. decreed that, whenever a person made a charge against the Jews of murdering the children of Christians,—a charge with which they were continually harassed, without being able to support it with the testimony of three Jews and three Christians, the accuser should himself suffer the penalty of an assassin: which was nothing more than just; because he who prefers a false charge of a crime, the penalty of which is death, is in heart a murderer, endeavoring to compass the death of an innocent person by a false accusation, and should therefore be punished as for the crime of murder. A similar spirit is recorded to the praise of Nicholas III. The monastic order of *Minorites* attempted to prevent the Jews, by forcible means, from observing the external rites and ceremonies of their religion. The Jews appealed to the pontiff, who thereupon issued a bull commanding the faithful to allow the Hebrews to enjoy the free use of their religion, and forbidding them to molest them in any way; and at the same time threatening severe penalties upon all who should disobey his edict. At the same time Nicholas showed that he earnestly desired the conversion of the Jews by legitimate means; and he allowed the Provincial of the Province of Lombardy to assemble the Jews whenever he thought proper, and preach to them, and use all the resources of moral suasion, to procure their conversion. In 1363 Urban V. proclaimed a bull, the import and purpose of which were similar to those of the bull issued by Nicholas.

But the experience of the Jews in Italy was not always so tolerable. Pope Eugenius IV. forbade them to practice money-lending, to exercise any public employment, or to eat and drink with Christians. He forbade them to build any new synagogues, or to enlarge or repair the old ones. He prohibited Christians from leaving the Jews any legacies in their wills. Some years later a popular tumult broke out against them at Trent, and all the Jews in that city were imprisoned, and afterward either tortured or executed. The preposterous charge by which this cruelty and injustice were excused, was that three Jews had murdered a Christian infant. Even had this accusation been true, of which there was not the slightest proof, the punishment of those only who had actually committed the crime would seem to have been equitable; but, according to the logic and the religion of that age and country, justice could not be satisfied except by the murder of hundreds of innocent people.

It should not, however, be inferred that the conduct of the Jews in Italy was always blameless. They often took advantage of their facilities as money-lenders to practice the most exorbitant usury; and the consequence was, the establishment of a peculiar institution by the Catholics, for the purpose of protecting the poorer classes of the community from their extortions. These institutions were the *Monté di Pieta*—Mounts of Piety—the purpose of which was to lend small sums to the poor, on the deposit of pledges, and at a rate of interest so low, that no profit remained after the expenses of the institution were paid. The originator of these establishments is said to have been a Franciscan monk named Barnabas; who, when Pius II. visited Perugia, preached before him, and in his sermon suggested this expedient to the Pontiff. Pius approved of the idea, and it was immediately carried into execution. It was called *Monté di Pieta*, because it was regarded as an act of piety to rescue poor Christians from the alleged frauds and oppressions of the acknowledged enemies of Christianity. The example of Perugia was soon followed by other cities of Italy, in which the exactions of the Jews had been most oppressive. The rate of interest which they generally demanded was a hundred per cent.; and it is not singular that the proposal to devise an expedient to remedy the evil, should be popular with the multitude. Mantua was the first city to establish the *Monté* after Perugia. They were placed under the management of twelve directors, four of whom were priests, chosen for life; the others were nobles, lawyers and merchants, elected for a term of two years each.

One of these institutions was erected at Florence, through the agency of a Franciscan monk named

Barnardino. He visited various portions of Italy, denouncing the Jews and their extortions, and urging the people and their rulers everywhere to establish *Monté* for the purpose of alleviating the evil. He was so violent in his denunciations at Florence, that the magistrates apprehended that a general massacre of the Hebrews might ensue, and ordered him to leave the city. After his departure, an institution of the kind was founded, which, for a time, was extensively patronized. The same was done at Sienna, Lucca, Rome, and Naples, and eventually in almost every town and city of Italy. They all flourished during a short period, but afterward sank into disuse and neglect. The reasons which led to this result are peculiar, and deserve to be noted. The *Monté di Pieta* were always subjected to certain peculiar regulations, which were necessary to confine their operations to the class of persons for whose benefit they were intended. It was requisite for every borrower to make an acknowledgment of his poverty, and also to prove that the security which he deposited was his own property. This requisition offended the pride of many who wished to use the advantages of the institution; and the borrowers from the Jews were exempted from such mortifying conditions. The jealousy of the rival order of the Dominicans, who condemned these *Monté* because they had been introduced chiefly through the agency of the Franciscans, helped to destroy them; for the Dominicans stigmatized them as *Monté di Impieta*, and used their influence to overturn their popularity. By the joint operation of these several influences, the Jews in Italy regained their former position and profits as the general money-lenders of the public, after the lapse of a series of years.

A favorable circumstance in their behalf occurred in the founding of the maritime city of Leghorn, which was effected by the enterprise of the Medici while they held possession of the sovereignty of Florence. A particular quarter of the new city was appropriated as the future residence of the Jews, within which they were allowed to have their synagogues, to elect a Senate for their separate government, and to erect schools, a hospital, and other desirable institutions. The result of this peculiar position and unusual protection was, that the Jews of Leghorn, many of whom were originally fugitives from Spain at the time of the banishment of the Hebrews from that kingdom, as already narrated, became very wealthy; and enjoyed a long era of security and prosperity, such as fell to the lot of very few of their brethren in other countries. They became, indeed, so rich and independent, that it passed into a proverb in Tuscany, that it was as safe to strike the Grand Duke as an Israelite. Their enormous wealth may be inferred from one remarkable circumstance: that, though they were compelled always to reside in the quarter of the city which had been originally appropriated to them, named the *Ghetto*, yet they actually owned a large portion of the rest of the city and the surrounding lands; and their commercial dealings were more extensive than those of all the other merchants of Leghorn put together.

In Naples the Jews experienced a much less agreeable fate, for they were exposed to the hatred of the populace, and to the exactions of the rulers. They were accused—whether falsely or not, it is impossible to determine—of having used their influence to induce the Sultan to deprive the order of the Minorites of their chapel in Jerusalem, and convert it into a synagogue. Whether the monks outbribed the Jews or not, is, of course, unknown; but Pope Martin V. and Joanna II. of Naples believed the charge, and compelled the Jews to pay a large sum to indemnify the Minorites for the loss of their chapel. In 1456, the Neapolitan Jews were subjected to another tribute of a different description, the payment of which was particularly obnoxious to their feelings. Europe was at that time filled with terror at the capture of Constantinople by the victorious arms of Mahomet II.; and Calixtus II. began to make pompous proclamations respecting the commencement of a war of extermination against the Turks. As this enterprise could not be carried on without immense revenues and the expenditure of enormous sums of money, the Pontiff victimized the Jews, and sent collectors throughout Italy, and especially into the Two Sicilies, levying a heavy tax on all the property, movable and immovable, of the obnoxious race; at the same time demanding from them all the proceeds of the usurious transactions in which they had been engaged for several years. These requisitions were enforced by all the terrors of the ecclesiastical and secular tribunals. It is impossible to conjecture how great a treasure was thus collected, but it must have been immense; and it remained in the coffers of the Pontiff, inasmuch as the war was never undertaken, and no call ever made for the designated use of the money.

While the Christian public of those times in Italy used the Jews to aid their commercial interests, they held them generally in abhorrence; and, whenever an opportunity occurred, inflicted upon them serious injuries. A single circumstance, which may be selected from many others, will illustrate this assertion. There lived at Sienna, about the middle of the fifteenth century, a celebrated Jewish physician, whose superior skill and learning in the healing art had acquired for him a very extensive practice among his own people; and sometimes, in cases of emergency, when all other doctors failed, he was called in to prescribe for Christian invalids, with much success. The son of a nobleman at Sienna having become dangerously ill, the father proposed, as a last resource, to send for the Jewish doctor; but the mother positively refused to permit it; and, it is recorded by cotemporary historians of repute, that the reason which she gave for so doing, was, because it was better and more Christian that her son should die, than that he should owe his recovery to health to the agency of one who belonged to the race which crucified the Saviour!

CHAPTER XVI.

RABBI ISAAC ABRABANEL—HIS TALENTS, LEARNING AND WRITINGS—JEWS AT GENOA—HEBREW PRINTING-PRESSES IN ITALY—HEBREW LITERATURE IN THE MIDDLE AGES—SOLOMON USQUE—LEO OF MODENA—JEWS IN THE PAPAL STATES—KARAITE JEWS IN RUSSIA.

THE most distinguished personage who belonged to the Hebrew race, during the latter portion of the fifteenth century, was Rabbi Isaac Abrabanel, sometimes called Abravanel ben Judah. He was the most learned and celebrated of all the Spanish Rabbis, and was descended from a family which was alleged to have been connected with the royal house of David. Abrabanel asserted that a certain Spanish king named Pyrrhus, who lived in the days of Nebuchadnezzar, to whose assistance he went with an army, brought back Jewish captives with him into Spain; a portion of whom having resided within the third wall of Jerusalem were of royal blood, and these he took to Seville. From some of these noble captives Abrabanel was believed to have descended. From Seville the family became dispersed into different parts of Spain and Portugal; but the principal members of it dwelt at Lisbon. There Rabbi Isaac was born in A. D. 1437. His parents were wealthy, and being regarded as possessing noble blood, were allowed by the haughty Spaniards to assume the title of Don, which was used only by those belonging to the nobility. Isaac received an excellent education; and, being gifted by nature with talents of a high order, he soon gave evidence of his superiority by his unusual and rapid proficiency. He began to expound the Scriptures publicly in the synagogue at Lisbon, at the age of twenty.

The superior talents and learning of Abrabanel soon gained for him a wide reputation; and the monarch of Portugal, Alphonzo V., reposed great confidence in his abilities and judgment. When John II. succeeded Alphonzo, Abrabanel fell into disgrace, together with all the ministry of the late king, who were charged with a plot to deliver the kingdom into the power of the Spaniards. Under these circumstances Abrabanel fled into Castile, having been stripped of all his property and even of his manuscripts, which were the result of the careful studies of many years. In Spain he applied himself to mercantile pursuits, especially to usury, in order to restore his reduced fortunes. He was successful, soon became wealthy, and lived in Madrid in considerable splendor. When Ferdinand and Isabella expelled the Jews from their dominions in 1492, confiscating all their propetry to the crown, Abrabanel, being ruined with the rest of his race, fled to Naples, and commenced anew the task of accumulating a competence. As was usual, his superior sagacity and intelligence succeeded; he became again rich, and even won the confidence and favor of the king. At Naples he wrote his famous Commentary on the Book of Kings at the age of fifty-six. When Charles

VIII. of France invaded the kingdom of Naples in 1494, and gained possession of the capital and all the principal fortresses, Abrabanel fled with king Ferdinand to Messina, in the island of Sicily where he was permitted to live in tranquillity and security during some years.

After the accession of Charles V. to the sovereignty of Naples, he banished the Jews from his Italian dominions; and while vast numbers of them took refuge in Turkey, Abrabanel sailed for Corfu. There he remained one year; thence he removed to Monopoli, a maritime town of Apulia, and continued his literary labors, which consisted in the preparation of commentaries on the Prophets of the Old Testament. He resided seven years at Monopoli, and during this interval he wrote his most celebrated works. In 1508 he visited Venice for the purpose of negotiating a commercial treaty between that republic and the King of Portugal. While residing at Venice he wrote his Commentaries on Jeremiah, Ezekiel, and the twelve minor Prophets; and there he died in 1508, at the age of seventy-one. His remains were taken to Padua, and buried in the ancient cemetery of the Jews without the walls of the city; but as if illustrative of the general fate of this people, when that city was besieged by the troops of Charles V. in 1509, the cemetery was entirely destroyed for the purpose of facilitating the operations of the besiegers, and all traces of Abrabanel's tomb were obliterated He left three sons, all of whom were distinguished. Judah, the eldest, was a learned Hebraist, an eminent physician, and a poet.

Joseph, the second, also possessed superior ability, but was more remarkable from the fact that he never deserted his father, during all his wanderings and persecutions, but shared them with him. Samuel, the youngest, who was also learned, grieved his father by becoming a convert to the Roman Catholic Church, and was baptized at Ferrara. The worst enemies of Abrabanel were compelled to admit his great learning, his superior sagacity, and his remarkable talents as a writer. Though some of his works were written in an incredibly short space of time, they all occupy a high place among the most esteemed productions of Hebrew literature.

A singular circumstance is recorded by Basnage in connection with the Jewish community settled at Genoa. At one time the port of Caffa was subjected to that city, which became the depot of their commerce in the Black Sea. The Jews became largely interested in that commerce, and engaged in the purchase and sale of slaves. Large numbers of boys and girls from Georgia and Circassia were brought to that port for sale by Russians and Tartars, whom the Jews bought and then sold to the Saracens and Turks. Their profits by this traffic were immense—sometimes as great as a thousand per cent. Many Jews became enormously rich, but their prosperity from this source was not of long continuance. The Dominicans, ever the mortal foes of the Hebrews, informed the Pontiff, Martin V., of the existence of this trade, and he ordered the bishop and the magistrates of Genoa to seize the property of all those who were known to have been engaged in the business, and appropriate it to the redemption of those who had been sold into slavery.

A remarkable peculiarity connected with the Jewish people in Italy, in the fifteenth century, was their literary activity. They established printing-presses in various cities, and published valuable editions of the works of their most eminent Rabbis. The first book printed by them issued from their press at Regghio, in Calabria, in 1475. It was the *Commentary of Solomon Jarchi* on the Five Books of Moses, and was printed in one volume, small folio. Only a single copy of this work is known to exist, though other editions of the same book are extant. The next work published was the *Abra Turim*, or Four Orders, a system of Hebrew jurisprudence by Rabbi Jacob ben Ascer; and it was executed in the town of Plebisacio, in the territory of Padua. Other presses, which had been established at Bologna, Mantua, Ferrara, and other cities, were kept in constant activity; and considering the infant state in which the art of printing was at that era, the Jewish publications were remarkable for the excellence of their mechanical execution. The most celebrated of the Hebrew printing establishments was located at the small town of Soncino, in the territory of Milan, over which the Soncinati family presided. They commenced their operations in 1484, and their first work was a portion of the Talmud, accompanied by the Commentaries of Maimonides, Jarchi, and other Rabbis. The most valuable of their publications was a complete edition of the Old Testament in Hebrew, containing all the points and accents, and a large number of valuable various readings.

Soncini, who became celebrated as a printer, illustrated the wandering and unsettled character of his people, by moving about continually from place to place, carrying his press with him. He first transferred his establishment to Brescia; thence he journeyed to Fano, and lived successively at Pesaro, Rimini, Thessalonica, and Constantinople, where he eventually died. At all these places he printed very valuable works, superior in execution to any other Hebrew publications of the time. Another celebrated press was established at Naples, the first issue of which was a Psalter, accompanied by the commentary of Kimchi. The skill displayed in the printing of this work was inferior to that of subsequent attempts, when Aben Ezra's Commentary on the Pentateuch was published. Various other works followed, such as Hebrew and Rabbinical Lexicons, the medical works of Avicenna, and editions of the Mischna. Daniel Bomberg distinguished himself at Venice by the issue of many Hebrew books of value, such as the *Targum*, with select commentaries of the Rabbis annexed, which were issued in four large folios.

From these and other literary enterprises which might be named, it is evident that the Jews in the fifteenth century were not destitute of a proper appreciation of intellectual cultivation, and especially of that cultivation which was appropriate to their race and condition. They cherished with a just and commendable pride their national literature, and, in so doing, they present a favorable contrast to the stupid prejudice which existed in the prevalent Church at that time against the study of the Hebrew language and literature. The ignorant priests asserted generally that those who paid any attention to the study of that tongue, even though it were for the necessary and useful purpose of expounding the Old Testament in its original language more critically and successfully, were in great danger of becoming converts to Judaism. They prevailed upon the Emperor Maximilian to issue an edict to the effect that all the books which had been printed at Hebrew presses throughout his dominions should be burnt. Before this preposterous order could be executed, the distinguished German scholar Reuchlin, who has justly been termed the Precursor of the Reformation, and was himself a learned Orientalist, succeeded in rescuing the most valuable works in Hebrew literature from the oblivion with which they were threatened by the ignorance and fanatical prejudices of those who should have been their protectors.

In the fifteenth century the Jews produced several eminent men in addition to Abrabanel, the chief of whom was Solomon Usque, the author of the celebrated work, entitled the "*Consolation of Israel.*" This author was a native of Portugal, and the book was written in the dialect which was spoken by the Jews in that country, in which many Asiatic words occur. It is written in the form of a dialogue, and represents a conversation which is supposed to have taken place between the patriarch Jacob and the prophets Nahum and Zechariah, in reference to the calamities and the destiny of Israel. The purpose of the work is to comfort and encourage the Jews under the afflictions which they endured, and the delay of the coming of the Messiah, by describing all these as resulting from the direct appointment and purpose of the Deity. Another important work was published at Venice by the Rabbi Joseph ben Joshua, describing the history of France as far as it refers to the wars which had taken place between that country and the Turks, and the several crusades. This writer is said to resemble Josephus, and to be very little inferior to him in the qualifications which he displayed for historical composition.

Rabbi Jahadah Arie, otherwise called Leo of Modena, was another Jew of eminence, who belonged to the era of which we now speak. He was remarkable for his intense hatred of Christianity; and, in his writings, did not use much caution and prudence in his allusions to that religion. His chief work was called "*The Mouth of the Lion*," which is a Lexicon of those words which occur in the Rabbinical writings, which are neither pure Hebrew nor Chaldee, and are, therefore, very perplexing to the learner. He also wrote a work on the manners and customs of the modern Jews, in which his hatred of Christianity is not disguised. He speaks of Christ as an impostor; and argued that the word *Jesus*, if reckoned according to the numerical powers of the letters which compose it, amounts to 616, which is the same number which is represented by the words "*Elohe nechar*," which signify *strange gods*. Leo was a resident of Venice, where he was chief of the synagogue, and where he died at a great age. In his enmity to Christians, he may be regarded as a good representative of an *ecclesiastical Shylock*.

The fate of the Jews in the Ecclesiastical States, during the fifteenth and sixteenth centuries, was one of continual vacillation and change, being entirely dependent upon the peculiar disposition and interest of the sucessive pontiffs. Alexander VI., who is generally admitted to have been the most infamous person of his time, disappointed the enemies of the Jews by protecting them, and by forbidding all persons to annoy them. Paul III. promulgated a bull, which annulled all the decrees of kings and other rulers which were favorable to those people, and ordering that converts from among them should be entirely separated from their relations, and that the latter should be subjected to the special scrutiny of the Inquisition. Julius III. ordered all the copies of the Talmud which could be found to be burnt. Paul IV. commanded every synagogue in his dominions to pay ten ducats annually for the instruction of converts to the Roman Catholic Church, forbidding the Jews, at the same time, to have more than one synagogue in one town. He also decreed that they should not engage in any mercantile pursuit, and should confine themselves to money-lending, requiring them to abstain from selling the pledges they had received for eighteen months, and then to restore the surplus to the borrower. The hardest blow of all, was a law commanding them to sell all their real estate within six months, forbidding them to acquire any more in future. The result of this law was, that, by forced sales, the Jews were robbed of nine-tenths of their real property, because it brought but one-tenth of its full value. This Pope forbade Jewish doctors to attend Christian patients; and he sent a Dominican to Cremona to burn a valuable library of Hebrew works which the Jews had collected and possessed there. Twelve thousand volumes were destroyed by this zealot, who combined the character of a thief and a barbarian into one infamous compound.

The succeeding Pope, Pius IV., exhibited more enlightened and charitable views. He annulled all the decrees of his predecessors respecting these people, and restored them to all the privileges which they had ever enjoyed in the Ecclesiastical States. The next Pontiff, Pius V., turned the tables, and accusing them of various crimes, including fraud, robbery, magic and licentiousness, he banished them from his dominions with the exception of those residing in Rome and Ancona. The reason why he permitted them to remain in those places probably was, because their financial resources and skill were indispensable to the papal court. Gregory XIII. allowed the Jews to return to the States of the Church, annoying them, however, by the special scrutiny of the Inquisition, forbidding them to read the Talmud and other Jewish books, and requiring them to attend the preaching of sermons from time to time, which were intended to convince them of the falsity of their religion. Sixtus V., on the other hand, perceiving the injustice and cruelty of all the oppressions and vexations to which the Jews had been subjected by his predecessors, removed all the disabilities under which they had labored, placed them on an equality in trade and other civil rights with the rest of his subjects, and imposed on them only the ordinary degree of taxation.

Having thus completed our survey of the most memorable events connected with the history of the Jews in the southern portion of Europe, we turn our attention northward, and notice their experiences and vicissitudes in other European communities. They existed in Poland at a very early period, probably in the eleventh century; and were allowed to possess very peculiar privileges and immunities. The first authentic account which we possess of them dates in the year 1264, when Boleslaus V. was Duke of Poland, and was their special patron. Their prosperity continued during the reign of his son, and increased during that of his great grandson named Casimer, whose favorite mistress was a beautiful Jewess named Esther. They have had synagogues, academies and Rabbinical schools in that country from a remote period; and among other singular laws which there existed was one by which, if a Jew became a convert to Christianity, and distinguished himself in the army, he became a nobleman. Many of the Polish nobility of the present day are descended from Jewish families; and during many ages the Jews in Poland have always been exempt from persecution and cruelty, except when the kingdom was invaded by the Russians and Tartars. A peculiarity of the Polish Jews is the existence among them of the sect of the *Karaites*, who are distinguished by their aversion to the Talmud, and the Rabbinical writings. They are supposed to have removed into Poland from Tartary originally, and King Stephen issued an edict in their favor in 1578. During the reign of Maximilian I. the Jews were complained of by many influential personages, and were accused of three grave offenses: of murdering Christian infants, of counterfeiting coin, and of extorting the most extravagant usury. He accordingly banished them from his dominions. In Styria the utmost hostility existed against the Jews; and the electors of that State inserted a clause in the constitution which each successive monarch was compelled to sign, which decreed the perpetual exile of the Hebrews from that country. During the reign of Michael, in 1672, the Jews in Poland were plundered of their wealth, being suspected of treason against the government, in favor of the Turks. The office of Chief Rabbi was abolished in Poland by King Stanislaus Augustus, though the Jews were promised exemption from poll-tax on condition that they would engage in the pursuit of agriculture. The Polish Jews have been remarkable for their peculiar position in the community, as being the middle class between the nobles and the serfs; and as engrossing to themselves a very large share of the pursuits of trade and traffic of every description.

The Israelites appear to have entered Russia first during the sixtenth century. At that time a Jewish physician from Venice, named Leo, visited the rude court of the Czar, and undertook to cure his son, who was dangerously ill. The patient unfortunately died; and the Czar was so much enraged that he ordered Leo to be executed. Some time afterward a Rabbi named Zacharias, who was skilled in astrology, visited the capital of Russia, and won over many of the ignorant priests and laity to a belief in his favorite science. What the particular purpose of the Jew was has not been recorded; but he excited a general commotion among the populace, which induced the superior clergy of the Greek Church to convene a Council, and publicly condemn the doings and doctrines of the adventurous Jew. It is probable that this people hade become numerous in Russia at the time of the accession of *Peter the Great*, and that they had acquired the character of sharp dealers in business; for Peter is said to have observed, on a certain occasion, that though the Jews were crafty rogues, his Russians were a match for them. In 1746, during the reign of Elizabeth, the Jews were expelled from Russia by an imperial ukase, because it was discovered that some of their leading men had been carrying on a secret correspondence with the exiles in Siberia. They also existed at this period in the Ukraine, where they engaged extensively in agriculture and literary pursuits; and where, in consequence of their superior intelligence, they were often placed in offices of importance and trust.

The Jews settled in northern Germany at a very early period; some of them doubtless accompanied the Roman armies and remained with the colonies which they founded on the banks of the Rhine and the Meuse. An edict, issued by Constantine the Great in 321, proves that they were then already established at Cologne. During the Middle Ages many German Rabbis were celebrated for their learning, such as R. Petachia of Ratisbon, and R. Moses of Spires. Occasionally important converts were made from among them by the Catholic clergy, such as Herman de Kappenberg, who became a monk in Westphalia, and who wrote a work setting forth the reasons for his change of religion. This event occurred in the twelfth century, and was the source of considerable triumph on the one hand, and of much mortification on the other; and various explanations were given by different parties, to account for an event which, in that age and country, was of very rare occurrence.

CHAPTER XVII.

JEWS IN HOLLAND—THEIR ORIGIN AND HISTORY—THEIR PURSUITS AND CHARACTER—MANASSEH—HIS MISSION TO ENGLAND—BENEDICT SPINOSA—HIS HISTORY AND DOCTRINES—JEWS IN BOHEMIA—JEWS IN ENGLAND—THEIR VICISSITUDES AND PERSECUTIONS IN THAT KINGDOM.

THE Jewish race has existed in Holland, and in the various districts of the Netherlands, from a very early period, and have there experienced at different times, the extremes of good and evil fortune. After the invasion of England by the Normans, the entire trade of those countries was in the hands of Jews; and when they were banished from Liege, that city became bankrupt, from the general loss and injury thereby inflicted upon its commerce. There were many Israelites living in Flanders at the period, and during the progress, of the Crusades. In the twelfth century they were banished from that country; but in the fourteenth, they were allowed to return. In Brabant they flourished in security until 1370, when they were accused of having dishonored a consecrated wafer, and were subjected to so much persecution, that they removed elsewhere. In Arnheim, a city of Guilderland, in the thirteenth century, they were in high honor; and the chief physician of the place was a Jew. A few years later, so rapidly had public sentiment changed respecting them, that a lady of rank was burnt at Cologne for having married a Hebrew, which was considered equivalent in infamy to having committed adultery. The Jews were forbidden by law to live in Utrecht, until the revolution of 1795.

As long as the United Provinces remained under the dominion of Spain or Austria, the condition of the Israelitish race in them was marked by danger and persecution. When the Jews were banished from Spain, as already narrated, many of them took refuge in Holland. But they were regarded with suspicion; and on several occasions the public officials interrupted their worship, and invaded their synagogues, in order to discover whether they were not plotting against the Government. At Amsterdam they gradually increased to a community of great numbers and wealth; and they erected three synagogues, which were distinguished for their size and splendor. One of these was called Beth Jacob, after Jacob Tirado, its founder. The next, which was erected was Newe Shalom, the Dwelling of Peace; the third was named Beth Israel, the House of Israel. At Amsterdam the condition of the Jews, for some centuries, was prosperous. In 1639 they established a Rabbinical school which attained to eminence; and they had also a number of printing establishments, from which many works were issued not only in the Hebrew language, but also in the Dutch, Spanish and Portuguese, all of which were connected with Hebrew literature.

In Holland, as elsewhere, the chief pursuit of the

Jews was money-lending; and many of them acquired immense wealth. But they did not confine themselves to this branch of business exclusively; and hence they attained to greater social consideration and respectability. They cultivated learning, and produced several writers of eminence who conferred lustre upon their race. The most distinguished of these was Manasseh ben Israel, who was descended from Abarbanel, and was born in 1604. He gave evidence of his superior genius at an early age, and when only eighteen years old he was chosen to succeed his preceptor, Isaac Usiel, as expounder of the Talmud in the chief synagogue. When twenty-eight, he published a work in the Spanish language called *Conciliador del Pentateucho*, in which he expounds a portion of the Old Testament, and endeavors to clear up its mysteries, and explain its meaning. So much ability is shown in this work that the eminent Protestant writer, Grotius, recommends it to the study of Biblical scholars. His other works refer chiefly to the resurrection, and the various rites and ceremonies of the Jews. It was his purpose to have written a history of his people, from the destruction of Jerusalem till his own time; but he did not live to execute his intention.

Manasseh distinguished himself by his efforts in behalf of his brethren. He visited England and presented a petition to Cromwell, who was then Lord Protector, requesting permission for the Jews to reside in that country. His petition was adroitly prepared, and was peculiar among other things for the skillful flattery which he addressed to the usurper.

He asserted that Cromwell was chosen by Providence to fill the high post which he held; he praised the humanity and intelligence of the English people; and put forth every argument to gain his point with the Dictator. Cromwell summoned a Council to deliberate upon the matter, consisting of two lawyers, seven citizens and fourteen preachers. He submitted to them two questions: whether it was lawful to admit the Jews at all; and if lawful, upon what terms and conditions it was just and expedient that they should be allowed to dwell in the Commonwealth? The lawyers decided without hesitation, that it was both lawful and expedient to admit the Hebrews; the citizens were of different opinions on the subject; but the Roundhead preachers were so prolix, obstinate and unyielding in their wranglings on the subject, that Cromwell became disgusted, lost his patience, and dissolved the Council. The result was that no definite answer was ever given by the Protector on the subject; and it was not till after his transient government ended with the resignation of his son and successor, Richard, and the advent of the money-spending Charles II., that the Jews were permitted to return to England.

Several curious incidents occurred in connection with this mission and petition of Manasseh, which illustrate the spirit and genius of the times. The republican writer, Harrington, in his well-known work called *Oceana*, proposed to sell Ireland to the Jews, as a place of residence, where they might not only be secure, but might exercise supreme authority. He also urged that by such a measure, England would be relieved of the difficulty and expense attendant on the government and control of that island. Many of the most enlightened men of that time, however, entertained the most absurd and despicable prejudices against these people. Sir Thomas Browne, in his famous work entitled *Religio Medici*, speaks of the Jews as the "contemptible and degenerate issue of Jacob." Bishop Hall, while asserting that Christians should pray for their conversion, calls them the "miscreant Jews." The most preposterous slanders were circulated in reference to them; such as that they had offered Cromwell five hundred thousand pounds for the possession of St. Paul's Church, for the purpose of using it as a synagogue. Another was that the Jews had sent a deputation to the Lord Protector, to inquire of him whether he was not the promised Messiah; and had actually searched and traced his family pedigree with great care at Huntingdon, to ascertain whether he was not in some way descended from Jewish ancestors.

Another eminent person who rose among the Jews in Holland, was Benedict Spinosa, the founder of the modern pantheistic philosophy. He was born in 1632, and was brought up to the trade of grinding optical lenses, at which he afterward continued to labor as a means of livelihood. Spinosa was a man of immense intellectual acumen and original powers of thought. His arguments and speculations are not surpassed and scarcely equaled for subtlety and profundity, by any other writer in the difficult science of intellectual and speculative philosophy. As soon as he began to call in question the doctrines of the Jewish system, as taught in the synagogue at Amsterdam, and to propound his own erroneous though plausible theories, he was expelled from the synagogue, and the greater curse or excommunication was published upon him. The persecution against him by the Jews ran so high that he was constrained to flee from Amsterdam. He took refuge first at Leyden, and afterward at the Hague, where he died at the age of forty-five. He was moral and blameless in his conduct, but his opinions were of the most execrable kind, though defended with extraordinary ability. He maintained that God and the universe are one and the same thing; that all things happen by the immutable law of nature and necessity; he attributed to the Deity the two qualities of thought and extension, and these only; and held that each individual was his own God—in fact, was God himself.

These blasphemous doctrines naturally excited the opposition not only of Christian writers, but also of the Jews. Prominent among the latter was Balthasar Orobio, who was a Spaniard by birth, originally a Roman Catholic, and finally a convert to Judaism. Previous to his open adoption of the Jewish faith, he had been Professor of Philosophy in the University of Salamanca. He also practiced medicine in Seville, where he excited the suspicion of the Inquisition by his equivocal conduct toward the Jews. Though he still professed to be a Christian, he was secretly a convert to the rival faith. He was imprisoned; and after his release he fled from Spain into France. He there obtained the post of

Professor of Physic at Toulouse; but having resolved to announce his conversion to the Jewish religion, he removed to Amsterdam, submitted to the rite of circumcision, and resumed the practice of medicine. He was a man of superior learning and ability. He held a public debate with the celebrated Limborch, the leading theologian of the Arminians or Remonstrants, in which he appeared to advantage, although neither party to the debate was converted. In his replies to the arguments of Spinosa, Orobio displayed superior ability. He possessed much greater learning than his opponent; though he was inferior to him in that depth of sophistry, that acumen of philosophical speculation, that rigor of logical thinking, in which Spinosa had few equals, and which, if they had been devoted to the propagation and defense of a true system of religion and philosophy, would have caused his name to be enrolled among the ablest and most illustrious benefactors of mankind.

The Jewish race existed in *Bohemia* from an early period; and previous to the year 1600 were more distinguished for wealth, numbers, and literary culture than the Jews of Poland. The rabbinical Academy at Prague was celebrated; and from its walls were sent forth during the sixteenth century, and later, many of the Jewish teachers who officiated in the synagogues of Germany, Poland and Bohemia. Some celebrated Rabbis flourished about this period in the last-named country; one of whom was David Ganz, who wrote a Jewish chronicle called *Temach David*, or Branch of David. Rabbi Bezaleel of Prague wrote an able work on the future coming of the Messiah. Rabbi Jacob Falk was an eminent teacher who lived during the sixteenth century in that city, who introduced among his brethren and scholars the habit of public disputations on religious questions, which was then prevalent in Christian universities. During the Thirty Years' War which desolated Bohemia, the Jews took the side of the Imperialists and assisted with great bravery in the defense of Prague against the attacks of the Swedes and the Germans. As a reward for their services, the Emperor Ferdinand III. allowed them various privileges. Some years later, a Bohemian Jew named Zechariah obtained permission from the Emperor to erect a synagogue at Vienna; but after its completion, the monarch was induced to deprive the Jews of its possession, and to convert it into a church, being persuaded by the Empress that her barrenness was caused by his protection to these unfortunate people. After their expulsion from the Austrian capital, the Empress conceived; and was fully persuaded that that lucky event was the reward of her piety and devotion to the Church. She and the Emperor remained under this assurance until her death in child-bed at length dissolved the illusion. The Jews were then allowed to return to Vienna, and to reside there under certain heavy restrictions and grievous burdens.

The first authentic record of the residence of Jews in England, is dated in the time of the Heptarchy, in the eighth century. In 740 Egbert, Archbishop of York, published an ecclesiastical canon forbidding

Christians to assist at Jewish festivals. Edward the Confessor promulgated a law in 1041 which declared all the Jews in the realm the serfs and property of the Crown. Many Jews accompanied William the Conqueror from Normandy; William Rufus protected them, and permitted the Rabbis to meet the bishops in a public debate in London, at the same time swearing by "the face of St. Luke," that if the champions of the Jewish faith defeated the Christians, he would abjure his religion, and turn Jew. The result of the disputation is not known, though the probability is, that neither party was convinced of the truth of their opponents. Rufus gave great umbrage to his subjects by farming out the bishoprics to the Jews; who, while making large profits by selling these dignities to aspiring churchmen, at a great advance upon what they paid for them, at the same time turned the religion and the Order which were thus disgraced into public ridicule and contempt. The Jews did not neglect the interests of learning, for during this bright period of their security and prosperity in England, they possessed three colleges in the University of Oxford, Lombard Hall, Moses Hall, and Jacob Hall, in which Hebrew literature was taught by learned Rabbis, not only to Jewish youth, but also to Christians. Yet it is a singular circumstance that, at this very period, they were allowed to have but one burial-ground in the kingdom, in St. Giles, Cripplegate, London, the most repulsive portion of the capital.

The greatest misfortune of the Jews has always been that, whenever they enjoyed a season of prosperity, their industry and sagacity, and sometimes also their avarice and rapacity, increased their wealth so enormously, as to excite the hatred and jealousy of the Christian population, which eventually broke forth in persecution and bloodshed. This process, so often and so constantly repeated, now recurred in England. Nothing is recorded of the Jews, except that they were free from calamities of every kind in England while Rufus reigned, and for ten years after his death, under the authority of his successors. At that time, the popular animosity began to take the form of slanders of the most atrocious kind; such as that they had secretly crucified several Christian youths at Norwich, at Gloucester, and St. Edmondsbury. Henry II. fined the Jews in the sum of five thousand marks—an enormous amount in that day—and banished all those who refused to pay their proportion. At a later period, when Henry resolved to make a crusade to the Holy Land, he levied a tax of seventy thousand pounds upon his Christian subjects, and one of sixty thousand upon the Jews. This proportion shows the relative wealth possessed by the several classes of the community; although the premature death of the monarch removed the necessity of its payment.

A great calamity overwhelmed the Jews in England at the coronation of Richard I. The ceremony took place in Westminster Hall, and they desired to be present on the occasion, and to testify their loyalty by offering rich presents to the new sovereign. The jealousy of the courtiers and the people opposed their admission to the edifice, and they induced Richard to give orders for their exclusion. The Jews of London wisely stayed away, but many who came from various parts of the country ventured to intrude into the Abbey, imagining that they would not be known or recognized. They were mistaken, for they were detected, beaten, and dragged from the church with great ferocity. The excited and insane populace took fire at the news, and a general assault of the private residences of the Jews followed. Their houses were usually very plain and unostentatious in their exterior, in order to avoid exciting the jealousy of the public; but the interiors were often furnished with all the resources of luxury and opulence. The king in vain attempted to suppress the tumult. The houses of the Jews were plundered, and then set on fire, and many were wounded and slain. The king punished three persons with death, but he dared not go further in avenging the wrongs of his Hebrew subjects.

The thirst for plunder and revenge spread rapidly from the capital to other portions of the kingdom. The Jews were subjected to similar outrages at Norwich, Stamford, Edmondsbury, and Lincoln. The most terrible disasters occurred at York. The excited populace attacked the house of a wealthy Jew named Benedict. His wife and children were murdered, and the building was burned. Terrified by such displays of fury, many of the Jews who resided in the city took refuge in the castle; the rest were massacred. The Governor of the citadel promised to protect the Jews who were in it; but they suspected his sincerity, and while absent in the town, they resolved to exclude him on his return. Exasperated by such treatment, the Governor applied to the Sheriff of the county for a military force, with which, aided by the mob, he attacked the fortress. The clergy distinguished themselves greatly by urging on the populace to acts of violence and vengeance. The Jews defended themselves with bravery, but they soon discovered that they would be unable to resist much longer, and deliberated upon the course which should be pursued under the circumstances. A council was held within the fortress. An aged Rabbi, of great learning and respectability, presided over the deliberations. "Men of Israel," said he, "the God of our fathers, to whom none can say What doest thou! calls upon us to die for our Law. Death is inevitable, but we may choose whether we will die speedily and nobly or ignominiously, after horrible torments and the most barbarous usage. My advice is, that we voluntarily render up our souls to our Creator, and fall by our own hands. The deed is not only reasonable, but according to the Law, and is sanctioned by the examples of our most illustrious ancestors." The aged hero then burst into tears, and said no more. One portion of the assembly were in favor of following his advice; another, the minority, declared that it was a hard and awful alternative. The Rabbi again spoke, and said, "Let those depart in peace who do not approve of my proposition." A few withdrew; the remainder commenced by burning their valuables in the court-yard of the castle; they then set the building on fire in a number of places, after which they slew their wives and children, and then each other. The aged Rabbi was the last survivor, and he took his own life by piercing himself to the heart.

The next morning the assault upon the castle was resumed, but the multitude beheld the flames arising from various places, and no one left to defend the battlements except the few who had preferred baptism and ignominy to death. The gates being opened, the populace poured in, and put every one to the sword without mercy. They then rushed to the cathedral, in the archives of which the bonds and mortgages held by the Jews against the Christians were preserved, and, having seized them, consigned them to the flames. By this summary method of repudiation they cancelled their obligations to the murdered Jews and their heirs to an enormous amount. It is said, that this was the only portion of these infamous and inhuman transactions which incurred the anger of the monarch, because, had the bonds not been destroyed, the claims which they represented would have reverted to his own coffers. The number of persons who perished in the castle was computed at a thousand.

CHAPTER XVIII.

RICHARD OF THE LION HEART—KING JOHN—HENRY III.—HIS TREATMENT OF THE JEWS—THEIR VARIOUS CALAMITIES—IMPOSTURE OF SABBATHAI SEVI—HIS EXTRAORDINARY ADVENTURES—SABBATHAISM—JACOB FRANK—HIS HISTORY AND TEACHINGS—THE SECT ESTABLISHED BY HIM.

WHEN King Richard of the Lion Heart returned to England from his captivity, he made several laws which were calculated to affect the condition of the Jews in his dominion very sensibly. He enacted, to prevent them from defrauding and being defrauded, that all the bonds and obligations which they should receive from Christians should be drawn up in the presence of four lawyers, two of whom were to be Jews, and two Christians, two public notaries, and two of the royal inspectors. He also ordered that all their deeds should be recorded in the proper office; that two copies of each deed and bond were to be made, one of which was to be kept in the public archives, in a chest which was secured by two padlocks, the key of one of which was to be held by the Jewish attorneys. Precautions such as these illustrate the suspicion of knavery which attached in that day both to the Hebrew speculator and to his Christian rival.

When John succeeded Richard on the throne, he at first appeared to be favorable to his Jewish subjects. He extended to them a number of privileges which they had not previously enjoyed, for the purpose of inviting others of the race to settle in his dominions. They were not restricted to any particular place of residence, and were allowed, in lawsuits with Christians, to have equal advantages. Their oaths were regarded as of equal weight with those of Christians. In their money operations they were permitted to receive all kinds of collaterals, except the sacred vessels of the churches. They were required to pay the sum of four thousand marks for the decree and the charter which guaranteed these rights to them. But John was a feeble and unprincipled prince, and soon his good feeling toward the Jews was turned to hostility and hatred. In 1210 he suddenly issued an order for the arrest of all the wealthier Jews in his dominions; he confiscated their wealth to his own use; and he put those to the torture who refused to reveal where their treasures were concealed.

An incident connected with this event in the history of the English Jews will serve to illustrate the barbarity and ferocity of the times. A Hebrew of Bristol, who was regarded as very wealthy, refused to reveal the place where his money was concealed; and the King having assessed him at ten thousand marks, he was informed that for each day that he refused to tell his secret he should lose a tooth, till all his teeth were gone; and if he still remained obstinate, his Majesty would then commence on his nails. The Jew refused to yield for seven days; but when the eighth tooth was about to be wrenched from his jaws, his obstinacy and avarice gave way, and he obtained his liberty and safety by paying the required sum. During this whole reign, the Jews were regarded merely as the chattels of the King, and subjected to repeated excesses of royal rapacity, being protected by no acknowledged rights and franchises of any kind. On one occasion all their money was seized, and their houses in London torn down, to furnish materials to the revolting barons to defend the city against an apprehended attack of the monarch.

Henry III. succeeded to the throne, and the Jews obtained more mercy. They were released from prison, and were protected from outrage, except that they were required to wear two strips of white cloth upon their dress, to distinguish them from the Christian population. In 1233 he built an almshouse in London for the reception of those Jews who professed to have become converts to the Christian religion, where they lived without labor or care, on the royal bounty. It is said that a good number of worthless Jews professed themselves converts in order to enjoy the lazy, easy life which this establishment afforded them. It is illustrative of the kind of piety which prevailed at that time, that the motive which induced Henry to establish an institution which was calculated only to afford a premium and an incentive to hypocrisy, lying and laziness, was that the King desired thereby to deliver his father's soul from the flames and torments of Purgatory. But in return for this charity toward one portion of the Jewish people, he acted as a thief and robber toward the rest, for soon afterward he extorted from them *one-third* of their whole property; and two years subsequent to this outrage he compelled them to pay the sum of eighteen thousand marks, and ten thousand more at the end of four years. He then robbed certain particular wealthy Jews in the most scandalous manner. The daughter of Hamon, a rich Jew of Hereford, was compelled to pay into the royal treasury the sum of five thousand marks—a mark was worth about five dollars of our money; and another wealthy Jew of York, named Aaron, was compelled to pay the sum of thirty thousand marks to the King during the period of seven years.

This grasping monarch played a practical joke of a serious character upon his Hebrew subjects, which was the cause of much malicious merriment to the Christian community at the time. The Jews were suddenly surprised and gratified by the announcement that they were to have a Parliament of their own, for the purpose of legislating on those matters which appertained to their own interests. The Sheriffs were ordered to return six of the richest Jews from each of the largest towns, and two from the smaller ones, who were to be summoned in regular forms of the Parliament of the realm. The order was obeyed; the joyous Jews complied with the royal requisition, assembled with all due solemnity at the appointed time and place; and were prepared to commence their deliberations. The "House" then received a message from the King, to the effect that, as his Majesty was greatly in want of money, it would be necessary, in the first place, for the Parliament immediately to furnish twenty thousand marks to meet the pressing exigency. The Hebrew legislators received this unexpected and disagreeable announcement with very wry faces; but, after some deliberation, and further threats from the King, they voted the amount. Immediately after this act of loyalty and compliance, the King dissolved the Parliament *sine die;* and those Jews who were slow to contribute their proportion of the requisite sum were arrested and thrown into prison till they paid the money.

One consequence of the robberies to which the Jews were thus subjected was, that they became robbers in return, and indemnified themselves for their losses by the enormous rates of interest which they extorted from those who borrowed money from them. Their usual rate at that time was fifty per cent.; and a cotemporary anecdote respecting some students of Oxford, who were compelled to have recourse to the Jews for money on one occasion, is recorded, which intimates that they regarded themselves as favored by the Hebrew money-lenders, inasmuch as they required but forty-three per cent. from them! Other troubles overwhelmed the Jews during the reign of this same monarch. The old story of crucified infants and insulted wafers was revived. A report was suddenly spread that the Jews of Lincoln had murdered a Christian child named Hugh, because he had wandered into their quarter, and sang hymns in honor of the Virgin. The body was found in a ditch; although no proof was ever adduced to show that the Jews were guilty of the charge. The remains were buried with great pomp; the unfortunate boy was canonized, and pilgrimages were made to his tomb from various portions of the kingdom. The work of revenge then commenced; a large number of Jews were arrested, and, after being cruelly tortured, were put to death.

During the reign of Henry III. the Jews were also charged, with greater probability of truth, with clipping and adulterating the coin of the kingdom. During one year two hundred and eighty Hebrews were executed for this crime alone, of whom, it is probable, a large number were guilty. Soon afterward the Parliament passed a law forbidding the Jews to engage in usury, thus depriving them of the chief means of their wealth. The claims which they then held against Christians for usurious interest were all cancelled, and they were allowed to receive only the principal. They were permitted, however, to engage in other occupations, such as farming, merchandise, and manual labor. In these employments the tables were turned upon them; and they were then compelled to receive such compensation for their labor and produce as the purchasers were disposed to give them. By this means the Jews soon became much impoverished; and as soon as it was perceived that they could no longer be made profitable to the royal treasury by repeated exactions, they were finally banished from the kingdom. This occurred in 1290; and they were permitted to take with them only a small portion of their property. As they withdrew into exile they were insulted by the populace; their synagogues were turned into churches, and during four centuries the Jews remained banished from England.

A very remarkable circumstance connected with the history of the Jews, in the seventeenth century, was the fact that several bold and skillful attempts were made by some among them to claim the honors and perform the functions of the promised Messiah. One of these was named Sabbathai Sevi. He was born in 1625, at Aleppo, and was the son of a poulterer. He was so studious in his youth, that he became so learned in the Cabala, that he was chosen a Rabbi in the eighteenth year of his age. He was ambitious of distinction, and endeavored to render himself remarkable by his extraordinary fasts, and his extreme austerity. Though he was twice married, he is said to have declined all sexual intercourse with his wives. His friends attributed this peculiarity to his piety; his enemies, to his impotency. At length he proclaimed that he was the true Messiah, and attempted, as a proof of the assumption, to work miracles. The neighboring Rabbis were filled with horror and disgust at his preposterous assumption, declared him worthy of death, and endeavored to induce the Turkish authorities to execute him. To save his life, he fled to Thessalonica, from which place he was also soon compelled to escape. At length he reached Jerusalem, where he proclaimed his pretentions to the character of the Messiah, and made many converts, among whom was Nathan Benjamin, a Jew of distinction. This person he called Elias, the forerunner of the Messiah. From Jerusalem he traveled to Egypt, and thence to Smyrna. He succeeded in gaining the populace of this city to his cause, although the Rabbis exerted their utmost to render him unpopular and despised. He next surrounded himself with great pomp, assumed the title of "King of the Kings of the Earth," conferred on his two brothers the titles of the Sovereigns of Israel and Judah, erected a throne, on which he sat before the multitude, heard causes and dispensed justice, and played at royalty and its functions generally. Meanwhile his fame extended; great excitement began to prevail among the Jews, both in Asia and in Europe, and the wisest and most dubious of the Israelites began to doubt whether there might not be some truth in the assertion, that at last the long-promised Messiah had appeared.

Having thus firmly established his pretensions at Smyrna, as the centre of his empire, Sabbathai determined to extend the area of his triumphs, and proceed to Constantinople; there to demand from the Sultan the crown and sceptre, which he asserted to be his own rightful possession. He was accompanied thither by a great multitude, who confidently expected that their leader would have no difficulty in making good his claims. The Sultan was absent at the time; but the Grand Vizier, who acted for him, seems to have treated the matter more as a jest, and to have sent a body of janissaries to take the vagabond in charge, and supervise his proceedings. Sabbathai pretended to make no resistance, and voluntarily took up his quarters in the castle of Sestos, where he was permitted to see his friends, and was treated with lenity. After a time, he was conducted to Adrianople, into the presence of the Sultan; but, instead of demeaning himself with the dignity which would have been appropriate to his lofty pretensions, he was overcome with terror, and excited merely the contempt and pity of the Moslem potentate. The Sultan asked him if he were the Messiah, to which he could make no answer. At length, to put his sincerity to the test, the Sultan informed him that he must either become a convert to Mahometanism, or submit to have three poisoned arrows shot into his person. Sabbathai did not hesitate long which alternative to choose. He declared that he was a believer in Mahomet, and in return for this act he was raised to the dignity of Pasha. His followers were naturally shocked and outraged at this apostacy; but he had an excuse for it, which was plausible enough. He declared that, according to the prophet, "the Messiah must remain some time among the unbelievers," and that Isaiah had predicted that the Messiah "should be numbered with the transgressors." But such an evasion, though propagated by the few adherents which still remained to him, was not able to avert the general contempt and ridicule to which his unfaithfulness gave rise. He was kept in confinement and obscurity in the castle of Belgrade until his death, which took place in 1676, when he was fifty years old.

Notwithstanding the apostacy of this pretender

there were some who upheld his claims even after his death, and asserted that he was still the true Messiah, and that instead of having died he had been translated, like Enoch and Elijah, to the heavenly land by a supernatural power. Some even of his most inveterate foes while living, espoused his cause after his death. A few years later this heresy appeared under a new form, and under the guidance of two new leaders, named Malaoh and Hajun. These were two Rabbis of Polish birth, who, in 1709, led a caravan of Jews from Bohemia and Moravia on a pilgrimage to Jerusalem, and they were the only survivors of the whole company. During this journey to the East they had become converts to *Sabbathaism*, and after their return to Europe they persisted in defending and propagating it in the Polish and German synagogues. Hajun composed and published several works, in which he expounded his doctrines, and also attacked the opinions and teachings of the Talmud and the Rabbins. Their followers extended from Smyrna to Amsterdam, and became very numerous in Poland. In 1722 the whole sect was solemnly excommunicated in all the synagogues of Europe; but Hajun persisted in preaching and expounding, so that his followers still increased. Among his converts were found persons of talent and influence, one of whom was Moses Meir, and another, of still greater talent and ability, was Moses Luzzato. These persons attained a local and temporary fame by the zeal with which they defended the doctrines of Sabbathaism. Yet the sect gradually faded away with the lapse of time, after having accomplished one of the most important and singular episodes presented by the whole history of the modern Jews.

In the year 1760 another extraordinary personage who appeared among the Jews was Jacob Frank, a native of Poland, and originally a distiller of liquors. He early conceived a great dislike to the Talmud, and at the age of thirty-eight he began to attack its doctrines and teachings publicly in the synagogues of his native country. He eventually caused a schism, and founded the sect of the "Frankists." Their chief peculiarities were the following:—They entirely rejected the Talmud as full of errors and absurdities. They regarded the Book of Zohar as of divine authority, and as the basis of their confession of faith. They also received baptism, and professed to believe in the doctrine of the Trinity. They were finally known by the name of "Zoharites," and they declared in their belief "that no religion can possibly exist without the knowledge of God; all other religion is an outward service of works; piety and the love of God are the effects of a profound acquaintance with His nature, and this must be sought in the study of His law, where it is found as within a kernel, from which it must be deduced by means of tradition; the doctrine of Moses and the prophets has an inward meaning far deeper than that of the letter, without which it is only a dead letter, and the source of errors and mistakes, the cause of the dangerous doctrines of the Talmud. According to the pure doctrine of the word of God, there is one only God, the creator and preserver of all things, but revealed in three persons. God has appeared from the beginning upon earth in human form, but after the entrance of sin he laid aside this form, and has since taken it again for the expiation of sin. He will once again appear in human nature finally to deliver man from sin. As for Jerusalem, it will never be rebuilt, and a terrestrial Messiah is not to be expected."

It is evident that the Frankists were more properly a Christian than a Jewish sect; and yet a corrupted offshoot of both, having a mixture of truth and error in their views, which rendered it impossible for them to be regarded with much favor by either sect. Their chief protector in the Church was the Bishop of Caments; and while he lived, they were exempt from ecclesiastical tyranny and persecution. But after his death, they were very severely treated in Poland, and many of them emigrated to Turkey. At the same time the Jewish community condemned and excommunicated them without reserve. A few of them eventually became Roman Catholics. A cotemporary writer thus narrates the personal incidents connected with the life of this remarkable man:—" Jacob Frank, who, from the first, had declared himself a Christian, continued to act as head of the sect, declaring that the Lord and the Prophet Elijah had appeared to him, commanding him to convert the Jews. He was looked upon with distrust by the clergy, though he declared himself an obedient son of the Church; and was for some time detained a prisoner at Czentoschow on account of his strange opinions, but afterward delivered by the Russians, when they took possession of the fortress in 1777. He then traveled through Poland, Bohemia, and Moravia, with a large retinue and great pomp, and established himself for some years in the capital of Austria, under the protection of the Empress Maria Theresa. From thence he went to Bruna, in Moravia, accompanied by a number of Jews and Jewesses, always living in the style of an Eastern prince, wearing a splendid uniform, and abundantly supplied from Poland with money for all his expenses. Many years later, when no longer admitted at Vienna, he fixed himself at Offenbach, in Hesse, where he lived in a kind of palace, always keeping up the character which he had assumed as head of a religious sect. There, numbers of Sabbathaist Jews from all countries resorted to him, presenting gifts and joining in the public prayers which he conducted with a great display of magnificence, accompanied by all sorts of singular ceremonies, the meaning of which has never to this day been explained. He died three years after his arrival at Offenbach, and was buried with great pomp according to the rites of the Romish Church, being followed to the grave by a great concourse of people as a public benefactor. A cross was erected over his tomb. For some time his daughter took his place in the guidance of the sect, which was, however, soon dispersed, especially when the pecuniary supplies began to fail.

CHAPTER XIX.

THE SECT OF THE CHASIDIM — JEWS IN POLAND — ISRAEL BESCHT — HIS HISTORY — SECT FOUNDED BY HIM — MOSES MENDELSOHN — INCIDENTS OF HIS LIFE — HIS WRITINGS — THEIR INFLUENCE — HIS LITERARY MERITS.

THE most extraordinary movement which occurred among the Jews in the eighteenth century was that of the sect termed the *Chasidim*, or the Pious, which took its origin in Poland. In that country the Hebrew community were very numerous at that period; and the founder of the new sect, who was named Israel Bescht, soon acquired many followers. The date of his birth is unknown; but he lived at Tluszty in Poland in the year 1740. He pretended to be the promised child foretold by the Prophet Elias, and named by him Israel, before his birth. The father of Bescht seems to have experienced both extremes of fortune, and to have been a remarkable man. It is said of him that, being robbed of all his property in Wallachia, the country of his residence, he was banished, and afterward being captured by pirates was sold as a slave in Africa; that he there attained the rank of general and prime minister in the State where he lived; and afterward being disgraced, was expelled again, utterly destitute. He was a hundred years old at the time of the birth of his son Israel.

The latter spent his youth in the careful study of the Cabala, and became very proficient in Hebrew literature generally. He declared that his soul often left his body and entered the land of spirits, and there learned the mysteries of the future state. He received the epithet of *Tzadik*, or the Righteous, in consequence of the peculiarities of his religious observances. He and his followers disciplined themselves with fastings and physical torments, and all sorts of self-denial and mortification, hoping thereby to commend themselves to the favor of Heaven. Sometimes they fasted seven or eight days in succession; and they abstained in general from all kinds of animal food, and from all food even which proceeded from animals, such as eggs, butter, cheese, and honey. They wore rough clothes made of hair next to their bodies; and even in the severest weather in winter, they rose at midnight and bathed in the half-frozen rivers. In winter they often rolled themselves in the snow naked; in summer, in beds of thorns and thistles.

The head of this sect, who exceeded all his followers in the extremes to which he carried his self-punishments, was revered by them as the representative of God on earth. The main peculiarity of his teachings consisted in enforcing the contemplation of God, and the strict fulfillment of their religious observances and penances, combined with a stoical repose and contemplation of soul, which ought not to be disturbed by the cares of this world. The most celebrated

Rabbis of the time did their utmost to oppose the spread of this sect, and hurled their anathemas against them; but they increased notwithstanding in Poland, Russia, Wallachia, and Moldavia. These Chasidim believed that Bescht had control over the heavenly bodies; that he could work miracles; that he could make barren women fruitful; that he could raise the dead, and could deliver the condemned from hell. They asserted that by a single word he could strike people dumb, and by a word enable the dumb to speak. His doctrines were set forth in several works which he wrote, and which were very singular productions.

One of these was published in 1814, at Berditschef, and was so much sought after by the open and secret patrons of the sect that several large editions were disposed of in several years. Another work written by Bescht, and published by his grandson, contains the rules of conduct and the doctrines which are held by the sect. In each of these books he makes the teachings of the Sohar the basis, and enjoins a contemplative and pious life; indifference to all worldly passions and pursuits; and entire obedience to the will of their chief, as the representative of the Deity. Bescht died in 1760, although his followers contended that he was transported to heaven, to dwell in the society of the angels, and to act as a mediator to reconcile the Jews who espoused his doctrines with God, and secure their ultimate entrance into his presence. The dignity or office of *Tzadik*, which Bescht held, expired with him, although it was regarded with great reverence by his deluded followers. His family were greatly esteemed; and his clothes, furniture, and every thing which had been connected with him, were preserved with great care, as memorials of extraordinary value, and as preservatives from the commission of sin to all who preserved them.

After the death of Bescht, his three most prominent disciples, who were his grandsons, were elected chiefs of the three divisions of the *Chasidim;* but this proceeding resulted unfavorably to the unity of the sect, for it led to their being divided into three rival factions. At this period their whole number had increased to forty thousand persons. It is undoubtedly true, that the origin of the singular doctrines held by this sect may be traced to the *Soofism,* or the quietist Theosophy of Oriental countries, as well as to the recondite teachings of the Cabala and Talmud. At the start, the Chasidim asserted that all opinions were derived from the Talmud; but the difference between the Cabalistic Sabbathaism and the Talmud was clearly demonstrated in 1755, when a member of the Chasidim, named Meschullam, burnt the Talmud publicly in the Jewish quarter of a city in Podolia. That the reader may form an idea of the doctrines entertained by this truly remarkable sect, we append the following extracts from their chief works:

"The foundation of faith is faith in the Zaddik, *i. e.* Bescht; to him the greatest reverence is due. Should it sometimes appear that the Zaddik's conduct is in opposition to the law of God, yet the people must believe that he does what is right; for the laws are given to the wise to interpret at all times according to their pleasure. The Zaddik is at liberty even to abrogate the law, and to institute new ones in its stead.

"In judging of the Zaddik, the Chasid is bound to renounce his reason and conviction, and implicitly to bow to the opinion of the Zaddik: so long as any one thinks that he possesses a judgment of his own, and is capable of acting for himself, so long is his attachment to the Zaddik not perfect. Those only can arrive at this excellent degree of piety who renounce their own reason, feelings and experience, and adopt in all things, implicitly, the will of the Zaddik.

"The Zaddik must be to the Chasid the first existing being. He must not only be to him more than all men, but more than God, because God has made over to the Zaddik the government of this world.

"When the prophet Isaiah says, 'All thy children shall be taught of the Lord,' he means all the children of the Zaddikim, for these teach God what he has to do."

That God takes pleasure in being contradicted by the Zaddik, the Chasidim prove in the following way:

"When a father orders his son to do any thing, and the son sees it would not be well to comply with the request, and convinces the father of his error, the father rejoices at the wisdom of his son, and willingly subjects his own opinion to that of his son. So it often happens with God and the Zaddik. Solomon refers to this in the Proverbs, xxvii., 'My son, be wise and make my heart glad, that I may answer him that reproacheth me.'"

"The Zaddik is a supernatural being."—*K. Shimlab*, s. 18.

"The Zaddik has power to appoint every one his place in heaven or hell, as he may see fit."—*Seph. Hammedath.*

"The most effectual means for barren women to become faithful is, to delight in hearing the Zaddik praised."—*K. Lik. Mehran*, 266.

"The only way for a sinner to obtain pardon from God is, unceasingly to endeavor with all his might to increase the income of the Zaddik."—*Seph. Hamid*, s. 14.

"Whoever makes the Zaddik a pleasure, his prayers will certainly be heard."—*Seph. Hamid*, viii. 10.

"Let every one take good heed in looking into any book upon human science, even should it be written by the most learned man in Israel. All profane sciences are dangerous to the holy faith. We have often mentioned this circumstance, but we cannot sufficiently warn the righteous, lest by a peep into such books he should lose his salvation."—*Lik. Mahran Tengana*, s. 39.

"All languages except the Hebrew are imperfect; for although in each language every thing has a name, yet this name is not the right one. That name only which God has given to every thing in Hebrew is the name of it."—*Lik. Amor*, s. 31.

The following prayer, written on parchment, and worn on the left side, was their charm for prosperity in business:

"May it please thee, O Lord God of Israel, to give charge to the following angels to go into the house of

N—, the son of N—, to go with him and make him prosper in all his undertakings, by day or by night, at home or abroad; in thy name, in thy holy zeal, make prosperous N—, the son of N—. Amen, Selah."

Cotemporary with the rise and progress of this sect there lived a man in Germany whose remarkable talents and writings constituted an era in the history of the Modern Jews, and which deserve a more minute consideration. This was the celebrated Moses Mendelsohn, to whom his admiring cotemporaries applied the same expression which had been used ages before in reference to Maimonides: "From Moses to Moses there arose none like to Moses."

Mendelsohn was born in 1729, at Dessau, in Anhalt, one of the minor German states. His father was a Hebrew caligrapher—a person who transcribed the Hebrew text of the Old Testament and other similar writings upon parchment. He was of a very feeble constitution, but early gave indications of superior talent. When thirteen years old he commenced the study of the Talmud under Rabbi Frankel; and he soon became proficient also in the writings of Maimonides, who remained through life his favorite author and exemplar. But the limited means of his father compelled him, at the age of fourteen, to leave home and remove to Berlin in search of some employment. There he starved for some time as a copyist and corrector of the press; meanwhile employing his leisure diligently in enlarging his knowledge and extending his studies in general literature and philosophy. He received much encouragement from Rabbi Israel, a Polish Jew, who had fled from persecution to Berlin, and from Aaron Emmerich, a Hebrew physician, who resided in the Prussian capital.

The first remunerative employment which Mendelsohn obtained was the post of tutor in a family of wealth; and his excellent conduct and disposition gained so completely the confidence of his patron, that in 1753 he entrusted to him the entire management of his affairs. His first publication—for he still assiduously continued his literary labors—was a series of essays on Natural Philosophy written in Hebrew, intended for the use of young Jews who were studying the Talmud. Already in this work some glimpses appeared of that peculiar intellectual freedom which afterward became his most remarkable quality; and some of the Rabbis in Berlin took offense at it. He would have suffered no little persecution had not suspicion and bigotry been lulled to repose by his exact obedience to all the requirements of the Oral Law. About this period he became acquainted with Lessing, Nicholai, and other German writers who were laying the foundation of the literature of their country; and the superior intelligence and congeniality of spirit which Mendelsohn exhibited gained their confidence and their intimacy. The society of these men tended to enlarge his views and prepare him more effectually for the part he afterward performed in German literature.

Mendelsohn's reputation was extended throughout Germany by the publication of his *Phœdon, or the Immortality of the Soul*, in which he displayed remarkable power of thought, and originality of conception.

His evident disposition for progress and intellectual freedom, as exhibited in this work, induced many Christians to imagine that he might readily be made a convert to their faith. Lavater, the celebrated physiognomist, was one of these, and he opened a correspondence with Mendelsohn on the subject. But the latter soon gave him to understand that he was in error, and addressed a communication to the pastor of Zurich, in which he defined more clearly his position as a liberal-minded and enlightened Jew.

In 1778 he prepared the report which the King of Prussia had required his Hebrew subjects to furnish him, on some particular points of the jurisprudence taught by the Rabbins, such as the right of succession, the nature of wills, etc. Not long afterward, he published his German version of the Pentateuch, accompanied by a commentary of his own. In this work he managed to combine the liberality and boldness of a philosopher, with a rigid adherence to the essentials of the Hebrew faith, so that, while scholars admired the work, the most bigoted Jews praised it. It therefore became generally used in the synagogues and schools throughout Germany; and was instrumental in promoting a knowledge of classical German among Jewish youth, who had previously been generally ignorant of that branch of learning.

The great peculiarity of Mendelsohn's writings was that, under the outward forms of Rabbinical Judaism, he endeavored to give a new impulse to his tribe in regard to their religion, to reform it, to develope it, and to adapt it to the progressive spirit and tendencies of the times. This purpose he more clearly exhibited in his answer to the work of Councilor Dohm on "The Amendment of the Political Condition of the Jews," in which Dohm had asserted that every amendment must proceed from a perfect liberty and equality of rights and relations in society conferred upon the Jew; from a total reform in the system of education under which they lived; from their free admission to all the learned professions; from an equal share of official employments in the service of the State; and also from the exercise of a rigid discipline by the synagogues over their members, by which means heresy would be crushed, and those who held heterodox opinions would be expelled.

Mendelsohn took particular offense at the last point thus urged by Dohm. He contended that the Synagogue should not interfere with freedom of thinking and acting among its members, thereby asserting one of the leading principles of Protestantism and of Christianity. But it is difficult to understand how he could entertain this doctrine, and at the same time assert, that those who were led by the exercise of free thought to abandon the Jewish religion, should be condemned and severely dealt with. This contradiction he attempts to explain by the following language, which is taken from the preface to his German translation of Manasseh's "Hope of Israel:" "Every society has certainly the right to expel any of its members who cease to conform to the principles of the society; but this rule could not in any way apply to a *religious* society, whether Church or Synagogue, because true religion exerts no authority over ideas and opinions, but being all heart and spirit, only desires to use the power of conviction; and Jews especially should take from Christians, among whom they live, an example of charity, and not of hatred or intolerance, and begin by loving and bearing with each other, that they might themselves be loved and tolerated by others."

The influence produced by the writings of Mendelsohn was to destroy all respect for the Talmud and the Rabbinical writers among the Jews who approved his opinions. This is the more remarkable, inasmuch as Mendelsohn professed, all this while, to be himself an admirer of those works; and this obvious inconsistency called forth a publication entitled "A Letter to Mendelsohn," in which this contradiction was clearly pointed out, and the assertion made that he was in reality a Christian, without having the courage to avow his true sentiments. He replied to this publication by his "Jerusalem: A Treatise on Authority in Matters of Religion," in which he contended that all religion was solely a matter of the heart, and should not be under any control, either by Church or Synagogue; while, at the same time, he insisted that the law of Moses was not a law of faith, but merely of statutes and prohibitions. The effect produced by these writings of Mendelsohn was precisely the same as that occasioned by the writings of Maimonides six centuries earlier; to render the Jews dissatisfied with their religion, and to drive them either to the adoption of Christianity on the one hand, or of total infidelity on the other.

Mendelsohn died in 1786. Some time before this period, the German philosopher, Jacobi, dedicated a treatise to him on the Pantheism of Spinoza; and he was incited by the charge contained in that work against his deceased friend Lessing, that he was a Pantheist, to refute it by the publication of a treatise entitled "Moses Mendelsohn to the friends of Lessing." In the hurried preparation of this production he overtasked his physical powers, and the exhaustion thus produced led to his premature death. Beside the works already mentioned, he wrote one called "Morning Hours," and several volumes of "Philosophical Writings." The German language and literature were indebted to his acute and powerful genius for much assistance in that development and improvement which took place at the period of his life and labors. He, together with Lessing, Jacobi, Nicholi, and a few similar spirits, were the predecessors of the still greater and more illustrious school represented by Goethe and Schiller. To the Jews Mendelsohn opened a new field in religion and in literature, which has ever since been occupied and improved by the most intelligent and cultivated minds among them.

His influence was exhibited to some extent in the opinions and labors of several distinguished persons who were his intimate friends and companions. The chief of these was Hartwig Wessely, a native of Amsterdam, where his youth was spent in a counting-house. He was very desirous of mental improvement from an early age, and employed all his leisure hours in study, the first fruits of which were his "Proverbs of the Fathers." He also composed a valuable work on "Hebrew Synagogues." In 1775 he removed to Berlin, and soon a congeniality of tastes and pursuits made him intimate with Mendelsohn, whose unfinished commentary on the Books of Moses he afterward completed. Hartwig distinguished himself more as a poet than in any other respect. His lyrical odes, his elegy on the death of Prince Leopold, his panegyric on the Emperor Joseph, and his heroic poem on Moses, all attest his poetical ability. He died at Hamburg in 1808, in the eightieth year of his age. He may be justly regarded as the founder of the modern Hebrew literature, as Mendelsohn may be considered that of German literature among the Jews of the eighteenth century.

CHAPTER XX.

JEWS IN THE AUSTRIAN EMPIRE—PERSECUTION—INDIVIDUAL WEALTH—THE OPPENHEIMERS—EMPRESS MARIA THERESA—JOSEPH II.—JEWS IN PRUSSIA—ELECTOR FREDERICK WILLIAM—EDICTS OF FREDERICK THE GREAT—REVOLUTION OF 1789 IN FRANCE—THE NATIONAL ASSEMBLY—TREATMENT OF THE JEWS BY NAPOLEON— THE GREAT SANHEDRIM.

THE history of the Hebrew people in the Austrian Empire, presents many diversified scenes of prosperity and adversity. At the end of the eighteenth century their number amounted to two hundred and fifty thousand, scattered among the Italian, German and Sclavonic States of the empire. In Italy, the Austrian sovereigns found it to be to their interests to protect the Jews; and they were sometimes employed by them on important missions, and even decorated with Orders of nobility. In Austria Proper, from the first establishment of the Duchy in 1267, the Jews were regarded as belonging to the sovereign of the country, and were often treated with great severity. The oath which they were compelled to take to the Duke was a singular one. The Jew swore upon the hide of a pig to be a faithful subject; and confessed expressly that a curse rested on himself and his children, because his fathers had crucified Jesus of Nazareth.

In Vienna persecution broke out against them in 1420, and also afterward in 1460, on both of which occasions their chief personages were pillaged and imprisoned. The jealousy of the people was aroused from time to time by the exorbitant rates of interest extorted by the Jewish money-lenders, and by the enormous wealth which many of them amassed. In 1553 Ferdinand I. formally granted them the right to reside in the Austrian capital, as they had previously lived there only by sufferance. He permitted them to trade in jewelry and horses; at a later date he expelled them. Maximilian II. recalled them, and allowed them additional privileges; and Ferdinand II. permitted them, about the year 1620, to erect a synagogue in Vienna. In 1644 false reports were spread through the city that the Jews were the secret spies of the victorious Swedes, and they were in great danger of pillage and murder. The storm passed by; but in 1688 they were accused of having set fire to the citadel, and the consequence was that conflicts occurred between them and the Catholic inhabitants, which resulted in the death of some of them. The Jews addressed a memorial to the Empress, the Infanta of Spain, setting forth their innocence, and imploring her protection. They accompanied this document with a magnificent present, which however was declined; and soon afterward an edict appeared, signifying the wish of the Empress that they should leave Vienna and the Duchy of Austria entirely. A single exception was made on this occasion in favor of Wolf Schlesinger, the agent for the Court, whose services as a financier were found to be too valuable to be dispensed with. In 1677 Sampson Werthermer and Samuel Oppenheimer removed to Vienna, as agents of the Court, and we find that in 1697 the Jews had gradually returned in such numbers as to form a distinct community.

Notwithstanding the prejudice with which the Jews as a people were regarded in Vienna, there were a few exceptions to this rule during the eighteenth century, and prominent among these was the family of the Oppenheimers, who have been already named. They were during several generations the favorite bankers of the profligate nobles about the Court, and men held in high esteem. When Professor Eisenmenger's celebrated work, entitled "Judaism Unveiled," was about to be published in Vienna, and seemed likely to incite the populace to fresh outbreaks of insane and brutal fury against the Jews, the Oppenheimers succeeded in inducing the imperial government to prevent its appearance, and all copies of the book which were found in Austria were confiscated and destroyed. The author was allowed to retain possession of but two copies, and those he carried with him to Berlin, where the work was afterward published through the influence of Jablouski, the distinguished Oriental scholar. It subsequently became widely circulated, and produced the most pernicious effects upon the public mind in reference to the Hebrew race.

The condition of the Jews in Austria improved

after the accession of the Empress Maria Theresa. That benevolent and enlightened Princess would not allow her government to become the tool of religious bigotry, and during her reign they enjoyed a happy interval of security and repose. At that time there were quite a number of wealthy Jewish families in Vienna who stood high in the favor of the Court, some of whom were even decorated with Orders of nobility. Prominent among these were the Arnsteins, Eskeles, Sinzheimers, Schlesingers, Zeidenderfers and Honigsbergs; and thus, being protected by the government, they established manufactories and workshops, in which they employed great numbers of the poor Jews. The Hebrew race generally had reason to regard the memory of the Empress with great gratitude and affection.

Matters even improved on the accession of the reforming Emperor, Joseph II., who ascended the throne in 1780. One of his first measures was an edict intended to ameliorate their condition. He opened to them all the schools and universities of the empire, and gave them liberty to take degrees in philosophy, medicine and civil law, from which they had been previously excluded. He enjoined upon them to establish primary schools of their own, and admitted them to equal rights and privileges in all commercial affairs, allowing them freely to establish manufactories of all kinds except gunpowder. At the same time he levied a toleration tax on them, but in all other respects placing them on the same footing with his Christian subjects.

Some time afterward he made them liable to military conscription, but as they were not nobles, none of them, according to the Austrian code, could attain high rank in the service. They were also released from the necessity of wearing a distinctive dress; were no longer excluded from festivals and public walks; were not compelled to reside in any particular section of the cities or towns; they were allowed even to wear a sword as a sign of gentility; and what was very peculiar, their children under fourteen years of age were protected against the proselyting zeal of the Roman Catholic priests. They continued to enjoy these advantages until after the death of Joseph II. The reactionary spirit then prevailed in the Austrian government, and many of these privileges were withdrawn.

In Prussia the condition of the Jews in modern times has generally been favorable. When Frederick William, the Elector of Brandenberg, surnamed the Great, administered the government of that country from 1640 to 1688, he was under immense obligations to two Jews who resided at Berlin, named Gompertz and Solomon Elias, who displayed the utmost zeal and integrity in his service. The consequence was that when the Jews were persecuted in Austria at that period, and they applied to Newman, the Minister of Brandenberg at Vienna, to know whether they would be received and protected in Berlin, the Elector sent word that forty or fifty respectable families would be favorably received. This number of families, therefore, removed to the Prussian capital, as well as to Potsdam and other cities; and these formed the nucleus around which all the Jewish population of Prussia has since collected. Many complaints were made to the Elector by his Protestant subjects against the spirit of charity and forbearance which he exhibited toward these people. Both Lutherans and Reformed disgraced the name of Protestantism by exhibiting a bigotry and fanaticism which they were in the habit of loudly condemning in the followers of the Church of Rome; but the Elector was too enlightened and too liberal-minded to be influenced by their representations.

In 1696 the number of Jews in Prussia had become so considerable that Dr. Beckman, a resident of Frankford-on-the-Oder; requested and obtained permission to print the Talmud, being convinced that the demand for the work which would follow, would justify the undertaking. At this period the jewelers of the court were two Jews, named Liebman and Reis, and they obtained permission to hold the services of their religion in their private dwellings; and soon afterward the privilege was extended, and they were allowed with their brethren to hold public worship. In the year 1699 a body of rules intended expressly for the Jews residing in the Electorate of Brandenberg were published and put in force. In 1712 these were modified by Frederick I., and no "vagabond Jews" were allowed on any pretext to enter the Prussian territory. But this measure was intended as much for the protection of the resident Jews as for the rest of the population; inasmuch as both were greatly annoyed and injured by the presence of those who came under the prohibited designation.

It was during the same reign that the synagogue at Berlin, one of the most elegant buildings of the kind in Germany, was completed with the royal approval, although great efforts were made by the members of the established church to prevent that result. During the reign of Frederick William, from 1717 to 1740, the Jews enjoyed more security than might have been expected from the semi-insane character of that prince. This statement is illustrated by his enactments concerning them. He never allowed them to be persecuted; he granted some of them especial favor, and others were received at Court with honor. But at the same time he compelled them to buy the wild boars which the King had killed in hunting, if his majesty slaughtered more than could be consumed at his own table. The Jews obeyed the royal mandate, but refused to eat the unclean meat, and bestowed it upon the hospitals. He also commanded that whenever a marriage took place among the Jews they should patronize the royal porcelain manufactory, by purchasing three hundred thalers' worth of its fabrics. At a later period this obligation was removed by the Jews buying four thousand thalers' worth of the porcelain at a single purchase.

The edicts of Frederick the Great in reference to his Hebrew subjects, were generally characterized by a spirit of toleration, though in this respect he was inferior to Joseph II. of Austria. He is said to have asserted that "to oppress the Jews never brought prosperity to any government." In 1750 he issued his "General Privilege," which abolished some of the ancient laws respecting this people, and modified others; but its main object was to prevent their increase in his dominions, and to improve the condition of those who already dwelt there. He guarded very carefully against the entrance of foreign Jews who were poor, and might therefore become a burden upon the community; but those who were wealthy were readily admitted. The "Privilegium" divided the Jews in Prussia into two classes: those who were tolerated by *inheritance*, and those who were tolerated *personally*. The former included those who were actually engaged in commerce, or occupied some office in connection with the synagogue. Their right of abode only extended to one child of the family. Those who were personally tolerated were those who had means of independent subsistence, though not engaged in commerce, and their right could not descend to their children. In 1740 those Jews who were tolerated by inheritance, purchased the right, by the payment of seventy thousand thalers, for a *second* child of the family to enjoy the privilege of residence, provided he possessed a capital of one thousand thalers.

The regulations imposed on marriage by Frederick were very severe; and all poor Jews who wished to marry were compelled to leave the country. No Jew in Berlin, or elsewhere in Prussia, was allowed to possess more than forty houses, nor were they permitted to own land. Their business was confined to trade in money or in goods, the result of which restrictions was, that their condition began to become more unfavorable as long as Frederick lived. His successor being conscious of this fact, endeavored after his accession to ameliorate these regulations; and the result was, that some of the Jewish community attained to considerable wealth, but the majority of them retained a degraded and dependent position, which continued till toward the close of the eighteenth century.

The revolution of 1789 in France, was the source of blessings to the Jews who resided in that kingdom such as it brought to no other of its inhabitants. Though banished from that country as already narrated, by the edict of Charles VI., a few had gradually returned. Some Portuguese fugitives had taken up their residence at Bordeaux and Bayonne; a few others had settled at Avignon, under Papal protection; and when Alsace and Mayence were conquered and annexed by France, some Jews were among the population thus acquired. In 1780 the Jews who resided in Alsace presented a petition to Louis XVI. complaining of the seignorial rights and impositions, by which they were compelled to pay not only for the royal patent of protection, but also a heavy sum to the lords of the soil, for the privilege of residing within their domains—a claim from which none were exempt, not even the aged, the sick, the children and the Rabbis. As these privileges when paid for were not hereditary, they had to be purchased separately for each member of a family.

They also complained with justice, of the restrictions which were placed upon their commerce; and of the attempts which were continually made by the Catholic clergy to convert their children to that faith.

They also demanded of Louis that a law should be passed forbidding the children of Jews to abjure their ancestral religion while under twelve years of age. The result of their appeal was that Louis abolished the capitation tax in 1784; and four years afterward a commission was appointed, with Malesherbes at its head, to propose a reformation of all the existing laws in reference to the Jews in that kingdom. Before this commission could execute or report their labors, the storm of the revolution burst over the country and swept away both commission and king. Two years before this date, in 1786, the Academy of Mayence had discussed the matter of the condition of the Jews in France, and had proposed prize essays on the subject. One of those written on this occasion proceeded from the pen of the celebrated Abbe Gregoire, and another from Horwitz, the librarian of the Royal Library at Paris, both of whom advocated the perfect equality of the Jews in the sight of the law, as dictated by the claims of truth and justice.

Soon afterward the Jews of Luneville and Sarquemines presented a memorial to the National Assembly, requesting that they should be put in possession of those rights which were guaranteed to them by the principles of the Revolution. The Portuguese Jews of Bordeaux had taken an active part in the early scenes of the Revolution, and had, therefore, claims which could not be ignored. The Jews of Lorraine also made known their demands to the Assembly, and condemned, in the bitterest manner, the outrages under which they had suffered for many ages during the existence of the monarchy. The Jews of Paris also presented their claims; and one peculiarity of their memorial was, that they demanded the suppression of the power and authority exercised by the Synagogue over its members. In 1790 the French Jews united in sending in to the Assembly a petition demanding their admission to full and equal rights with other citizens. This requisition at first met with some serious opposition. Even among the stern advocates of universal liberty, the ancient prejudice against these people had not been entirely eradicated. But the exertions and influence of Mirabeau and Rabaut St. Etienne prevailed; and in 1791 the Hebrew population of France were admitted to all the rights of citizenship. Five years afterward a similar law was enacted by the Dutch Republic.

During the supremacy of Napoleon, the condition of the Jews in France remained on the same footing as during the Reign of Terror. He was disposed to protect them, though at the same time he punished them whenever he thought their peculiarities were injurious to his interests or to the popularity of his government. Thus in 1808 he issued an imperial edict, by which he ordained: that in the provinces along the Rhine, where the reputation of the Jews was bad from their excessive usury, every Jewish creditor who should sue a debtor, should procure a certificate from a neighboring magistrate alleging that the said plaintiff was a person of good character, and was not accused of usurious dealings. The operation of this law, however was restricted to the period of ten years.

Two years prior to this edict, in 1806, Napoleon conceived the idea of turning the peculiar talents of his Hebrew subjects to his own advantage. He had doubtless discovered that their skill as financiers was unrivaled; that their commercial correspondence and intercourse throughout Europe was more rapid and reliable than any other; that the secret ramifications of their trade in various countries gave them a great advantage over all their rivals in the world of traffic; and he purposed to convert them into devoted auxiliaries by more favorable measures and more ostentatious protection. As a preliminary step, he astonished Europe by summoning a meeting of the Grand Sanhedrim, to which deputies consisting of the most eminent and learned Rabbis were to be sent, not only from all portions of France, but from all those adjacent countries over which the influence of Napoleon exended. The alleged purpose for which this convention was called was to "*convert into religious doctrines* the answers given by this Assembly, and likewise those which may result from the continuance of their sittings." This statement is rather indefinite; and and was doubtless made intentionally so, in order that Napoleon might have an opportunity afterward to develop or to alter his ultimate intentions.

This Sanhedrim convened on the 28th July, 1806; and Abraham Furtado, a distinguished Portuguese Jew of Bordeaux, was chosen president. The Assembly consisted of a hundred and ten members; and among these there were not only men who were then eminent for their abilities and learning, but some who afterward attained distinction in a succeeding generation, such as Gaudchaux, Cremieux, Avigdor, Rodrigues, Cologna, and others. After the meetings were fully constituted, and were prepared for the transaction of business, Napoleon appointed three commissioners to wait upon them. These were Mole, Portalis, and Pasquier; and they were intrusted with twelve interrogatories, which the Sanhedrim were required to answer, as the first and most important duty which devolved on them.

CHAPTER XXI.

STATEMENT OF JEWISH DOCTRINES BY THE SANHEDRIM—CONDITION OF THE JEWS IN FRANCE—ADULATION OF NAPOLEON BY THE JEWS—THE JEWS IN THE NETHERLANDS—THE NEW BATAVIAN REPUBLIC—SCHIMNIELPENNINCK—ADMINISTRATION OF LOUIS NAPOLEON—THE HOUSE OF ORANGE.

THE inquiries which were propounded to the Sanhedrim at Paris, by the Commissioners of Napoleon, were as follows:

1. Is polygamy allowed by the Jewish law?
2. Is divorce recognized and permitted among them?
3. Are Jews allowed, by their regulations, to intermarry with Christians?
4. Would the Jews in France regard the French people as strangers, or as brethren?
5. In what relation would the Jews stand toward the French, according to the Jewish law?
6. Do those Jews who are born in France consider it their native land? and are they bound to obey the law and customs of the country?
7. Who are the electors of the Rabbis?
8. What legal powers do the Rabbis possess?
9. Are the election and authority of the Rabbis grounded on law, or merely on custom?

10. Are the Jews forbidden to engage in any business?

11. Is usury to their brethren prohibited by the law?

12. Is it lawful, or unlawful, to practice usury with strangers?

To these twelve searching inquiries the Sanhedrim, after due and careful deliberation, sent the following answers:

1. Polygamy is unlawful, being declared such by a decree of the Synod of Rabbis held at Worms in 1030.

2. Divorce is allowed by the Jewish law for various causes; but on this subject the Jews cheerfully obey the decisions of the civil laws of the land in which they may happen to reside.

3. Intermarriages with Christians are not forbidden; but as differences and disputes often arise as to the ceremony of marriage and the education of children, such unions are generally regarded as inexpedient.

4. The Jews in France recognize the French people, in the fullest sense, as their brethren.

5. The relation of the Jew to the Frenchman is the same as the relation of the Jew to the Jew, the only distinction between them being that of religion.

6. The Jews, even while they were oppressed by the French monarchs, regarded France as their country. How much more readily will they do so, after they have been admitted to equal rights.

7. There is no definite and uniform rule in reference

to the election of Rabbis. They are usually chosen by the heads of each family in the community.

8. The Rabbis have no judicial power; that belongs exclusively to the Sanhedrim. As the Jews of France and Italy enjoyed the equal protection of the laws at that time, there was no necessity to confer any jurisdiction or authority on their teachers.

9. The election and authority of the Rabbis are governed solely by custom.

10. There is no law which forbids the Jew to engage in any kind of business. The Talmud enjoins that every Jew shall be taught some trade.

11 and 12. The Mosaic law forbids unlawful interest; but that was a regulation intended for an agricultural people. The Talmud allows interest to be taken from brethren and strangers, but forbids usury.

Napoleon expressed himself satisfied with these answers of the Sanhedrim. It was evident to him, from the spirit of the replies, that the Rabbis were disposed to acknowledge the supremacy of his government, and to make their laws and usages subservient to his authority. He formed a regular plan for the organization of the Jews throughout his empire. Every two thousand of them were to establish a Synagogue and Consistory, to which one principal and two inferior Rabbis should belong, with three householders of the town where the Consistory was held. This body were to select twenty-five notables, or representatives, as their council, for which office all usurers and bankrupts should be regarded as ineligible. The duty of this Consistory was to watch over the conduct of the Rabbis, taking care that they taught nothing contrary to the answers given by the Great Sanhedrim to the questions of Napoleon. The Central Consistory was to be located at Paris, and to be the supreme tribunal of the Jews in the empire. It was to have the power to appoint and depose the Rabbis, whose duty it also was to make the decrees of the Sanhedrim public; and it had authority to inculcate obedience to the laws; to encourage the Jews to enter into military service; and to pray in the synagogues for the welfare of the Imperial family.

In 1807 Napoleon convened another great Sanhedrim at Paris. To this assembly the Rabbis from various other countries, especially from Holland, were invited, in order that the principles promulgated by the body might acquire general authority among the Jews. The Rabbi Segre, of Vercelli, was chosen President. Great pomp attended their proceedings; and their deliberations resulted chiefly in confirming the judgments and opinions previously given. The organization of the Synagogues, as proposed by the Emperor, was approved by the Sanhedrim. According to a statistical account published by the Great Consistory of Paris at this time, there were then eighty thousand Jews in France: of these, one thousand two hundred and thirty-five were landed proprietors, not including the owners of houses in towns; there were two thousand three hundred and sixty workmen; two hundred and fifty manufacturers; seven hundred and ninety-seven military men, among whom were officers of all ranks, from Marshals of the empire downward. Among the Marshals were doubtless reckoned Massena and Soult.

The Jews throughout France were at first highly gratified at the interest taken by the Emperor in their affairs, and at the regulations which he had made in reference to them. But their joy was soon afterward diminished by an edict which he issued in those provinces which bordered on the Rhine; by which he forbade them to lend money to minors without the knowledge of their parents or guardians, or to wives without the knowledge of their husbands, or to soldiers without the permission of their officers. This decree also made void all acknowledgments of indebtedness for which the "value received" could not be proved. It also required all Jews engaged in commerce to take out a patent, and those who were strangers in France to invest some property in land or agriculture. Nevertheless, in Westphalia, Napoleon exerted a favorable influence by supporting the benevolent endeavors of a Jew named Jacobson, who devoted himself to the diffusion of education among his brethren, and who was the means of establishing elementary schools, and an institution for the proper instruction of teachers among them.

A singular circumstance connected with the relation of the French Jews to Napoleon I., was that, on the occasion of celebrating the birth-day of the Emperor, some of his Jewish admirers profanely blended the cipher of Napoleon and Josephine with the name of Jehovah—a word which the Jews venerate with great solemnity; and also elevated the imperial eagle above a representation of the Ark of the Covenant. Such an exhibition of profane adulation of power was offensive to every right-minded Jew. From the time of the first Napoleon to the present, the condition of the Hebrew race in France has not been greatly varied. They have ever since retained their social and political equality, notwithstanding the numerous revolutions of government which have taken place. Many of them have attained distinction in finance, war and literature. In 1830, M. Merilhou, the Minister of Public Worship, declared, as the result of his observation and experience, during the forty years after the emancipation of this oppressed people, that "in the offices of State, under the French banners, in arts, sciences and manufactures, they had, during the quarter of a century, given ample refutation to all the calumnies of their oppressors." One singular result followed this prosperity, which deserves to be named. The freedom which the French Jews have so long enjoyed from tyranny and persecution, has led to greater indifference on their part to their religion. In France there are more of what are termed "infidel Jews"—that is, Jews who, though Hebrews by birth, are believers in no religion whatever—than in any other country. Their feelings and sympathies have been absorbed in the great movements which have been going forward in that country; and in becoming more thoroughly Frenchmen, they have at the same time become, in the same degree, less identified with Judaism. In France, in recent years, a school of thinkers has arisen among the Jews, who have pretended to erect upon the Mosaic law a new and universal religion, which should supersede all others, Christianity included. Prominent in this school of French Jews was the learned Parisian J. Salvador, the author of an able History of the Roman Dominion in Judea. But the views of this faction, though propagated with ability, have never attained any very decided success or diffusion.

When the French armies invaded the Netherlands in 1795, they were the means of introducing into that country, by degrees, a complete emancipation of the Hebrews. Yet, strange as it may appear, the Dutch Jews entertained very different sentiments in reference to the great popular movements of that era from those of the French Jews; and received, with considerable caution, the progressive and radical ideas then propagated. The greater majority of the Jewish synagogues in the Netherlands were upon principle opposed to revolutionary movements. The Spanish and Portuguese Jews who had settled in that country were attached to monarchical principles, were prejudiced in favor of the aristocracy, and were devotedly attached to the House of Orange. Even the Jews of the German and Polish synagogues in Holand were not disposed to exchange their ancient Israelitish nationality for the new political character offered them by the revolutionary government. It is true, however, that a small number of persons belonging to both synagogues, who were distinguished for their talents and enterprise, exhibited a sympathy with the prevailing, far-extending spirit of the age; and established a political association under the title of *Felix Libertate*, for the diffusion of the new opinions and the defense of those rights which were guaranteed to them in common with their co-religionists. This difference in political sentiment, however, occasioned a schism in the synagogues; and the partisans of the new ideas founded an independent and separate Synagogue, named *Adath Jeshurum*, which maintained a distinct existence until the reign of William the First.

In 1795 the new Batavian Republic was founded; and those persons who resided within its limits were divided in their sentiments in reference to the political equality of the Jews. Among them there were many admirers of the Revolution of 1789 in France, and of that of 1705 in Holland. Yet these regarded the Christian religion as the established faith in the latter country, and therefore had objections to the complete naturalization of the Hebrews as equal to all other citizens in the sight of the law. This opinion was defended by many eminent members of the Protestant Churches. Prominent in this class was Van Hametsveldt, a distinguished pastor and professor. He was opposed to allowing the Jews the right to vote in the National Assembly in the year 1796, on the ground that they were aliens; and must be such, in consequence of the fact that, as he believed, the Jews would all be converted to Christianity and would soon return in a body to Palestine. The opposite opinion was entertained by a very eminent and influential citizen, named Schimmelpenninck, who afterward became the "Grand Pensionary." He and his party ultimately triumphed in the Assembly, and obtained the passage of a law by which the Jews were entitled to election to seats in that body. Soon afterward several Jews were chosen as members of the municipal government, and the Courts of Amsterdam, and also of the National Assembly at the Hague. Under the government of Louis Napoleon, the brother of the French Emperor, and afterward under the restored House of Orange, the Jews of Holland became reconciled to their new political rights. Nevertheless they never felt much sympathy with the Great Sanhedrim at Paris, to the meetings of which they refused to send any deputies from among their Rabbis. It was only from the synagogue of Adath Jeshurun that three deputies were sent to that tribunal. These were Charles Asser, an eminent Dutch jurist; De Lemon, a distinguished physician, who was subsequently, in 1813, confined in the Castle of Ham, on account of a supposed conspiracy against the government of the first Napoleon; and M. Littwak, a celebrated Polish mathematician, who resided at Amsterdam.

After the restoration of the House of Orange to the government of Holland, the principle of the absolute equality of all the inhabitants of the country in the eyes of the law, was proclaimed and recognized by the several constitutions of 1815, 1840, and 1848. The result of this impartial and just distribution of rights was, that the Jews soon became promoted to offices of importance and responsibility, such as governors of towns, members of the judicial body, and representatives in the National Assembly. Many Israelites have obtained eminence and distinction in Holland, in consequence of the equal protection of the laws which they enjoyed in that country during the progress of the present century. Among their prominent men were Dr. Jonas Meyer, the author of the "Judicial Institutions of the Chief States of Europe," who was distinguished as a jurist, and Drs. Heilbron and Davids, whose reputation as physicians was European.

CHAPTER XXII.

JEWS IN NORWAY AND SWEDEN—ABROGATION OF ANCIENT LAWS AGAINST THEM—THE POET WERGELAND—JEWS IN RUSSIA—UKASE OF ALEXANDER I.—POLICY OF NICHOLAS I.—THE KARAITES—JEWS IN POLAND—THEIR PECULIAR CHARACTER—THE CONGRESS OF VIENNA—JEWISH RADICALS—BRUNO BAUR—LUDWIG BORNE.

IN former times a law existed in Norway and Sweden which forbade a Jew to settle in either of those kingdoms, without the express permission of the monarch. The result of this regulation was, to restrict the number of Jews in those countries to a very small number; and accordingly, we find that, at the commencement of the present century, among a population of four millions, there were only about nine hundred Israelites. The dynasty of Bernadotte has been more favorable to them than the old hereditary sovereigns; and some amelioration has, in recent times, taken place in the regulations and disabilities which attended their abode in that country. In 1848 a bill was introduced into the Legislative assembly, with the approval of King Oscar, for their benefit. Previous to this, a popular poet of Norway, named *Wergeland*, had distinguished himself by his efforts to procure the abrogation of those ancient laws against the

Jews which existed in the kingdoms of Norway and Sweden. After his death, the Jews expressed their gratitude by erecting a monument in his honor, cast in the foundry of an Israelite, after a model prepared by an artist of the same race. The same spirit of amelioration has existed for some years in the neighboring kingdom of Denmark; and the German and Portuguese Jews residing there have had an augmentation of their privileges. On the 29th of May, 1814, a royal edict was issued, which contributed greatly to their temporal interests, and to the improvement of the administration of their synagogues. Yet a considerable difference of political rights between Jews and Christians still exists to this day, in all the countries of the Scandinavian peninsula.

In Russia the Jewish population have experienced, at different times, various kinds of treatment. In 1824, the Emperor Alexander I. issued a ukase commanding all the Jews who resided in his Polish provinces, to remove, except those who would engage in regular mercantile business, or in the medical profession. They were ordered to give up their usury, their small trading, the management of distilleries, and similar employments, and to make arrangements to migrate to a region of country where they could engage in agriculture. As an inducement to lead them to embrace this offer, it was ordered that they should be exempted from all taxes for a certain period.

The reason of these regulations in regard to the Polish Jews seems to have been, because Alexander became jealous and suspicious of the vast number of them who had gradually congregated in Poland; and to have feared that, at any future outbreak against Russian tyranny on the part of the Poles, the Jews might join the ranks of the insurgents. He was guided by the same motive in ordering that the Rabbis should be stripped of the power which they exercised among their Polish brethren, and that it should be distributed among the elders of the various congregations. Alexander also attempted to improve their peculiar religion and literature by introducing among them a much more liberal and extensive course of education. After that monarch's death, his stern successor, Nicholas, exhibited the same spirit of distrust and illiberality toward the Jews in his dominions. In November, 1827, a ukase was issued forbidding them to traffic through the interior provinces of Russia; and they were not allowed to reside, even for a short period, in any of the cities of Russia Proper, without permission from the Government. That permission was never granted, except in cases where the presence of the Jews was directly useful to the interests of the State. And in cases where they had been allowed to reside for a time, and afterward been ordered to retire, if they were not prompt to obey, they were treated with great rigor, were placed on the same footing as vagrants, and none were ever permitted to afford any shelter under very heavy penalties.

At a subsequent period of the administration of Nicholas I. another vexatious law was passed, requiring all those Jews who lived in the country to reside in the towns. It was also decreed that all those who did not possess real estate should enjoy none of the rights of citizenship. This was equivalent to depriving them of all opportunities to carry on commerce and trade. Subsequently a new tax was imposed on them, called the Sabbath Tax; which was professedly intended for the support of the schools. An incident which occurred on one occasion in the presence of the Emperor Nicholas, illustrates the spirit which characterized that arrogant and narrow-minded despot, who was only fit to be, what indeed he was, a bungling imitator of Napoleon Bonaparte in small matters. At a naval review held before him, two sailors displayed such superior skill, that he immediately promoted them to the rank of officers. Some one informed the Emperor that they were Jews, upon which he immediately ordered them to turn Christians, and began to insult and threaten them. Upon this treatment, and rather than comply with the demand of the sovereign, they both plunged into the waves and were drowned.

The special contempt entertained by Nicholas toward the Jews is further illustrated by the following incident:—Once, on his passage through Riga to Warsaw, the Jews resident in Riga embraced the opportunity to present him a petition. He was on the point of embarking on the river Dwina to visit Mindare. The Czar declined to receive the petition, and the Jews exclaimed in despair: "Where are we to go?" In reply, Nicholas merely pointed to the water, as if he would have said, "Go and drown yourselves!" at the same time ordering the boatmen to row off. After the Polish revolution of 1831, the vengeance of the Czar fell heavily on those Jews whom he suspected, justly or unjustly, of complicity with its movements. He ordered all those who were engaged in smuggling and second-hand traffic to be transported to the Caucasus. Old men, women and children were dragged away, surrounded by crowds of Cossacks. A large number perished from exposure; and when the survivors reached the end of their journey, a conscription of their children was levied, and all those who were over six years of age were carried off into military or naval service.

The subjection of the Jew to the Christian in Russia is shown on various occasions. The former are oppressed in a number of ways, are robbed and defrauded without much protection from the laws, and are insulted with impunity in the relations of social life. If a Christian enters a coffee house or hotel, and finds a Jew sitting there, he imagines that both his honor and his religion require that he should insult him. At the festival of Easter, it is frequently dangerous for the Jews to show themselves on the streets. Within the Russian dominions are found several communities of those Jews called *Karaites*. One of these occupy a mountain residence in the Crimea, called *Djufut Kale*, or the Jews' Castle. It is reached by a steep and narrow path. The houses of this town are built in Oriental style, with windows facing inward from the streets. There are two synagogues in the place, and a burying-ground, which is called "The Valley of Jehoshaphat." Some of the tombs are said to be very ancient, dating five centuries ago. The inhabitants of this fortified town number five thousand. They observe the Jewish ceremonies with great strictness, and many of them possess vast wealth. They are said to possess a curious Tartar Targum, or version of the Old Testament. It consists of four volumes in quarto, and is complete, with the exception of the two books of Chronicles. The other abode of the Karaite Jews in the Russian dominions is on the shores of the lake at Troki, in Lithuania, and the inhabitants claim to be the descendants of a colony who settled there four hundred years ago. They once addressed a petition to the Empress Catharine II., in which they affirmed that their ancestors had no part in the crucifixion of Jesus Christ. They urged this as a reason why they should be exempted from the persecuting vengeance of Christians.

The *Journal des Debats* published the following letter from St. Petersburg, in February, 1840:

"A new tax has been imposed on the Russian Israelites. An imperial ukase, which has been published on the proposition of the Senate, commands that for every head of horned cattle slaughtered by the Jewish butchers, according to the Jewish rite, a tax of twenty-one silver roubles (£3 10s.) shall be laid; and that moreover all the portions of the animal which are considered unwholesome or impure by the Israelites, and which the Jewish butchers formerly sold to the Christians, shall hereafter be buried under ground, or destroyed in any other manner, in the presence of police agents. In consequence of these two measures

—of which the latter is founded on the fact, that Jews are not justified in selling to Christians a food which they consider unfit for us—the pure meat, according to the Jewish doctors, will cost the exorbitant price of fifty silver kopecks, or 1s. 6d. per pound weight; so that the less wealthy class of the Israelites, who form five-sixths of the population of Russia, will find themselves compelled to abandon the use of meat, as the Russian Jews, who are most rigid in the observance of the ceremonies of their religion, will never consent to use food forbidden by their priests. The purpose of the ukase appears to be to destroy the religious distinctions which exist between the Israelites and other subjects of the Russian autocrat."

It is probable that, since the unprincipled despot who issued this decree has descended into the grave, its provisions are not enforced with that degree of inhumanity which would have been grateful to his feelings.

One of the most remarkable portions of the Jewish race in modern times is that community of them who live in Poland. In that country they abound in greater numbers than in any other, and there their peculiarities are more singular. Throughout Poland the Jews are the only agents and brokers, and no business of importance can be transacted without their interposition. The land-owner sells his corn to the householder or merchant through a Jew; servants, tutors and governesses, are employed by their agency; estates are sold, and money loaned and borrowed, only through a Jew. Formerly they were the only persons who rented and worked the salt mines of Poland; but the Austrian Government has since interfered with this franchise. Polish noblemen generally employ a Jewish broker in their establishments; and when the former makes a journey the latter accompanies him, for he has rarely sense or prudence enough to prevent him from ruining himself by some preposterous act of extravagance.

The increase of the Jews in Poland and their position there can readily be accounted for. For ages only two classes of persons existed in that nation: one of which consisted of the nobility—a very turbulent, reckless, wasteful race, who lived in luxury and tyrannized over those around them; and the other, the working community, whose spirit was cringing, servile and mean, and who lived in terror of the higher class. Between these two an immense chasm necessarily existed, which there was no middle class to fill. The nobles were resolved to keep all others below them. The peasants were destitute of sufficient spirit to rise. As long as the old Sarmatian kingdom existed, and the wants and mercantile relations of the community were few and simple, it was not necessary that this cavity should be supplied. But as a taste for commerce and other elements of civilization became gradually more diffused, the existence of a third class, occupying a position between the other two, became absolutely necessary. Thus, when the Jews were driven as exiles from other countries, they found a welcome in Poland, and a place in the nation prepared for them.

The Jews were well adapted to fill this vacant place to their own advantage. The Pole is headstrong and passionate; the Jew is timid and patient. The Pole is extravagant and generous; the Jew is prudent and thrifty. The Pole is ignorant of the art of financiering, and is helpless when pecuniary settlements are to be made; the Jew is good at figures, and is able to count with accuracy. The Pole is improvident, and if he have enough wherewith to live with pomp and with luxury to-day, never thinks of the hour of reckoning, or how to-morrow is to be provided for; the Jew is prudent and full of resources. These and other contrasts of character adapted the Hebrew race admirably to attain prosperity among the Poles.

These things led to many strange relations and events in the history of the Jews in Poland. Sometimes they have enjoyed the most extraordinary privileges, and have been elected as deputies to the Diet at Warsaw. At other times they have been made the victims of the rapacity and cruelty of their aristocratic masters. It is said that one very remarkable feature of the Polish Jews is their beauty; and travelers have narrated how, amid filth and rags, they have observed countenances of the most astonishing loveliness. The rich Polish Jews live in luxury; but nowhere are the poor of that race sunk into greater depths of degradation than in that country. Hence in Poland, where the Jews number several millions, greater contrasts are presented in their condition than in any other land. A recent traveler describes as follows one of the scenes and relations which formerly prevailed in Poland, the singularity of which makes it worthy of repetition:

"It was formerly a common custom for the Polish nobles to keep Jews at their castles as fools. Even now these Jewish jesters are often met with in great families; they bear every kind of insult and ill-treatment with patience and servility. They are treated just like house-dogs, eat and sleep in their master's rooms, but are the butts and scape-goats of the whole family, on whom each throws his own sins, and vents his own ill-humor. In a certain Polish household there lived lately a *house Jew* of this kind. He had received the brilliant name of Prince Friedrich, and was never called by any other. He was as elegantly dressed as the master of the house, and was fed by every one like a pet parrot. Each member of the family was continually popping things into his mouth, which he was compelled to swallow:—if he was in favor, it was a lump of sugar; if they wished to teaze him, rhubarb and magnesia, and sometimes a rap of the knuckles at the same time. He was obliged to be alternately rocking-horse, dancing-bear, draught-ox and jackass for the children, as they and their play required. On Sundays they dressed him up and masked him, now as a negro, now as a Brahmin, now as a he-goat, and now as Jupiter, or Pluto. The master himself often played tricks upon his fool, even more *piquant* than those of his children, for they did not always pass off without bloodshed. One day the Jew met him in the castle-court, just as he returned from the chase, in a great ill-humor, having shot nothing. "I hope the gnadige Herr has had a good day's sport," said the fool, bowing low. "The devil! Jew! I haven't so much as shot one chattering magpie. My gun is still loaded. But stay—I think I can bring down a magpie yet! Up into the tree, sirrah! Up! no flinching! Higher, higher, or I'll give you the ball in your head! Up into that branch—now sit still, magpie!" So saying, he discharged the contents of his gun into the leg of the screaming Jew, who fell down from the tree into the court-yard, and the nobleman rode past him laughing heartily, and fully content with his day's sport. The Jew was taken up, cured, fed with honey and bonbons, and remained in the house as before."*

Glimpses, such as these, of days not very remote, give us an insight into some of the phases of European life and character which formerly existed; and while we pity the barbarity and misfortunes of others, we are justified in congratulating ourselves that we live in more enlightened times, and under more rational influences.

When the Congress of Vienna in 1815, settled the affairs of Europe, the condition and interests of the Jews were not such insignificant matters as to be beneath the notice of the statesmen who figured in that assemblage. They acted upon the principle that they must not disturb more than was necessary the then existing order of things. The sixteenth Article of the Federal

* Kohl's Travels in Austria, Hungary, Bohemia, &c. London, 1844, p. 461.

Acts of the Germanic states, published on the eighth of June, 1815, compelled the Congress to adopt some measures for the improvement of the social condition of the Jews, and to obtain for them the enjoyment of civil rights; at the same time imposing civil duties connected with and resulting from those rights. This proposal met with intense opposition from many quarters. The prejudices against the Jews seemed to be intense, varying in their nature and degree according to the different circumstances of the thirty-eight states into which the Germanic body was divided. Their condition in different principalities was already very dissimilar. Hence, in the Grand Duchies of Baden and Hesse they were prosperous and protected, while in Hanover, they may be said to have lived more under the *surveillance* of the police than under the charge of the government. In the end, the Congress committed the disposal of the subject, in a very great measure, to the legislation of the respective states which formed the confederation.

When this subject came up subsequently for discussion in the legislative assemblies of the several states, it was found that three distinct parties existed, who might be termed the Conservative, the Historical, and the Revolutionary. The Conservative school, on this question, were opposed to all change or amelioration of the condition of the Hebrew race within their limits. They contended for the continuation of all the ancient disabilities, whatever they might be, which then existed, on the ground that the Jews had no rights; that they were aliens; and that both religion and law justly regarded them in that light. The Historical school took the ground that their rulers should be guided by the lessons of history on the subject; that the Jews had long been persecuted, but unjustly; and that the infliction of former wrongs did not justify their repetition. They held that Jews, being born in a certain country, gave them a just and equal claim to the protection of its laws; and that a safe and judicious extension of their rights to any equality with those of other citizens, was the dictate both of prudence and humanity. The Revolutionary party were, in this case, the fanatics and fools of the day and the occasion; violently demanding that the lessons of history should be discarded; that religion and revelation should be wholly ignored; and that a total reconstruction of society should take place, in which, amid universal equality, liberty and fraternity, the Jew should secure his equal rights.

The most famous and pernicious of the Revolutionary party was Bruno Bauer, a prominent infidel writer of Germany, and the forerunner of the equally famous D. F. Strauss, whose "Life of Jesus" proved so terrible a blow to the interests of Orthodoxy in Germany some twenty years ago. Bauer declared that he did not wish the emancipation of the Jews as Jews, but their total extinction in a new race of pantheistical humanity. Against this and other tenets of Bauer, the most learned and esteemed Israelites of Germany —such as Drs. Philipson, Hirsch, Freund, Holdheim, and Solomon—opposed themselves, and condemned his theories without reserve. Nevertheless, he found an immense number of partisans among those Hebrews who, having been long weary of the religion of their forefathers, were eager to adopt any plea for abandoning it and embracing something else. Among the number of these was the well-known writer, Ludwig Börne, who, in 1819, defended the Jewish religion with earnestness, but afterward became thoroughly disgusted with it. He received baptism—not, as he explained, for the purpose of becoming a Christian, but as an indication that he had abandoned the Jewish faith, and wished to abolish all religious differences among the Germans. The King of Prussia approved of the measures proposed by the Historical school; and, in 1847, after the National Assembly had discussed and rejected the proposition to emancipate the Jews from all disabilities in his dominions, issued an edict, on the 23d of July, by which he conferred an equality of rights and imposed the same duties on his Hebrew subjects, reserving only a few points in which the constitution of his government erected an impassable barrier to their universal equality.

CHAPTER XXIII.

JEWS IN BADEN—IN THE FREE CITIES OF GERMANY—PERSECUTIONS—
MORE RECENT HISTORY OF THE JEWS IN ITALY—ENACTMENTS OF LEO XII.
—PAPAL TYRANNY—PIUS IX.—CHARLES ALBERT—DUKE OF MODENA—
RECENT HISTORY OF THE JEWS IN TURKEY—SULTAN MAHMOUD—THE
KARAITES IN TURKEY.

THE experience of the Hebrew race in the various states and kingdoms which constitute the Germanic Confederation, has already been briefly referred to; and has been of the most diversified description. The majority of these rulers have had sufficient humanity and intelligence to treat the Jews with some degree of justice; a few have accorded to them the full enjoyment of their legitimate privileges. Thus, the Grand Duke of Baden issued an ordinance in 1809, admitting the Jews to full civil rights, exempting them from heavy taxes, and giving them the liberty to enter all the liberal professions. The same wise and enlightened policy was imitated by the King of Prussia, in 1812; by the Duke of Mechlenberg-Schwerin, in 1813; by the King of Bavaria, in 1814. The German Jews were not ungrateful for these and other acts of generosity; and when the country was overrun by the French, under Napoleon, many of them enlisted in the service of their country against its oppressor, and distinguished themselves in the field of battle. During the conflicts for German liberty, in 1813–1815, no less than seventeen hundred Jews served in the Austrian army alone. At Waterloo, thirty-five officers of the Allies, who were Jews, were slain; and a large proportion of the ablest physicians and surgeons who were in the camp of the conquerors belonged to that race.

But the German Jews have turned the toleration which they have received to good account in other departments of mental labor. They have produced many men of eminence in all the learned professions, and in the Fine Arts. They have paid special attention to the study of Oriental languages—the Hebrew, Arabic, and Syriac, especially; and the results of their labors have been appropriated by Christian theologians to good account in the exegesis and interpretation of the Scriptures. It is a circumstance worthy of note, that many of the chief patrons of the arts, especially of music, throughout the continent of Europe, are Jews. Some of the most eminent performers in Opera have belonged to this race; and enthusiastic audiences, even in our own country, have applauded with rapturous demonstrations of delight, the wonderful powers of favorite vocalists, little imagining that they were lavishing their adoration at the feet of idols in whose veins coursed the blood of the despised Jew.

The great trading towns of Germany—Hamburg, Bremen, Lubeck, and Frankfort—have been more jealous of their Hebrew population than the larger governments; doubtless because they found them more direct rivals in their commercial pursuits. The higher classes of citizens who resided in those towns entertained feelings of hostility toward their Jewish neighbors for another reason. During the disasters which resulted from the tyranny of Napoleon, many of them were compelled to sell their estates, which were purchased by the Jews; who, with their property, incurred their hatred. In those times, castles, palaces and domains, which had descended during many generations in the same family, became alienated as the possession of the Hebrew speculator; and this was a calamity not to be forgiven. Other Jews had become rich by the contracts into which they had entered with the French government and Emperor; and German patriots regarded all such transactions with special horror. The enormous wealth accumulated by many German Jews, through these means, was often displayed with provoking and imprudent ostentation; and this weakness increased the popular indignation in certain particular quarters. Thus, in 1820, a riot against them occurred at Meiningen, which was followed by similar scenes at Wurtzburg, Hamburg, and other places in Northern Germany; during which, acts of violence and plunder were perpetrated against them. The authorities exerted themselves to suppress these acts of insubordination with but partial success. Nine years afterward, when a proposition was discussed in the Chamber of Wurtemberg, in favor of extending the civil rights of the Jews, the populace of Stutgard surrounded the Hall of the Deputies, and filled the air with shouts of "Down with the Jews! Down with the friends of the Jews!" Notwithstanding this exhibition of adverse popular feeling, the bill was eventually passed, and became the law of the kingdom of Wurtemberg. One of its provisions was the admission of the Jews to all the learned professions; and the result was, that many Hebrews of talent and learning soon showed themselves in the chairs of professors, and in the Chamber of Deputies. Among the former was David Frederick Strauss, whose " Life of Jesus" was the most deadly blow ever inflicted on Christianity in modern times.

Nowhere have the Jews experienced a more diversified fate than in the territories of the Pontiff, varying according to the peculiar disposition and prejudices of the successive Popes. The most numerous bodies of Israelites in the Papal dominions are at Rome, Ancona, and Ferrara. They have always enjoyed a certain degree of protection; and at the accession of each new Pontiff, the Jews have always sent a deputation to congratulate him, and, in return, he generally confirmed the privileges which they enjoyed, by uttering the somewhat equivocal expression: *Confirmamus sed non approbamus;* We confirm, but do not approve. The most liberal patron whom they have had among the modern popes was Pius VII., from 1816 till 1825; during which interval they enjoyed ample protection and equal franchises.

On the accession of Leo XII., however, their fortune turned. He and his advisers brought forth a number of old and obsolete bulls, heavy with curses and execrations against the Jews, and proceeded to put them into execution. By these they were prohibited to acquire any real estate; they were again required to live in particular quarters of the city, and nowhere else; their gates being closed by the police at sunset. As Jews who rigidly adhere to the rights of their religion do not touch fire on their Sabbath, Christian servants were forbidden to enter their houses from Friday evening till Saturday evening; and every Jew in whose house a Christian servant was found in violation of this rule, was fined three hundred scudi. Before a Jew could make any journey, he must not only obtain the usual passport, but also the permission of the Inquisition. At the celebration of the greater festivities of the Church, the Jews were required to remain at home, and not show themselves abroad. On every Saturday a certain number of Jews were ordered to attend a church for the purpose of hearing a discourse from a priest, directed against their religion in particular; and if the required number of Hebrews was not present, the Jewish community was fined thirty *bajochi* for every person who was absent. If the Christian nurse of a Jewish child declared that she had baptized the infant according to the Christian rite, the law was, that the Inquisition immediately took the child from its parents, and gave it to other persons, for the purpose of having it brought up under the control and instruction of the Roman Catholic religion and priesthood.

It was the existence of this extraordinary law which led to the events connected with the famous Mortara case; but we should be in error, were we to imagine, that that was the first and only instance of the kind which has ever occurred, in which Jewish children have been torn from the bosoms of their families in the Papal dominions. A case of this description happened at Rome during the pontificate of Gregory XVI., about the year 1835. There lived at that time in Rome a young Jewess, aged about eighteen years, who was the heiress of a considerable amount of property. Her father was deceased; but her mother, who survived, had married again. The girl was suddenly taken by night from the house of her parents by the Papal police, and removed to a convent, in spite of the tears and protestations of her family, on the ground that she had been baptized by an Italian nurse when an infant; and that, therefore, she had ceased to be a Jewess, and had been made a daughter of the Church. After her removal, the work of her conversion was begun: and the most questionable means were employed to accomplish that result. She was assailed by false visions, mechanical delusions, and all the tricks which are known to have been resorted to for the purpose of imposing on the conscience of mankind. The result was, that she became an easy victim, and then her property was the object of pursuit. Her relatives were not only required to transfer it to her new spiritual friends, but also an additional sum to which she would have fallen heir at the death of her mother. The Papal government afterward offered to find her a Catholic husband, and to dispose of her destiny under the auspices of the Church.

Pope Pius IX. has exhibited a more charitable sentiment toward his Jewish subjects. In 1847 he issued new regulations in reference to them. On the evening of the 17th of April, in that year, the *Ghetto* of the Jews at Rome was solemnly and publicly opened, thus removing the wall of distinction and separation which had previously existed for ages between the Christian and Hebrew population of the "Capital, or Center of Catholicity. Previous to that time the Jews who resided in Rome were compelled annually to send four Elders of the Synagogue to the Pontiff to supplicate permission, in public, for their people to dwell there. Pius IX. abolished this preposterous custom, and carried his liberal sentiments so far that, when reorganizing the ancient "Order of Virtue and Merit," which had been instituted by Pius IV., he substituted a star in place of the cross which had formerly been used on the badge; thus removing an obstacle which had till then prevented the Jews from becoming members of the Order.

In 1848 this liberal example was followed by Charles Albert in his dominions, who proclaimed from his head-quarters at Vogherd, perfect equality of political rights to his Hebrew subjects. The Duke of Modena, at the same period, permitted the Jews in his territory to publish a monthly periodical. There are seven Jewish communities in his dominions—at Modena, Corregio, Carpi, Novelara, Riggio, Finale, and Scandiano. These are generally wealthy, although they labor under some singular restrictions, such as that they are excluded from all the learned professions except medicine, and are confined as to their residences within their Ghettos. The Jews are numerous in Mo-

19

dena, having nine synagogues and an excellent school. The distinguished General Ventura was born among and belonged to the small Jewish congregation at Finale. The eminent engraver, Jesi, bore the same relation to the community of Jews at Corregio. Of all the Italian states, the Jews possess the least toleration and equality in Naples. There they are regarded by the government as strangers; and neglected, except for the purpose of being tyrannized over, and enjoy no recognized civil rights, not even the privilege of erecting or establishing synagogues. In Florence, on the contrary, their condition has always been more tolerable. In that city they have a distinct quarter assigned to them, as in all the Italian capitals, but they have the privilege of residing in other portions of the city. Many of the Florentine Jews are extremely wealthy, and they possess several large and handsome synagogues. In former times the Hebrew printing presses which were established here were celebrated for the beauty and excellence of their work; but these have long ceased to exist.

The history of the Jewish people in the dominions of the Sultan exhibits that diversified character which has marked their fate in all other climes. We possess but few records of them during the middle ages; but after the taking of Constantinople by the Turks in 1453, the Ottoman conqueror found a numerous community of Hebrews already established in his new territories. And when, at a later day, as already narrated, the Jews were banished from Spain and Portugal, and many of the fugitives took refuge in Turkey, they there found their brethren in great numbers, in possession of many synagogues, and holding an important and recognized position in the nation. In Constantinople, Tiberias, Jerusalem, Damascus, Aleppo and Salonica—all being within the limits of the empire—many Israelites were established, and these became central points of Hebrew literature and theology. When the Spanish exiles settled in these places they erected synagogues of their own, retained their own liturgy, language, and customs, and they were known and distinguished by the name of the cities from which they had come, such as Toledo, Lorca, and Lisbon.

The social and political condition of the Jews in Turkey continued to be favorable during the lapse of many generations. During this interval they were free from persecution, enjoyed equal liberty and protection in commerce, manufactures, agriculture, and the acquisition and possession of real estate; although they were subjected, like all the subjects of the Sultan, to those temporary exactions which their caprices or necessities occasionally impelled them to impose. Often the financial affairs of the Sultan were committed wholly to their care, and frequently the chief physicians of the court and harem were Jews. One reason why this people obtained such toleration in Turkey doubtless was, because there existed several other religious communities in that empire who divided between them, and thus weakened, the hostility or contempt of the followers of Mahomet. These were the Greek and Roman Catholic Christians; and upon them the true

Musulmans looked down with as much derision as they did upon the descendants of Abraham, and rejoiced to see them frequently arrayed against each other.

The recent sovereigns of Turkey, especially the bold reformer Mahmoud, and the equally liberal and enlightened Mehemet Ali, the late Viceroy of Egypt, ameliorated the condition of their Jewish subjects, by extending the benefits of the laws equally to Jews, Greeks, Catholics and Mussulmans. The Sultan issued an ordinance to that effect; and this movement was produced by the fact that the state of affairs in the East, the importance and numbers of the Israelites who dwelt there, and the requisitions and progress of public opinion, demanded a liberal policy in reference to that people. This remark applies to Egypt as well as to Turkey. When Dr. Duff, well known as a Missionary in India, passed through Alexandria, on his way thither, in 1839, he obtained an interview with Mehemet Ali; during which the subject of the Jews in Egypt and Syria was adverted to. Mehemet then asserted that his treatment of the Jews in his dominions should always be liberal, and that he would place them on a perfect equality with his Mahometan subjects, socially and politically. This declaration was afterward fulfilled in the main. The Viceroy gave every facility to the Jews within his jurisdiction to return to the Holy Land, which many of them at that time desired to do. He also allowed them to become cultivators and possessors of the soil, and rendered them more secure in the enjoyment of their rights and privileges.

One of the most remarkable features connected with the Jews in the Turkish capital, is the existence there of the sect called Karaites. They have a synagogue in that city, and their peculiarities are so striking as to deserve special description. The chief mark of distinction between them and the other Jews is, that they reject the Talmud, and receive the Old Testament Scriptures as the only proper source of authority and instruction in religion. Their name indicates this distinction, for Karaite means *Scripturist;* while the general body of Jews are called *Rabbinists*, or *Pharisaical*, from the fact that they receive, as of great authority and importance, not merely the Talmud but other writings of distinguished Rabbis. They also differ in the manner in which they interpret the Scriptures; the Talmudist being disposed to extort recondite and mysterious meanings, while the Karaite maintains that the Scripture is its own best interpreter; and that the most certain process by which to elicit the meaning of a passage is to depend upon the grammatical and philological rendition of the words, at the same time paying due regard to the scope and connection, and to the light derived from parallel passages.

The consequence of this method of interpreting the law is, that the Karaites obey all its requirements literally without any figurative evasions. Thus it is commanded in the law of Moses: "Ye shall kindle no fire throughout your habitations on the Sabbath." (Exod. xxxv. 3.) The Talmudic Jews do not generally regard this rule as of binding obligation; and hence, as a traveler narrates, the Jews in the Polish villages illumine their houses with a profusion of candles during the Sabbath night; and they evade the injunction as to having fires by interpreting the word "*ye*" as applying to themselves, and not to their servants. Hence they order their domestics to kindle their fires. The Karaites, on the other hand, obey this injunction literally; they have neither light nor fire in their dwellings during the Sabbath, and eat nothing but cold food during its continuance. They also spend the Sabbath rigidly in religious exercises, and in total abstinence from worldly business or pleasure. The gates of their quarters, wherever they reside, are shut on Friday evening, and remain so till Saturday evening, according to the injunction contained in Neh. xiii. 19.

The Karaites also reject some of the peculiar opinions of the Rabbinical Jews, such as the belief in the transmigration of souls, and the power of talismans. They are very strict and exemplary in their domestic affairs, and are remarkable for their honesty in their dealings with others. They are singular in their abstinence from all lawsuits; for while other Jews in certain localities, are noted for their continual litigation in civil courts with each other, the Karaites are rarely or never known to sue or to be sued. Justice compels all those who have written concerning this sect to admit, that, wherever they have existed—and they are nowhere numerous—they have presented a remarkable example of sincere devotion to their religion, and consistent practice of its precepts.

CHAPTER XXIV.

RECENT PERSECUTION OF THE JEWS IN DAMASCUS—THE SCHEREEF PASHA—HISTORY OF TOMASO—ORIENTAL JUSTICE—SYMPATHY WITH THE SUFFERERS IN EUROPE—MEETING OF THE LONDON JEWS—RABBI SOLOMON HERSCHELL—SIR MOSES MONTEFIORE—JEWS IN PALESTINE—PRESENT CONDITION OF THE JEWS IN JERUSALEM.

It would be a reasonable expectation that the scenes of extreme cruelty toward the Jews, which we have heretofore described as having occurred in various countries, should be confined to former periods; and that such revolting excesses would be unknown in the present age. But that reasonable supposition is contradicted by facts; and we will proceed to narrate events which took place in Damascus, in February, 1840, which show that the progress of time and the diffusion of light have not divested religious bigotry of its malignant cruelty.

There lived at that time in Damascus a Roman Catholic priest, named Tomaso, a native of Sardinia. He supported himself chiefly by the practice of medicine, being particularly skillful in vaccinating children. The Jews of Damascus regarded him very favorably; nor had any ill feeling ever occurred between them. Tomaso was usually attended by a servant, a native Catholic, named Ibrahim; and both of them suddenly and mysteriously disappeared on the night of the 5th of February, 1840. Tomaso generally lodged in a cell in the convent of Capuchin monks which existed at Damascus. As soon as it was ascertained that he and his servant were missing, the French Consul was informed of the fact, and the cell which they usually occupied was examined. Every thing was there found to be in perfect order; and even a large sum of money, which Tomaso had accumulated, was undisturbed. What had become of the missing men, was an inscrutable mystery; but the suspicions of the Roman Catholic and Mahometan population were immediately centered upon the Jews of the city, and the most detestable means were then adopted for the purpose of gratifying their hatred, under the disguise of promoting the ends of justice.

The first step was to inform the Governor of the city, the Schereef Pasha, of the facts. This was done by the French Consul, who was the recognized protector of all the Latin priests who resided in Damascus. The inquiry which was instituted took a twofold form: to ascertain where and when the missing persons were last seen, and to ascertain whether certain Mahometan conjurors, who were resorted to, could discover their fate. After practicing their incantations for a time, they decided that Tomaso and his servant had been murdered by the Jews in their own quarter of the city; and to confirm the truth of this charge, it was actually proved that the missing men had been seen, at eleven o'clock of the day on which they had disappeared, in the Jewish quarter, posting up the notice of an auction which was to take place. It was also alleged that they had not been seen anywhere after that time.

The result of these conclusions was, that the Jews were charged with the murder of the priest and his servant; and the motive for the horrid act was alleged to be, that they might procure human blood for the feast of unleavened bread, which happened to be near at hand. To rebut this charge, an elderly Jew of respectability named Katasch, then came forward, and testified that he had seen Tomaso as late as five o'clock of the day on which he disappeared, and in the Christian quarter of the city. Having made this statement, he was immediately arrested and imprisoned. On the 8th of February, while the whole affair was still involved in obscurity, a Mahometan named Tulli, whose character was bad, and who was at that time in prison for debt, asserted that, if he were at liberty, he possessed the means of arriving at the truth of the matter. The French Consul obtained his discharge, after which he set himself to work to make discoveries. At his suggestion, Schereef Pasha sent for the chief Rabbi, Yacoob Anthabi, and for two other inferior Rabbis, and informed them that, if they did not discover the murderer of Tomaso within twenty-four hours, they should all be beheaded. The Rabbis departed, and immediately summoned all the Jews of Damascus to the synagogue. They then pronounced the most solemn and severe anathemas against every one who might have any knowledge of the facts of the case and would not reveal them. The result was, that a young Jew informed the Rabbis that he had seen Tomaso on the fifth day of the month, in the Christian street, precisely at the time and place designated previously by Katasch. He was also taken before the Pasha, to whom he solemnly repeated this statement. The Pasha exclaimed, in a great rage: "Who has bribed you to give evidence in favor of the Jews?" and ordered him to be whipped. The result was, that he was scourged with such extreme cruelty, that he was carried from the Pasha's presence lifeless, and afterward expired.

The Jewish barber, upon whose door Tomaso was last seen affixing the notice of the auction, was then arrested and examined. He named six poor Jews who had visited his shop during that day, all of whom were immediately arrested and put to the torture. As nothing could be extorted from them, they were afterward discharged. On the 12th of February the barber also was tortured, first by being whipped, and then by having an instrument affixed to his head, which crushed it so violently as to press his eyes out of their sockets. The unfortunate wretch persisted, amid his agonies, that he knew nothing of the matter. He was informed by the Mahometan Tulli that he was expected to criminate some of the wealthy Jews; and that, by so doing, he would immediately obtain his own release. He was subjected to the torture a second time, but he refused to implicate those in a horrible crime whom he knew to be innocent; and his agonies were continued and increased by his inhuman persecutors, with the approbation of the French Consul, until at length his resolution gave way, and he declared his willingness to make some revelations on the subject.

Accordingly, he stated that he had seen Tomaso on the evening of the fifth of February, in the Jewish quarter, in company with a wealthy Jew, named Arari, and his three nephews, with three others whom he named. The seven were all persons of great consideration among the Hebrew community, and all denied the barber's statement as wholly unfounded and untrue. These persons were immediately arrested and imprisoned. They were afterward subjected to a species of torture which consisted in compelling them to stand on their legs, without change of position, for the long period of three days and three nights. As this process failed in extorting any confession from the sufferers, the barber was again threatened with torture unless he made some additional revelations. Overcome by the thought of such horrors, he declared that on the night of the fifth of February he was sent for to the house of Arari, for the purpose of bleeding him; that there he saw Tomaso lying bound in a corner, and the seven Jews sitting around him; and that they offered him twelve hundred piastres if he would bleed the monk to death. When he refused the proposition, they agreed to give him two hundred piastres if he would keep the matter secret. To that proposal he had consented, and then went home.

After having obtained these forced confessions from the barber, the seven Jews were subjected to the most cruel tortures to constrain them to acknowledge the murder. They all persisted in their declarations of innocence. The chief of them, Arari, an aged man, seventy-five years old, having received the twentieth blow, began to foam at the mouth, and fell into convulsions. The rest were similarly tortured, but without obtaining any confessions from them. On the 17th of the month, sixty-three Jewish children were arrested and frequently questioned, for the purpose of ascertaining whether they had heard or seen any thing connected with the fate of Tomaso. The most ingenious management was in vain resorted to to induce them to implicate their relatives, but in vain. The tortures of the seven wealthy Hebrews were resumed from time to time, and every variety of suffering inflicted on them. Sometimes they were whipped; at other times their eyes were pressed out of their sockets; they were compelled to stand upright for four days without relief; they were dragged by the ears about the courtyard of the prison, till the blood gushed out from the roots; thorns were driven under their finger-nails; lighted candles were held under their noses till the flames arose into their nostrils; and their beards were burnt from their faces. Yet all these horrors were perpetrated in vain; and after the occurrence of scenes of barbarity which were not exceeded in the darkest eras of history, the persecutors were compelled at last to desist, without having attained a particle of evidence, which deserved credence, to throw light upon the mysterious end of the priest and his attendant. The truth doubtless was, that not one of the Jews possessed the least information in reference to the case, or had any connection with it in any possible form.

Such extraordinary barbarity very naturally excited the indignation of the public—first, in the adjoining countries; and afterward, as the revolting details became more extensively known, throughout Europe. No person of the least humanity could become cognizant of them, without feeling some sympathy for the unfortunate victims of such ferocity. This sentiment became general throughout Western Europe. Sir Robert Peel introduced the subject in the British Parliament, and demanded that the English Government should interfere in the case. Lord Palmerston, who was then in the Cabinet, announced, in reply, that the matter had already engaged the attention of the ministers, and would be further agitated. About the same time, the Jews of London assembled, and took the matter into consideration. The Rothschilds had received a letter from the Jewish congregation of Constantinople, setting forth the facts of the case, stating their inability to afford any relief, in consequence of the hostile relations existing between the Turkish Government and the ruler of Syria, and asking the interference of the British Jews.

In consequence of this appeal, the Israelites in London convened in their chief synagogue in Duke's Place. Several of the Rothschilds were present, and Sir Moses Montefiore presided. Resolutions were offered and approved to this effect:—"That the meeting acknowledge with deepest gratitude the prompt interference of the British Government in behalf of the Jews of the East; that they deem it important that some gentleman of rank and talent, delegated by the Jews of London, do accompany M. Cremiex, the delegate from the Jews of Paris, to co-operate with him; that Sir Moses Montefiore, from his high moral character, influence and zeal, is particularly fitted to be the representative of the British Jews, for such purpose, at the Court of the Pasha of Egypt; after whose appointment and acceptance, it was further resolved, that the meeting, impressed with the generosity, zeal and devotedness of Sir Moses Montefiore, in accepting their appointment, do tender him their gateful thanks, in token of their admiration of his conduct."

It would appear that these cruel scenes at Damascus had arisen from the existence of a suspicion which prevailed not only in the East, but also even in Europe, that the Jews secretly practiced the use of the blood of murdered Christians at their feasts, when unleavened bread was eaten; and hence, when persons were missing or murdered at those seasons, the suspicion of foul play on the part of the Jews was immediately excited among the ignorant populace, which then led to acts of violence and murder. It was important to contradict this slander, and the false impression produced by it, in some authoritative way; and this the Jews of London proceeded to do. At their instance Dr. S. Hirschell, the chief Rabbi of the British Jews, addressed a letter to Sir Moses Montefiore, in which he stated that he had been an incumbent of the office which he then occupied for forty years; that he had been a Rabbi in Germany previously; and yet, that he could solemnly declare, that no such rite or custom had ever existed within his knowledge. He added, that his ancestors had been Rabbis for more than ten successive generations; that the instructions appertaining to their office had been carefully transmitted from father to son; that he had been thoroughly informed of all the usages and rites pertaining to the Jewish religion; and that it was absolutely certain that, if any such custom or practice as the use of the blood of Christians by the Jews, under any circumstances, existed, he would have become aware of the fact. And yet he solemnly declared that no such custom or rite had ever been practiced, with or without the sanction of the Jewish law; and he concluded by invoking on himself all the anathemas and curses contained in Leviticus and Deuteronomy, if his statement were not strictly and absolutely true. A similar declaration was made in a letter from Dr. David Meldola, presiding Rabbi of the congregation of Bevis Marks, in London; a person who was descended in the same manner from a long line of Rabbinical ancestry, and enjoyed similar opportunities of knowing the facts.

While these movements were taking place among the English Jews, an interest was felt in the subject by a large portion of the British public. A meeting of merchants, bankers and others, was held in the Egyptian Hall, by which resolutions were passed expressing sympathy with the sufferers, and giving utterance to their feelings of horror at the use of the torture for the purpose of compelling suspected persons to confess. They also resolved to send copies of their resolutions to all the British ministers and diplomatic representatives throughout the East, expressive of the sympathy of the British public with the suffering Hebrews, and their hope that a speedy and final termination might be put to them.

The Mission of Sir Moses Montefiore to the Pasha of Egypt was productive of good results. An end was put to all further proceedings at Damascus against the suspected Jews, and the mind of Mehemet Ali was so operated upon, that not long afterward he had an opportunity of showing his impartiality and justice toward them. A young Christian, named Michael Bahun, having suddenly disappeared at Cairo, and having been last seen in the Jewish quarter of the city, a report was raised that he had been assassinated by the Jews, that they might obtain his blood. A complaint was made to that effect before Mehemet Ali by the brother of the young man; and an intense excitement began to prevail. The Grand Rabbi, having heard of the event, summoned the chief Jews of Cairo, proceeded with them to the palace of the Viceroy, and requested him, in the name of the Jewish community, to put an end to the calumny. Mehemet Ali was too enlightened a man not to perceive the absurdity of the charge which had been made against the Israelites; and he gave orders that a thorough search should be made for the missing person. Steps were immediately taken to execute this order. For some time no discoveries were made. A reward was offered to any one who would produce the man. At length, four months after his disappearance, Michael Bahun was brought to the Grand Rabbi, and the secret of his concealment revealed. He had fled from Cairo into Upper Egypt on account of debt, and had been sojourning in the Convent of St. Anthony. This result at once disabused the public mind in reference to the murderous propensities and cannibal appetites of the terrified Hebrews; and the latter, together with French, Tuscan, and Austrian Consuls at Cairo, expressed to Mehemet Ali their admiration for his enlightened opposition to the absurd prejudices of the public.

From the time that Palestine fell under the sceptre of Mehemet Ali, and became incorporated with the government of Egypt, the condition of those Jews who dwelt at Jerusalem has been much more tolerable than while they were subjected to the arbitrary dominion of the Sultan. The "Holy City," associated with so many thrilling, glorious and melancholy recollections to the Jew, contains six synagogues, and about ten thousand persons of that race. The following particulars in reference to their condition, and the most striking peculiarities of the ancient capital of Judea, are taken from the pages of a recent traveler in Palestine:

"The Jews inhabit a particular portion of the southern part of the city of Jerusalem, the Haret-el-Youd, between the foot of Zion and the enclosure of the mosque of Omar, and are not the least interesting of the objects presented to the traveler in the Holy City.

"This extraordinary people, the favored of the Lord, the descendants of the patriarchs and prophets, and the aristocracy of the earth, are to be seen in Jerusalem to greater advantage, and under an aspect, and in a character totally different from that which they present in any other place on the face of the globe. In other countries the very name of Jew has associated with it cunning, deceit, usury, traffic, and often wealth. But here, in addition to the usual degradation and purchased suffering of a despised, stricken, outcast race, they bend under extreme poverty, and wear the aspect of a weeping and mourning people; lamenting over their fallen greatness as a nation, and over the prostrate grandeur of their once proud city. Here the usurer is turned into the pilgrim, the merchant into the priest, and the inexorable creditor into the weeping suppliant. Without wealth, without traffic, they are supported solely by the voluntary contributions of their brethren throughout the world. I think I am warranted in stating, that the number of Jews now in Jerusalem is greater than at any other period in modern times. The population of any Eastern city is with great difficulty accurately ascertained, owing to the total absence of statistical or municipal tables, as well as to the immense floating population, hundreds arriving at night, and passing out in the morning; besides, here the number of pilgrims varies daily. The entire resident population of the city is about thirty-five thousand; of which ten thousand are Jews, ten thousand Christians, ten thousand Mahometans, and about five thousand foreigners, or partial residents, including the garrison. As a rough guess would but little approximate to the truth, and as many contradictory accounts have been published of the number of Jews resident in Jerusalem I have used every means of procuring correct information on this subject. The Latins and the Jewish Rabbis themselves, whom I severally consulted, both agreed in stating that the number is greater now than at any other period in latter times of which they have any record, and that at the lowest calculation it amounted to the number I have stated. The period is not very distant when the Turkish law permitted no more than three hundred Jews to reside within the walls.

"A vast concourse of this people flocked to Jerusalem at the time that Syria was occupied by the Egyptians, and afterward on the conquest of Algiers. Within these two or three years, however, the extreme scarcity of provisions has deterred others from going there, and the number has not been so great as heretofore. With all this accumulated misery, with all this insult and scorn heaped upon the Israelite here, more even than in any other country, why, it will be asked, does he not fly to other and happier lands? Why does he seek to rest under the shadow of Jerusalem's walls? Independently of that natural love of country which exists among this people, two objects bring the Jew to Jerusalem—to study the Scriptures and the Talmud—and then to die, and have his bones laid with his forefathers in the valley of Jehoshaphat, even as the bones of the patriarchs were carried up out of Egypt. No matter what the station or the rank—no matter what, or how far distant the country where the Jew resides, he still lives upon the hope that he will one day journey Zionward. No clime can change, no season quench, that patriotic ardor with which the Jew beholds Jerusalem, even through the vista of a long futurity. On his first approach to the city, while yet within a day's journey, he puts on his best apparel; and when the first view of it bursts upon his sight, he rends his garments, falls down to weep and pray over the long-sought object of his pilgrimage, and, with dust sprinkled on his head, he enters the city of his forefathers.

"In Jerusalem alone, of any place upon the earth, is the Hebrew spoken as a conversational language; for, although the Scriptures are read, and the religious rites performed in Hebrew, in the various countries in which the Jews are scattered, yet they speak the language of the nations among whom they are located. And, as the last link of that chain which binds them to home and to happiness, they, like other oppressed nations, cling to it with rapturous delight. And it is the only door by which the missionary there has access to the Jew; for they have themselves said to me, 'We cannot resist the holy language.'

"Most of the Jews are learned, and many spend the principal part of their time in studying the Scriptures or the Talmud, while others are engaged in discussing the law and disputing in the synagogues, or in weeping over Jerusalem. They are particularly courteous to strangers, and seem anxious to cultivate intercourse with Franks."

CHAPTER XXV.

RECENT STATE OF THE JEWS IN PERSIA—SCENES AT ISPAHAN—THE TEN LOST TRIBES—THE RIVER GOZAN—JEWS IN INDIA—JEWS IN MALABAR —INTERESTING DOCUMENT—JEWS IN MOROCCO AND TUNIS—SINGULAR PERSECUTIONS—EXAMPLE OF HEROIC FORTITUDE.

DURING the early portions of the present century, the condition of the Israelites who dwelt in Persia was one of great suffering, and exhibited scenes not unlike those which occurred at Damascus. This remark is particularly applicable to those Jews who resided at Shiraz. The Persian Government and the Mahometans used every opportunity to oppress and degrade them. By these means they were reduced to the most abject and melancholy situation. Their dwellings were huts, marked by low, narrow entrances, which no one could enter with an upright position. They were always seen in the streets clothed in rags. Their occupation was generally searching for broken glass and old clothes, which they sold again. In the streets they were constantly seen begging. The celebrated missionary, Rev. Joseph Wolff, thus described what he himself witnessed in the streets of Shiraz: "On my entering the Jewish quarter at Shiraz, I saw old and young men, and old and young women, sitting in the street and begging; their heads were bowed to the ground and fainting; and, stretching out their hands, they cried after me with a feeble voice, 'Only one pool; I am a poor Israale, I am a poor Israale!' I distributed some trifle among them, and several of the Jews said to me, 'Are you arrived? We have heard that you are a son of Israel, and have brought with you the Gospel in Hebrew. Give us the Gospel!' I told them that I intended to visit them in their houses; and whilst I was speaking with them, I heard the poor Jews and Jewesses crying, 'I am a poor Israale! one pool, only one pool; I am a poor Israale!'"

Scenes such as these clearly indicate the extreme poverty and degradation to which the tyranny of the Persians had reduced the Jews among them. These events occurred in the year 1825; and, that the Hebrews were thus degraded by the influences which surrounded them, is evident from the particular impositions and cruelties to which they were subjected. They were often compelled to work for the dominant race without payment. They were protected by no law; for often, while the father of a family was abroad, endeavoring to earn something, if he happened to have a daughter who possessed any personal beauty, his house would be entered by the agents of the prince or governor, and his child forcibly abducted, and placed in the harem of her ravisher. On a single occasion, as many as eight young Jewesses at Shiraz were stolen from their parents by the direct orders of the Shah. At Ispahan five of them were subjected to the same outrage, and taken to the harem of the sovereign.

When a community are made the victims of such outrages, without enjoying any protection from the law of the land, their social degradation will soon become complete. Accordingly, we find that their condition was so perilous and exposed to constant injury at Shiraz, that the Jews did not venture, even when able to do it, to dress themselves decently, lest, becoming suspected thereby of being in possession of some property, they would be robbed of it. They never dared to show themselves in the streets on Fridays, that being a sacred day with their Mahometan neighbors. Whenever a public slander or report was started against them, the whole community became at once intensely incensed, without examining into the truth or falsehood of the charge; and while the popular frenzy continued, they were liable to, and often actually suffered, the extremes of popular fury.

An illustration of this fact is furnished by the traveler to whom we have already referred. He writes as follows:

"Six or seven years ago, a poor Jewess, who had a bad hand, asked the advice of a Mahometan physician, who told her to kill a dog and dip her hand in the blood. She did so, and it happened to be at the time of Bairam, one of the Mahometan feasts, when they offered a sacrifice. One Sayeed, *i. e.* one of the descendants of Muhamad, the prophet, assembled the Mahometans in the great mosque of Imam Resa, at Meshed, and exclaimed: "People of Mahomet, the Jews have sacrificed on the holy day of Bairam a dog, in derision of our religion. I therefore shall only pronounce two words, which will tell you what to do, and these two words are, 'Allah daad.'" The meaning of these two words is "God has given!" Upon this, thousands of Mussulmans rushed to the houses of the Jews, shouting "Allah daad!" burnt, destroyed and plundered their houses, and killed thirty-five of them! The rest of the Jews, smitten with consternation, to save their lives cried out, "There is God, and nothing but God, and Mahomet, the prophet of God!" A few good old men, however, exclaimed, "Hear, Israel! the Lord our God is one Lord! The law of Moses is truth, and the prophets are truth!" and immediately their heads were struck off! The anniversary on which the Jews were massacred is now called by the Mahometans, as well as by the Jews of Meshed, "The year of Allah daad!" *i. e.* the year in which the Jews were given into the hands of the Mussulmans! I have lived in one of the houses of these poor Jews, where they in secret worship the God of their fathers in their own way. It was on the Day of the Atonement, when most of them, especially their women, fasted the whole day. The poor Jewesses tell their children, "Never forget that you are of the seed of Israel, and remember the day of Allah daad!"

A few years since much attention was excited among those who were interested in the history and fate of the Hebrew race by the supposition that the descendants of the *Ten Lost Tribes* had at length been discovered in a previously unknown country in the heart of Asia. At that time some Jewish merchants made their appearance at a fair in Leipsic, who brought with them valuable shawls made of the finest wool of Cashmere and Thibet, and who dwelt in Bucharia, a region of country situated in the centre of Asia. It was asserted that the location of this country corresponds with that referred to in those passages of Scripture which describe the original wanderings and destination of the Ten Tribes of Israel.

Thus we read in the seventeenth chapter of the second book of Kings, that "in the ninth year of Hosea, the King of Assyria took Samaria and carried Israel away into Assyria, and placed them in Halah and in Habon, by the river of Gozan and in the cities of the Medes." It is also said in another passage that the Lord "put away Israel out of his sight, and carried them away into the land of Assyria unto this day." These passages are connected with another contained in the Apocryphal book, second Esdras, thirteenth chapter, in which it is said that the Ten Tribes were carried beyond the river; and so they were brought into another land, where they took counsel together, that they would leave the multitude of the heathen, and go forth into a further country, where never mankind dwelt; that they entered into the narrow passages of the river Euphrates when the springs of the floods were stayed, and went through the country a great journey, even a year and a half.

Now it is supposed that the river *Gozan* thus referred to is the same as the Ganges, which has its sources in the countries from which the merchants in the Leipsic fair came. The region beyond Bucharia was unknown in ancient times to the rest of Asia and Europe, and its distance from Palestine is so great, that to reach it would require a journey of many months at the slow pace at which a numerous caravan or company would necessarily travel. To confirm this supposition, a Christian missionary at Bombay, named Sargon, made some inquiries in 1822, of Jews who visited that city; and he even undertook a journey to Cannanore, for the purpose of obtaining definite information on the subject. He there met with Jews who were descended from some who had removed thither from Bucharia, and from them he learned that the people in question called themselves *Beni Israel;* that they were numerous among the hordes of Tartary and Cashmere; and that these had originally come from Bucharia. Their peculiarities he found to be chiefly as follows:—They had Hebrew names, to which, however, local terminations had been generally added. They understood the Hebrew language, although their ordinary tongue in daily intercourse was the Hindoo. They had idols, which they worshiped; yet the Hebrew language was introduced into their religious exercises and ceremonies. They practiced circumcision and observed the great day of Expiation, though they did not keep the Sabbath. They also spoke of the Arabian Jews as their brethren. They made frequent use of the phrase prevalent among other Jews: "Hear, O Israel, the Lord our God is one Lord!" They had no priest, rabbi or levite, but simply a reader, who conducted their religious ceremonies. They also had traditions of a Messiah, and expected his speedy appearance among them to lead them to Jerusalem. These peculiarities seemed to many persons conclusive of the fact that these isolated and distant Jews were the descendants of the Lost Tribes. It is an inquiry of interest not only to Jews themselves, but also to all those who are fond of historical researches in regard to the development and progress of the human race.

Another interesting community of Jews in the East is that in *Malabar*. They existed here previous to the first settlement of the Portuguse, in 1498. They are divided into the White and Black Jews. The former are the descendants of emigrants who came thither after the destruction of the Temple by Titus; the latter are the offspring of some of the natives of Malabar. The number of those who are said to have reached this coast after the fall of Jerusalem was about ten thousand; and several centuries passed away, of which no record exists. In the year A. D. 379, the Emperor of Malabar granted the Jews a document or charter, which guaranteed to them a reasonable share of liberty and protection. This charter was afterward engraved by them on a copper plate, and is so remarkable a document, that we herewith present a translation of it:

"Swastri Sri! the King of kings hath ordained it! when Raja Sri Bhaskarah Irava Varma was wielding the sceptre of royalty in a hundred thousand places, in the thirty-sixth year, above the second cycle, he vouchsafed, during the time he sojourned in Mavil Cottah, to perform a deed, the subject of which is as follows:—From Yusuf Rabba and his people, in five degrees of persons, we exact the tribute of due and deference to our high dignity, and of the usual present to our Royal person. To these we allow the privileges of bearing five kinds of names, (colors;) of using day lamps; of wearing long apparel; of using palanquins, and umbrellas; copper vessels; trumpets and drums; of garlands for the person; and garlands to be suspended over their roads; and we have relinquished all taxes and rates for these; and also for all other houses and churches in other cities; and independent of this bond to him, we have made and given a copper instrument for these latter, separate and distinct. These are to be enjoyed after these five modes of descent, viz., by Yusuf Rabbi himself, and his heirs in succession—thus his male children, and his female children, his nephews, and the nephews of his daughters, in natural succession, an hereditary right, to be enjoyed as long as the earth and moon remain, Sri!"

Then followed the witnessing of the grant, and other official appendages.

Under the guarantees of this edict the Jews of Malabar lived during many centuries, until the arrival and supremacy of the Portuguese in the fifteenth century. Then, as usual, their persecutions began. They were robbed, assailed and outraged in every possible manner. They were forbidden to observe the rites and ceremonies of their religion, which, if practiced at all, were practiced in secret; and they enjoyed no recognized protection or justice from the courts of law. Subsequently, the Portuguese burnt their synagogues and houses; and among the valuable books which were thus lost, there was one called Sepher (book) of

Jashar, which continued the history of the Jewish community in Malabar, from the time of their emigration to the country till that period. In January, 1663, Malabar was wrested from the Portuguese by the Dutch under Admiral Van Goes; and then the condition of the resident Jews became ameliorated. With the end of the supremacy of the Portuguese in that fertile clime, the sufferings and perils of the Hebrews terminated; and they have since been permitted to enjoy the blessings of security and peace.

We turn from the Jews of Malabar to those of Morocco and Tunis. In the latter State they are numerous in proportion to the rest of the population, being about a hundred and seventy thousand. All the Israelites are placed by the Bey, under the authority of a Governor, who has power to imprison them for offenses, and even to inflict severer penalties upon them. Their synagogues are presided over by a council of five Rabbis, to the principal of whom the epithet *Ab Beth Din*, the "Father of the House of Judgment," is applied. The majority of them are poor, having been oppressed for ages by the exactions and tyranny of their Mahometan rulers.

The Hebrew race are also numerous in the empire of Morocco. They originally removed to that country when expelled from Spain and Portugal by the bigotry of the sovereigns of those States, as we have already narrated. At first they were allowed protection and security, and the followers of the False Prophet exhibited more charitable tempers toward them than the disciples of Him of Nazareth. But the Jews gradually excited the hostility and the envy of their Moslem neighbors by their avarice and knavery in their business transactions; for they generally applied themselves in their new homes to money-lending and commerce, and, being more sagacious and shrewd than the native population, they usually gained the advantage. The result was that a feeling first of enmity, and afterward of contempt, arose in the minds of both rulers and people toward them, which was soon displayed in the passage of rigorous and cruel laws in reference to them, and a general spirit of persecution and intolerance.

There are, probably, about four hundred thousand Jews in the empire of Morocco. They are engaged chiefly in the pursuits of merchants, artisans, tradesmen, brokers, and interpreters. Their services are generally required in all transactions which take place between Europeans and the native Moslems. The existing laws in reference to them, display the spirit of hostility and distrust which characterizes the feelings of the latter. The Jews are forbidden to read or write Arabic, on the plea that they are unworthy to read the Koran. They are forbidden to mount a horse, because that animal is supposed to be too noble for them. Whenever they pass a mosque or holy place, or even the palaces of the great, they are required to remove their shoes, and go barefoot. They must not approach a well while a Mahometan is drinking from it. They are compelled to dress in black, because that color is regarded as the meanest; they must pay heavy taxes, and an extra assessment for the privilege to wear shoes and employ mules; the Jew who raises his hand to strike a Moslem is punished with death; and they alone perform the functions of executioners and grave-diggers.

The result of the existence of this hostile feeling is, that the Jews have been subjected, from time to time, to occasional outrages of the worst description, enacted in accordance with the extreme ferocity and cruelty which are prominent traits in the character of the monarch and people of Morocco. By the laws, they are never permitted to bear testimony against a Mahometan in a court of justice; yet the evidence of any two Moslem witnesses is sufficient to convict a Jew, even on the gravest charge. It sometimes has occurred, within the present century, that this law has been employed to compel Jews to renounce their religion and to become Mahometans, by being represented by two persons of the latter faith as having repeated the standard phrase of the Moslem: "There is no God but God, and Mahomet is the Apostle of God." When thus charged, it is vain for the Jew to protest against his forced conversion; and should he persist in so doing, and refuse to abandon the religion of his forefathers, as the law requires under such circumstances, death is his only alternative. An instance illustrative of this fact occurred some years ago, which deserves to be briefly narrated.

A handsome young Jewess was represented by two Moors as having repeated their confession of faith, as above given; and she was accordingly summoned before the tribunal of the Caadi. She resolutely denied the charge; but the testimony of the two Moslems was sufficient to overpower all her asseverations. She was ordered to announce her conversion to Islamism, or suffer the penalty of death. She appealed, by the assistance of her friends, to the Sultan; and with the facts of the case, the report of her beauty was also conveyed to that potentate. After hearing the representations of both sides, the Sultan confirmed the decree of the Caadi, and commanded the young woman to be sent to his seraglio. It is difficult to say whether the entire proceeding was not a plot to bring about her abduction for that express purpose; but certain it is, that every effort was made, by alternate threats and promises, to induce her to profess herself a convert to the Mahometan faith, which was nothing more than a preliminary step to her abandoning herself to the embraces of the despot. She resisted these purposes, however, with the utmost resolution. She had determined to suffer death, rather than become an apostate from the religion of her forefathers, and the paramour of a licentious tyrant. When this result became apparent, the Jews offered a large sum of money for her release; but the offer was refused. Baffled in the attainment of his prey, the Sultan was determined to be revenged. The young Jewess was accordingly condemned to death. The last scene is said to have been one of the most affecting, of which the imagination can conceive. On the day of the execution the fair and innocent victim was led forth to the scene of death. An immense crowd surrounded the spot, in whose breasts pity seemed strangely to have overcome, to some extent, the power of bigotry. Even the Morocco soldiery, the most brutal and ferocious in the world, are said to have displayed proofs of sympathy. Again, on the scaffold, and for the last time, her life was offered her on condition that she should renounce the religion of her forefathers, and profess that of her persecutors. Her only reply was to ask for a few moments to be spent in prayer. She then submitted herself to the hands of the executioner with heroic firmness; her throat was instantly cut with a scimiter, and her body was thrown upon a pile of wood to be consumed!

It must be admitted that cases of devotion and heroism like this are rare and remarkable among any people, or in any age; nevertheless, when they do occur, they demonstrate that some of the noblest attributes of human nature still exist, to redeem the race from the abhorrence and degradation which their prevalent vices and deformities so justly incur.

CHAPTER XXVI.

THE HEBREW RACE IN THE UNITED STATES—EARLY SETTLEMENT OF JEWS AT NEWPORT—THEIR ADDRESS TO GENERAL WASHINGTON—HIS REPLY—PECULIARITIES OF AMERICAN JEWS—EMINENT LIVING ISRAELITES—JEWISH THEORY RESPECTING THE DEATH OF CHRIST—CONTRAST BETWEEN THE CONDITION OF THE JEWS IN THE UNITED STATES AND IN THE DOMINIONS OF THE POPE.

IN the preceding chapters we have traced the history and the vicissitudes of the Hebrew race from the fall of Jerusalem down to the present time, in the various countries in which they have resided, as far as any authentic materials existed to guide us in the narrative. In concluding the work we will glance briefly at their history in the United States, and at some of their present personal and religious peculiarities.

In no couutry of the world have the Jews ever enjoyed the same advantages and the same equality of rights as in this Confederacy. Even in France—where they are more protected and favored than in any other European community, in consequence of the results produced by the struggles of the Revolution and the frequent changes of the government—they do not now enjoy the same perfect and absolute political, social, and religious equality which they possess, and to which they are entitled, in this land. The consequence is, that nowhere else are they as influential, as much esteemed as an integral portion of the community and an important element in the body politic, as in the United States. The earliest details of their existence in this country are somewhat uncertain and obscure. It is probable that the first settlement of them on the new continent was made in New York, then termed New Amsterdam, about the year 1660. These first Hebrew immigrants were Portuguese and Spanish Jews, who were driven from their native country, in the first instance, by the cruelties of the Inquisition. Their first asylum was in the Batavian Republic. Thence they removed to New York, where, as they had been informed, they should be free from all kinds of impositions and exactions. Another settlement of Jews took place at an early period at Newport, in Rhode Island, where they were esteemed for their industry, wealth, and social standing. Their residence at this place dates prior to the American Revolution; and an interesting event connected with their history, which deserves to be mentioned, is the fact, that in 1790 they addressed a letter to General Washington, congratulating him upon his public services to his country, and expressing other very appropriate and patriotic sentiments. This address, dated August 17th, 1790, together with Washington's reply, were published at that time in the *Gazette of the United States;* but they have long since become forgotten and unknown. We accordingly insert them here. We are indebted for this rare and interesting document to Rev. Dr. Fischell, a learned Rabbi of New York, who has in preparation a history of the Jews in the United States; a work which will display superior ability and research, and supply a want which is felt by all who are interested, not only in Jewish history, but also in the general annals and antiquities of our country:

"*To the President of the United States of America*—Sir:—Permit the children of the stock of Abraham to approach you with the most cordial affection and esteem for your person and merit, and to join with our fellow-citizens in welcoming you to Newport.

"With pleasure we reflect on those days—those days of difficulty and danger—when the God of Israel, who delivered David from the peril of the sword, shielded your head in the day of battle; and we rejoice to think that the same Spirit who rested in the bosom of the greatly beloved Daniel, enabling him to preside over the provinces of the Babylonish empire, rests and ever will rest upon you, enabling you to discharge the arduous duties of CHIEF MAGISTRATE of these States.

"Deprived, as we heretofore have been, of the invaluable rights of free citizens, we now (with a deep sense of gratitude to the Almighty Disposer of all events)—behold a Government erected by the MAJESTY OF THE PEOPLE—a Government which to bigotry gives no sanction, to persecutors no assistance, but generally affording to ALL liberty of conscience and immunities of citizenship, deeming every one, of whatever nation, tongue, or language, equal parts of the great governmental machine. This liberal and extensive Federal

Union, whose base is philanthropy, mutual confidence and public virtue, we cannot but acknowledge to be the work of the great God who ruleth in the armies of Heaven and among the inhabitants of the earth, doing whatever seemeth to Him good.

"For all the blessings of civil and religious liberty, which we enjoy under an equal and benign administration, we desire to send up our thanks to the Ancient of Days, the Great Preserver of men, beseeching Him that the Angel who conducted our forefathers through the wilderness into the promised land, may graciously conduct you through all the difficulties and dangers of this mortal life; and when, like Joshua, full of days and full of honors, you are gathered to your fathers, may you be admitted into the Heavenly Paradise to partake of the waters of life and the tree of immortality.

"Done and signed by order of the Hebrew congregation in Newport, Rhode Island."

To this letter Washington replied as follows:

"*To the Hebrew Congregation in Newport, Rhode Island* —GENTLEMEN:—While I receive with much satisfaction your address, replete with expressions of affection and esteem, I rejoice in the opportunity of assuring you that I shall always retain a grateful remembrance of the cordial welcome I experienced in my visit to Newport from all classes of citizens. The reflection on the days of difficulty and danger which are past, is rendered the more sweet from a consciousness that they are succeeded by days of uncommon prosperity and security. If we have wisdom to make the best use of the advantages with which we are now favored, we cannot fail under the just administration of a good Government to become a great and happy people.

"The citizens of the United States of America have a right to applaud themselves for having given to mankind examples of an enlarged and liberal policy—a policy worthy of imitation. All possess alike liberty of conscience and immunities of citizenship—this now no more that toleration is spoken of, as if it was by the indulgence of one class of people that another enjoyed the exercise of their inherent rights. For happily the Government of the United States, which 'gives to bigotry no sanction, to persecutors no assistance,' requires only that they who live under its protection should demean themselves as good citizens in giving it, on all occasions, their effectual support.

"It would be inconsistent with the frankness of my character not to avow that I am pleased with your favorable opinions of my administration and fervent wishes for my felicity. May the children of the stock of Abraham, who dwell in this land, continue to merit and enjoy the good-will of the other inhabitants, while every one shall sit in safety under his own vine and fig tree, and there shall be none to make him afraid.

"May the Father of all mercies scatter light, and not darkness, in our paths, and make us all in our several vocations useful here, and in his own due time and way everlastingly happy."

There are at present nearly two hundred thousand

Jews in the United States, of whom not more than fifteen thousand are natives. Forty thousand reside in the city of New York, where certain particular localities are almost entirely appropriated by them as their residences. Ten thousand of them live in Philadelphia. The remainder are scattered throughout the length and breadth of the land. They do not belong to any one political organization, but occasionally they make public demonstrations of their peculiar sentiments by holding meetings and publishing memorials. Illustrations of this kind occurred on the occasions of the Damascus massacre in 1840, and the more recent Mortara case. All their associations are purely of a religious and charitable nature. In New York they possess twenty institutions of this description, among which are a hospital for the sick, and an asylum for orphans of both sexes. Several institutions of the same kind have been established in Philadelphia, where Jews have been known to exist for more than a century.

In the United States, the Jews chant the ritual in their synagogues in the Hebrew language, though discourses are delivered in English. All the festivals and fasts as originally instituted by Moses, are observed by the majority of them. Among these occasions the Feast of Passover commemorates their deliverance from Egypt; that of Pentecost, is the anniversary of the Revelation of the Law on Sinai; that of the New Year, the creation of the world; the fast of Atonement is observed as a day of humiliation. The meat which they eat is always that of animals which chew the cud and are cloven-footed, the killing of which is superintended by an officer appointed for that purpose, and who also takes care that the animal was not diseased. It cannot be denied that the Hebrew population of the United States are charitable toward their less favored brethren in the Old World, inasmuch as they send frequent contributions to those who are there persecuted and distressed. They remit large sums annually to Palestine, and more recently liberal contributions have been sent to support those Jews who fled from Morocco to Gibraltar at the commencement of the war between that country and Spain. In every community in which the American Jews are found, some of them occupy highly creditable positions, both socially and professionally; and the day of stupid prejudice and malignant bigotry against this ancient people has now passed away forever in this land and home of the free.

A remarkable feature in the history of the Jews in recent years, is the fact, that from among them have proceeded many of the most eminent artists and savans of the age. They are in all countries the most efficient and liberal patrons of the musical drama. The opera in New York may be said to be entirely under their management; and the same remark is true, to some extent, both in Paris and London. Among the distinguished artists who are Hebrews by birth, may be enumerated Meyerbeer, the great composer; Scribe, the French writer of tragedies, comedies and vaudevilles; the Rothschilds, bankers; Rachel, the *tragedienne;* Sir Moses Montefiore, the English philanthropist; Halevy, the musical composer. M. Strakosch is a Polish Jew,

Jullien a French, and the Seguins, English Jews. Among other eminent Hebrew artists are Madame Laborde, Mad'lle Calvè, and Thalberg the pianist. Nordheimer, the grammarian and philologist, was a Jew; Messrs. Benjamin and Yulee, United States Senators, and Lewis C. Levin and Henry M. Phillips, of the House of Representatives, belong to the same race.

Any community of people who can boast such an array of distinguished names cannot fail, eventually, to take a prominent place in the social and intellectual world, in proportion as prejudice and ignorance give way to the progress and diffusion of light. In regard to their religious sentiments, we have already noticed the fact that the writings of Mendelssohn have had the tendency to introduce a spirit of freedom and inquiry which is in opposition to the conservative tendency of the more rigorous and orthodox. But both parties, the radical and conservative, adhere to the great cardinal doctrine that the promised Messiah is yet to come, and will establish a temporal kingdom of superior power and splendor at Jerusalem. They generally entertain the belief that Christ was a wise man, and even a good man, except that his claims to being the Messiah were false. The theory of some of them in regard to his crucifixion is peculiar, and deserves to be mentioned. They hold that, according to the Jewish law and custom in Palestine, it was unlawful to execute a malefactor of any kind on the Sabbath day; or even to permit such an one to remain on the scaffold or instrument of death during any part of that holy time. The Jewish Sabbath begins at sunset on

Friday, continuing till sunset on Saturday; and as Christ's crucifixion was delayed by several causes till a late hour on Friday, he was taken down from the cross as the end of the day approached, before he had time to expire. In other words, they do not believe that Christ was really dead when removed to the sepulchre; but think that he was there resuscitated by his friends through the use of the expedients usually employed under such circumstances. Thus they account for his subsequent appearance to his disciples, alive and well, with the evident marks of the crucifixion still remaining upon his person; and they contend that no argument can be drawn from this fact in support of his claims as the true Messiah.

The greatest contrast to the felicity and freedom of the Jews in the United States, which exists in any country, is that presented by their present condition in the States of the Pope. We conclude by quoting the interesting statement of a cotemporary writer on this subject:

"It appears that at Rome the Israelitish community is compelled to pay annual contributions to the Convent of the Converts and the House of the Catechumens. When Paul IV. had suppressed Jewish congregations, only tolerating Israelites in the three cities of Avignon, Ancona and Rome, the community of the last city was compelled to pay the portion of the suppressed ones; and Clement VIII. imposed upon them still more taxes, fixed their annual contribution at eight hundred scudi, three hundred of which he assigned to the Convent of the Converts, which sum has still annually to be paid to it. The five hundred scudi given to the House of the Catechumens were afterward increased to one thousand one hundred, owing to the following circumstances:—A convert to Roman Catholicism, named Massarono of Mantua, wrote a book against the religion of his former brethren. Urban VIII. compelled the Jewish community to reward him with an annual pension for life of six hundred scudi, and when he died it was decreed that this sum should be paid in perpetuity to the House of the Catechumens, in addition to the five hundred paid before. Moreover, whenever an Israelite, from whatever country, goes to this house for the purpose of embracing Christianity, the Jewish community of Rome is charged with the expense of his maintenance during his state of preparation for baptism."

The beneficent diffusion of light and freedom throughout the nations of Christendom, which forms the fairest feature and greatest glory of the present age, opens to the Hebrew race a future of boundless hope. The extraordinary powers and capacities which they possess, and which have survived the crushing persecutions of so many dark and troubled centuries, will henceforth obtain an opportunity of full development, and will thus increase, as time advances, the marvels of their history, which already constitute one of the most wondrous pages in the book of time.

APPENDIX.

AN EXPOSITION OF THE HEBREW LAW AND COMMONWEALTH.*

THE Law is laid down in the Books of Exodus, Leviticus, and Numbers, and repeated with modifications in the book of Deuteronomy, but in neither case in any systematic order. (*Exod.*, xx.-xxiii., xxv.-xxxi., xxxiv.-xxxv.; *Levit.*, i.-viii., xi.-xxv., xxvii.; *Numb.*, v.-x., xviii., xix., xxvii.-xxx.; *Deut.*, iv., etc.)

The Mosaic laws must be viewed throughout as enacted for a people who stood in the peculiar situation of having been chosen by Jehovah out of the nations to preserve the knowledge and worship of the true God, and to exhibit in their history the providential dealings of God with his people.

The whole law rested on two fundamental principles, one of which was religious, and the other partly religious and partly political.

The first fundamental principle of the Mosaic law is the worship of Jehovah as the one true God; and consequently an uncompromising opposition to polytheism and idolatry, which were at that time the prevailing religious errors. Other nations, while acknowledging the supreme God as the creator, associated with him subordinate deities, to whose agency they looked for temporal blessings. All such worship was prohibited by the first words of the Law, 'I am Jehovah, thy God, which brought thee out of the land of Egypt, out of the house of bondage. Thou shalt have no other Gods *with* me.' (*Exod.*, xx. 2, 3; *Deut.*, iv. 35, 39.) The second commandment is an equally decisive prohibition of idolatry of every kind. *Exod.*, xx. 4, 6.) To render this fundamental law the more binding,

---

* From the English version of the "*Mosaisches Recht*" of J. D. Michaelis, D.D.

Jehovah, who was already the founder of the nation of Israel by delivering them from Egypt, was represented as their king, with the consent of the people themselves, and thus idolatry became high-treason. (*Exod.*, xix. 4-8; *Deut.*, vi. 22-24, xxxiii. 5; 1 *Sam.*, viii. 7; x. 18, 19; xii. 12; 1 *Chron.*, xxix. 23; *Isaiah*, xxxiii. 22.)

The land of Palestine too was represented as the property of God, held under him by the people, who consequently had not the power to alienate it forever. (*Levit.*, xxv. 23.) This fundamental principle was carried out in the form of government which is commonly called a *theocracy*, that is, a government under the direct superintendence of God. The laws were given by God, and could only be repealed by his command. (*Deut.*, iv. 2; xii. 32); the judges were selected usually from the caste of the priests, and are represented as holy persons, sitting in the place of God, to whose decision they submitted difficult cases by means of the Urim and Thummin. (*Deut.*, i. 17; xix. 17.) God often made known his will concerning state affairs through the prophets, of whom a constant succession was promised (*Deut.*, xviii. 15-22); and he promised to reward the people with prosperity if they kept the law, and threatened to punish them with calamity if they broke it. In these particulars the Israelites were distinguished from other nations as being under the more direct government of God; but nevertheless they had a well-defined civil constitution, as we shall presently see.

The second fundamental principle of the Mosaic law is the discouragement of intercourse between the Israelites and other nations. This principle was not carried so far as to prohibit the settlement of foreigners in Palestine, or of Israelites in foreign countries; but both practices were discouraged, and the latter much more than the former. Each man had his hereditary possession in land, which, as he could not sell it, he of course forfeited upon settling in a foreign country; and many of the practices enjoined upon the people were such as could hardly be observed in a strange land. To prevent their indulging in conquest, and thus running the risk of becoming subject to foreign powers, Moses confined them within certain boundaries, and also prohibited their choosing a foreigner as king. (*Deut.* xvii.)

This state of isolation was well suited to a nation who were sufficiently numerous to people the country assigned to them without the aid of foreigners, and who had neighbors, such as the Sidonians, who were able to conduct their commerce for them. But above all, this arrangement was necessary for the preservation of the worship of Jehovah among them, prone as their history proves them to have been to follow the idolatry of the surrounding nations.

The nature of the occupations followed by the citizens of any state affects the whole complexion of its institutions. Among the Israelites, trades do not appear to have been followed to any extent as the means of gaining a livelihood. Mechanical labor was probably left to the slaves who, in the houses of the wealthy, appear to have carried on extensive manufactures (1 *Chron.*, iv. 21), and to the women (*Prov.*, xxxi.); though in the building of the tabernacle we find some of the more noble mechanical arts practiced by freemen. Hence it followed that there were no cities dependent on trade or manufactures, and no separate classes of citizens, or burghers, and peasants. The cities of Palestine were only fortified villages, and most of them appear to have been small.

Neither was commerce the occupation of the Hebrew people. The necessary internal commerce was provided for by the three great feasts, to celebrate which all the men were assembled at Jerusalem thrice a year, and which, in this respect, answered the purpose of modern fairs. But foreign and maritime commerce was not at all encouraged by the Mosaic institutions, many of which tended directly to obstruct it, especially the making each man a landholder and cultivator, and the law against lending money on interest. Besides the example which Moses had before him in the case of Egypt, of a powerful and civilized nation, flourishing almost without foreign commerce, he was probably influenced by the following reasons in discouraging it. It would tend to introduce idolatry, to tempt many citizens to leave the country, to foster luxury, and to invite the Israelites in quarrels with other nations; while on the other hand they had all the advantages of commerce within their reach through the Sidonians and the Asiatic trading caravans. In later times Solomon pursued commerce to a great extent, though his seamen were not Israelites, but Phœnicians.

The practice of freebooting to obtain a livelihood, so common among the Arabs, and by no means unknown among their Hebrew brethren (*Judges*, ix., xi.), was discouraged by Moses, both by the allotment of land to every citizen, and by the little encouragement which he gave to hunting.

The real foundation of the Mosaic polity was in agriculture. The whole territory of the state was so divided that every Israelite (that is, every head of a family except those of the tribe of Levi) received a portion of land, which became the inalienable property of himself and his heirs. They had previously been a nomadic people, and a trace of that condition was long after preserved in the extent to which they pursued the breeding of cattle.

This freehold basis, as we may call it, prevented the formation of classes of burghers and nobility. There was no distinction of *caste*, except in the case of the Levites (the descendants of Levi), who were devoted to the offices of religion and learning; but even they could not be said to form a class of nobility, for they had no landed property, but were supported by the tithes of all the land.

In consequence of the equality of the citizens, the *constitution of the republic* had a democratic character. When Moses made known any laws, he called together the whole "congregation of Israel." When we consider that the number of adult males was then about 600,000, it becomes probable that those whom Moses addressed on such occasions were certain persons deputed to represent the rest. Such persons are mentioned in *Exod* xix. 7, 8, and *Numb.* i. 6; and in other passages there are enumerations of the classes of persons of whom these representatives consisted, namely, *elders*, *heads* or *captains of tribes*, *judges*, and *officers* or *scribes*. (*Deut.*, xxix. 10; *Josh.*, xxiii. 2; xxiv. 1.)

The lowest rank of officers in the republic were the *heads of tribes* and *heads of families*. These orders were a remnant of the patriarchal state, and are still kept up among the Bedouin Arabs.

Each of the twelve tribes had its chief. (*Numb.* ii.) The tribes were subdivided into greater and lesser families, called *families* and *houses of fathers*, which had their respective heads. (*Numb.* i. 2; *Josh.* vii. 14.) These heads of families are in all probability the persons called *elders* in *Deut.* xix. 12; xxi. 1-19; and *Josh.* xxiii., xxiv. It is uncertain whether the elders were chosen with reference to their age, as the word would seem to denote if it were not constantly used in other languages as a title of office or of honor, without reference to age, as in the Roman *senator*, the Greek *presbuteros*, and the Arabic *sheik*. It is equally uncertain in what way the heads or princes of tribes were chosen. The princes of tribes are found as late as the reign of David.

Thus the twelve tribes formed twelve distinct commonwealths, governed by the princes of tribes, and under them by the heads of families; and they sometimes acted as separate states, carrying on war independently of each other, even as late as the time of the kings. (*Josh.* xvii. 11-15; *Judges* iv. 10; xviii.-xx.; 1 *Chron.* iv. 41-43; v. 18-23.) The descendants of Levi were not reckoned among the twelve tribes, but were scattered over the territory of their brethren; and the number of the tribes was made up by the division of the descendants of Joseph into two tribes, which were named after his sons Ephraim and Manasseh. (*Numb.* i.) A certain number of persons appears to have been necessary to constitute tribes and families. (1 *Chron.* xxiii. 11.)

These twelve tribes were united in one republic, which generally, though not always, had a chief magistrate, whether a lawgiver as Moses, or a general as Joshua, or a judge as those whose history is recorded in the book of *Judges*, or a king as Saul and his successors. With regard to the judges however, it is highly probable that some of them ruled not over all Israel, but only over single tribes. The twelve tribes met in general diets (*Josh.* xxiii., xxiv.), and united in war against a common enemy. We have striking instances of the independence of the separate tribes in the fact that David reigned sevaral years over the tribe of Judah alone; in the revolt of ten of the tribes from Rehoboam; and in the standing rivalry between the tribes of Judah and Joseph, which led to that revolt.

The next rank of officers, the *judges*, did not represent their tribes. Before their appointment Moses was sole judge, and it was to relieve him from his burden of that office that a class of judges was instituted. (*Exod.* xviii.) There was a judge over every ten persons, another over every hundred, and another over every thousand. From each of these orders there was an appeal to the one above, and from the last to Moses himself. Moses further ordained that when the people were settled in Palestine, judges should be appointed in every city. The choice of them appears to have been left to the people, as Moses lays down no rules for their election. In subsequent ages it generally happened that they were Levites.

In *Numb.* xi. 16, we have an account of the appointment of seventy men out of the elders of the people to assist Moses. These are commonly supposed to have been judges; and the foundation of the Sanhedrim, so well known in the later Jewish history, is traced to their appointment. Michaelis takes a very different, and, we think, more correct view of their office. He considers that they were a senate chosen to take part with Moses in the government, and that the institution was but temporary. We do not find them mentioned in the subsequent history of the people, and the real Sanhedrim was not founded till after the Babylonish captivity.

The *scribes* were an order of officers quite distinct from the judges. This office was instituted during the Egyptian captivity. (*Exod.* v.) They were to be appointed in every city. (*Deut.* xvi. 18.) In the time of the kings they were generally taken, like the judges, from the tribe of Levi. Their name is derived from a root, which still exists in Arabic (*satar*), meaning *to write*. From this and other circumstances it is concluded that they were the officers who kept the genealogical registers and apportioned the public burdens to every individual. They also conveyed to the people the general's orders in time of war. (*Josh.* i. 10.)

Such was the Israelitish state, consisting of the congregation of the people, governed by the heads of families, the princes of tribes, the judges, and the scribes. To this Democratic constitution the tribe of Levi formed a counterpoise. They had no landed property, but received the tithes of all the other tribes. Besides these they received the first fruits of all produce, probably about a sixtieth part of the whole crop; they had a part of every sacrifice; and while the people were in the wilderness every beast killed for food was offered as a sacrifice, and afterward the priest received a portion of every slaughtered beast that was not brought to the altar; they had everything that was devoted to God, and the redemption fees of the first-born of men and unclean cattle, a share of the spoils taken in war, and some minor articles. A calculation of these items would show that their revenues were enormous, and far more than is needed for the support of a body of religious instructors. But this was not the office of the Levites; and the circumstance of their living in cities of their own made the discharge of such an office impossible. They were indeed, in a different sense, the ministers of religion; for they performed all religious ceremonies, preserved copies of the law, explained it in doubtful cases, and were bound to read it over to the people once every seven years; but a body of religious teachers or *doctors* did not exist till after the Babylonish captivity. The Levites were the *literary class* of the nation, and filled all the learned professions. Difficult questions of law were to be referred to them for judgment. (*Deut.* xvii. 8-13; xxi. 5.) In the wilderness they formed a guard to the tabernacle and to Moses. The occasion of their obtaining the priest's office is related in *Exod.* xxii. 25-29.

The head of the Levitical order was the high-priest, who was always taken from the family of Aaron. He possessed great influence in the state. He was the supreme legal authority. In *Deut.* xvii. 12, he is placed on a level with the judge or chief magistrate; and when there was no king or judge, the high priest was the chief magistrate, as in the case of Eli.

Moses did not determine what should be the nature of the *supreme magistracy*. Before his own death he appointed a successor in the person of Joshua, who was a *military leader*, and whose office it was to put the people in possession of Palestine.

Joshua was succeeded by the *judges** at intervals of time. The office is mentioned by Moses (*Deut.*, xvii. 12), but he gives no command for the appointment of the judge. The judges seem to have been somewhat analogous to the Carthaginian suffetes. They were not the ordinary and permanent magistrates, but they governed Israel in times of trouble. There was no regular succession of them, and it is by no means clear that all of them governed the whole nation.

The judges were succeeded by *kings*, of whom there was a regular succession from Saul to the Babylonish captivity.

Though Moses evidently desired that the state should remain a free republic under the supreme government of Jehovah, and though when the people actually asked for a king, God, by Samuel, represented their desire as both foolish and sinful (1 *Sam.*, viii.); yet as Moses foresaw that they would wish for a king, in imitation of the surrounding nations, he gave the people power to choose one, and prescribed his duties. (*Deut.*, xvii. 14–20.) This is one of the many instances in which Moses shows one of the highest qualities of a good legislator, in making the best provisions which the circumstances allowed, instead of attempting to carry out his views of what was best where the character of the people made those views impracticable. The following are the chief laws respecting the king. The election of the king was left to the people (*Deut.*, xvii. 14), with the restriction that he must be an Israelite by birth, not a foreigner (ver. 15); the appointment must be one which had the sanction of God (ver. 15), whose will on this subject was made known through a prophet, as we find from history. (1 *Sam.*, ix. x.) He was not to keep a strong body of cavalry, nor a great number of horses (ver. 16). This law was well suited to the physical condition of Palestine, a mountainous country, which could be defended without cavalry, and where the keeping up of such a force could only arise from a spirit of conquest. This, like some others of the Mosaic laws, was disregarded by Solomon, who had an enormous number of horses. The king was forbidden to lead the people back to Egypt (ver. 16), which probably

---

* This supreme magistracy must not be confounded with the ordinary judges mentioned previously.—*Smucker.*

means that he was not to attempt to reconquer the land of Goshen. (Michaelis, vol. i., pp. 64–67.) He was not to take many wives, 'that his heart turn not away' (ver. 17), as happened to Solomon, whose wife seduced him to idolatry. Another reason of this law was probably to discourage polygamy by the example of the king. This law was constantly broken by the kings of Israel. He was not to collect excessive quantities of gold and silver (ver. 17). He was to be well acquainted with the law, of which he was to have a copy written out at his accession, which he was to read daily (ver. 18, 19). On his obedience to these commandments depended the continuance of his kingdom (ver. 20). Besides this fundamental law, there was an agreement or covenant between the king and the people, which was sworn to by every king at his accession. (1 *Sam.*, x. 25; Michaelis, *Art.* 55.) The kingly power was therefore not unlimited; but we find that the government of the kings had always a tendency to despotism, which may be ascribed to the want of an hereditary military noblesse, and to the notion which prevailed among the Israelites, in common with other Oriental people, that it was the office of the king in person to be supreme judge. As to the latter point, it certainly was not the intention of Moses that the burden of deciding causes should rest upon the kings, and very mischievous consequences resulted from their assuming the office.

The king had the power of enacting new laws, provided they were not at variance with the fundamental principles of the constitution, and of dispensing with the punishment prescribed by Moses. He had the power of life and death over the priest, even the high-priest; and it was part of his duty to reform abuses in religion. These powers, which are not mentioned in the Mosaic code, are inferred from the constant exercise of them by the kings. Such matters probably formed part of the covenant between the king and people mentioned above. It is uncertain whether he had the right to declare war at his own pleasure.

On the subject of the royal revenues Moses left no ordinance. They consisted of presents (1 *Sam.*, x. 27; xvi. 20), of tithes from all the land (1 *Sam.*, viii. 15), and of a demesne which was probably acquired by confiscations. The kings had a right to demand bond-services of the people (1 *Sam.*, viii. 12–16 ; 1 *Kings*, v. 13–18), which at first however were chiefly performed by the Canaanites who remained in the land. In later times a poll-tax was exacted on pressing occasions. They took advanvantage of the neighboring Arabian deserts to rear cattle. (1 *Chron.*, xxvii. 29–31.) Solomon derived a considerable revenue from foreign commerce.

The monarchy was hereditary, for the election by the people mentioned above referred not to every individual, but to the family from which the king was to be taken. The crown did not necessarily descend to the eldest son ; thus David appointed which of his sons should succeed him, and the people evidently expected him to do so. (1 *Kings*, i. 20.) But this right of selection was afterward abrogated.

The *foreign relations* of the Israelites were of a simple character. Although, as stated above, it was a fundamental principle of the Mosaic law to avoid foreign intercourse, yet alliances with foreign nations were not forbidden. The alliances which were afterward made, in the time of the kings, with Assyria and Egypt were sufficiently imprudent in their own nature to account for their being opposed by the prophets. There were, however, some nations whom the Israelites were commanded to exterminate—those Canaanites, namely, who dwelt in the land which they were to possess ; this command was never perfectly obeyed, and in later times it was mitigated. Other nations, as the Amalekites, Ammonites, and Moabites, were represented by Moses as the hereditary enemies of the people of Israel, on account of injuries which they had done them, and which it was their duty to revenge when an opportunity occurred. The laws regulating war against other nations (*Deut.*, xx.) were exceedingly severe, but not more so than the international law then recognized is sufficient to account for, and the cruelties exercised by their heathen enemies are known to have been greater than any that the Israelites can be charged with. If a city resisted after being summoned to surrender, all the men in it were to be put to death, and the women and children made slaves. This law however only applied to the cities 'which were very far off;' but as to the cities of the Hittites, Amorites, and others, which were given as an inheritance to them by God, they were commanded to save alive nothing that breathed. The spoil was to be divided among the soldiers, except in some cases, when it was devoted to God and destroyed. Horses were to be hamstrung. The fruit-trees in the enemy's country were to be spared.

During the three great festivals, when every male went up to Jerusalem, there was a suspension of arms, the assurance being given by God that during these periods no man should desire their land. (*Exod.*, xxxiv. 24.) Michaelis endeavors to show that this truce was observed by all the surrounding nations except the Canaanites, who were therefore destroyed.

Embassies were only resorted to on particular occasions, and the persons of ambassadors were sacred. When the Israelites wanted to pass through the territories of other people, Moses asked permission of the inhabitants.

The foundation of the *civil law* of Moses is laid in the command, 'Thou shalt love thy neighbor as thyself.' (*Levit.*, xix. 18.)

1. *Laws relating to Property.*—Moses ordained that after the conquest of Canaan the land should be divided by lot in equal portions among the Israelites, and should then be inalienable forever. This law was invested with a religious sanction, by representing God as the proprietor of the whole land, which the people only held as tenants under him. (*Levit.*, xxv. 23.) The land might be sold *nominally*, but as it reverted to the original owner ro his heirs, in the year of *jubilee*, which was every fiftieth year, such a sale amounted only to the sale of the crops for fifty or fewer years. Land so sold might be redeemed on certain conditions before the year of jubilee. (*Levit.*, xxv. 25, &c.) The law against the alienation of land admitted of exceptions, the chief of which was that land vowed to God, if not redeemed before the jubilee, became the property of the priests. (*Levit.*, xxvii. 16.) Moses however plainly intended that land sold or vowed should always be redeemed before the jubilee.

A provision was made for avoiding litigation respecting the crops upon the ground at the jubilee, by the institution of the *sabbatical year*, during which there was to be neither sowing nor reaping, but all the land was to lie fallow. Every seventh year, and likewise the year of jubilee, was a sabbatical year. A promise was annexed to the law, that the crop of the sixth year (or perhaps we should read of the *six years*) should be sufficient to afford food while the land lay fallow. (*Levit.*, xxv. 20–22.) Michaelis is of opinion that the tendency of this law was to increase the national wealth by affording a strong inducement to store up corn during the six years of plenty, part of which might be sold at an increased price to the neighboring commercial nations in the seventh year, but this seems a very unsatisfactory explanation of the matter. He also mentions other incidental advantages, as he considers them, of this institution. (Mich., *Arts.* 74, 75.)

The laws of the jubilee and sabbatical years do not appear to have been long observed; indeed it is plain from *Levit.*, xxvi. 34, that Moses expected them to be disregarded. From 2 *Chron.*, xxxvi. 21, it appears that up to the Babylonish captivity there had been seventy sabbatical years neglected. This would carry us back nearly five hundred years, namely to the reign of Saul or David, as the time at which the observance ceased.

A man's property descended to his sons, of whom the eldest had a double share. (*Deut.*, xxi. 17.) The exclusion of daughters from the inheritance was established long before the time of Moses. (*Gen.*, xxxi. 14.) No provision is made in the law for the support of unmarried daughters. On the occurrence of a case in which a man died leaving only daughters, Moses made the law that in all such cases the daughters should inherit their father's property, but that they should not marry out of their own tribe. The husbands of such heiresses were reckoned as the sons of their father-in-law, and took his name. Failing daughters, the inheritance passed to a man's brethren; failing them, to his father's brethren; and failing them, *to the next of kin* of the deceased. (*Numb.*, xxvii. 1–11.) But the law gives no directions as to determining *who* are the next of kin; probably this was already determined by custom. The Mosaic law contains nothing on the subject of wills; but we find that the right of bequeathing property other than land existed both before and after his time, and he nowhere prohibits it.

2. *Laws relating to Persons.*—The laws of Moses inculcate the most complete filial obedience. (*Exod.*, xx. 12; compare *Ephes.*, vi. 1-3.) The power of fathers over their sons was great, and does not appear to have ceased as they grew up. We have here a remnant of the patriarchal state. Flagrant acts of disobedience were punished with death (*Exod.*, xxi. 17; *Levit.*, xx. 9), which however could only be inflicted by a judicial process, and not at the pleasure of the father. (*Deut.*, xxi. 18-21.) Fathers, and even mothers, chose wives for their sons. Next to the father, the first-born had the greatest power over the family, though it does not clearly appear in what this consisted, nor whether it was exercised in his father's lifetime. Though whatever opened the womb was *a* first-born (*Exod.*, xiii. 12), yet it is clear from *Deut.* xxi. 15, and 1 *Chron.*, v. 1, 2, that *the* first-born of a family was the first-born to a man of all his children, and not the first-born by each of his wives.

Marriage Laws.—Among the Hebrews, as among other Oriental nations, wives were generally bought (*Gen.*, xxix. 15-30; xxxiv. 12; *Hosea*, iii. 1-2), and in certain cases their price was fixed by law. (*Exod.*, xxii. 16, 17; *Deut.*, xxii. 28, 29.) Some wives were not bought, and these enjoyed greater freedom than the others. In certain cases concubines were allowed. (*Exod.*, xxi. 7-11; Michaelis, *Arts.* 87, 88.)

The marriage law of Moses had in general a tendency to promote marriage, and this chiefly by his sanctioning the notion, which he found already prevailing among the people, that it was highly honorable for a man to have posterity who might perpetuate his name, and by his engrafting upon this notion the law of *levirate marriages,* by which it was enacted that when a man died leaving a widow, his brother should marry her, and raise up children to his brother; that is, children who were to be accounted as belonging to the first husband, and who were enrolled in the genealogical registers in his name.

The Mosaic law prescribes no marriage ceremonies. We may conjecture from history (*Gen.*, xxix. 22-28) that ceremonies much resembling those of the Arabians in the present day

(Lane's *Modern Egyptians*, vol. i., c. 6) were already in use, which Moses had left as he found them. He connected no religious ceremony with the solemnization of matrimony. The bridegroom might put away his wife if the *signa virginitatis* were wanting. (*Deut.*, xxii., 13–21.) A right understanding of this law is very important to the explanation of the doctrine of Christ concerning divorce (*Matt.*, v. 31–32), which has had no small influence on the marriage laws of Christian countries. (Michaelis, *Arts.* 92, 93.)

Moses permitted polygamy, as is proved by the laws in *Exod.*, xxi., 9, 10, *Levit.*, xviii. 18, *Deut.*, xxi. 15-17, by the constant practice of it both before and after his time, connected with the fact that he nowhere prohibits it, and by the small number of the first-born compared with the whole number of males, namely, about 1 in 42. (*Numb.*, iii. 43.) But he permitted it only as a matter of policy, "on account," as Christ said, "of the hardness of the people's hearts," that is, the difficulty of rooting out inveterate customs, and perhaps for other reasons, which are pointed out by Michaelis. (*Art.* 96.) Some of his laws have a strong indirect tendency to prevent it, for example, the buying of a wife; and notwithstanding some striking examples of its practice, as that of Solomon, it does not appear to have prevailed extensively among the Israelites. (Mich., *Art.* 95.) After the Babylonish captivity it ceased entirely. Moses however set limits to the practice of polygamy, not allowing *many* wives. (*Deut.*, xvii. 17.) Moses prohibited marriages between certain near relations, some of which, those namely between parents and children, brothers and sisters, he considered as opposed to natural morality, for he calls them *abominations*, and represents them as sinful in themselves. Other marriages between relations were probably forbidden only for reasons connected with the character and habits of the people. (*Levit.*, xviii. 20; Michaelis, book iii. c. 7.)

Of *divorces* Moses was no favorer, at least if we may judge by the way in which he speaks of the marriage bond in *Gen.*, ii. 24; but he allowed it to a greater extent than he altogether approved, 'because of the hardness of their hearts.' (*Matt.*, xix. 8.) The law of divorce is in *Deut.*, xxiv. 1-4. If a man disliked his wife, he might put her away by giving her a writing of divorcement. She might then marry again; but if her second husband put her away or died, she might not return to her first husband. (Mich. *Arts.* 119, 120.) No provision is made for the support of the divorced wife. In certain cases the husband forfeited his right of divorce. (*Deut.*, xxii. 19, 29.) The support of a widow after her husband's death was provided for, if she had no children, by the law of levirate marriages; if she had children, it was left to filial piety.

Laws respecting Slaves and Servants.—Moses found slavery already existing among the Israelites and their neighbors. He permitted it to continue, under certain restrictions, and his laws on this subject are conceived in the most merciful spirit. (See especially *Deut.*, xxiii. 15, 16.) Slaves were acquired by capture in war, by purchase, and by the marriage of slaves. Of purchase there were four kinds: 1, when a slave was transferred from one master to another; 2, when a man under the pressure of poverty sold himself for a slave; 3, when parents sold their children; 4, when an insolvent debtor, or a thief unable to make restitution, was sold as a punishment. The value of slaves was of course variable, but in two cases it was fixed by law. (*Exod.*, xxi. 32; *Levit.*, xxvii. 1-8.) Besides the slaves of private individuals, there were others who belonged to the public; these were employed in menial labors for the service of the sanctuary. Slaves might have property of their own. A master might beat his slave, but not so as to kill him (*Exod.*, xxi. 20, 21); if he even maimed him, the slave was to be set free. (*Exod.*, xxi. 26, 27.) A Hebrew slave possessed this advantage over a foreign one: he was entitled to his freedom in the sabbatical year and in the year of jubilee, and he might be redeemed before the year of jubilee, while the stranger might be held in slavery forever. The manumitted slave received presents from his master. (*Exod.*, xxi. 2-11; *Levit.*, xxv. 39-55; *Deut.* xv. 12-18.) Slaves had to conform to some of the principal religious ceremonies observed by the Israelites.

Besides the slaves, there were day laborers, who were to share in the rest of the Seventh-day, and in the spontaneous produce of the sabbatical year, and whose hire was to be paid every day before sunset (*Levit.*, xix. 13; xxv. 6; *Deut.*, xxiv. 14, 15.) The statute in *Deut.*, xxv. 4, besides its literal meaning, probably meant also that servants were to share in the food prepared for their masters.

The Goel, or Blood-Avenger.—There was a custom of ancient standing among the Israelites, and which exists to this day among the Arabs, which made it the duty of the nearest relation of a murdered person to pursue the murderer and kill him with his own hands. This relation is called in Hebrew *Goel*, in Arabic *Tair*. This usage, which was probably of high antiquity, is dangerous to any state, from the haste and passion in which vengeance is exercised, and from the hereditary feuds which it causes between families. Moses dealt with this as he dealt with other long-established customs of which he disapproved, not making the vain attempt to root it out, but surrounding it with provisions calculated to mitigate its evils. Six cities of the Levites were appointed as cities of refuge for the manslayer, and every facility of access to them was provided. If he escaped to one of these, he was safe from the avenger of blood. (*Exod.*, xxi. 12, 13; *Numb.*, xxxv.; *Deut.*, xix. 3.) But these cities afforded no asylum to the willful murderer, who, when proved to be guilty might be torn even from the altar. (*Exod.*, xxi. 14; *Deut.*, xix. 11-13.) At the death of the high-priest, the person who had taken sanctuary might leave the city of refuge in safety. These laws seem to have acted as an effectual check on the practice of blood-avenging, for an instance of it rarely occurs in the later history of the Israelites.

The Mosaic law commanded kindness to be shown to strangers, who, unless they belonged to certain nations that had been guilty of flagrant outrages against the Israelites, might 'enter the congregation of Jehovah,' that is, might be naturalized in Israel. Moses inculcates veneration for old age, and kindness to the deaf and blind. (*Levit.*, xix. 14, 32; *Deut.*, xxvii. 18.) He made laws in favor of the poor (*Deut.*, xv. 11), besides adopting usages already in existence for their benefit; though many of his laws discourage begging. He recommended the people to lend to them (*Deut.*, xv. 6-14), he gave them the right of gleaning, and of collecting the spontaneous produce of the earth during the sabbatical year (*Levit.*, xix. 9, 10; xxv. 5, 6; *Deut.*, xxiv.19–21; *Ruth*, ii. 2–19), and the remains of the second tithes and firstlings, which were sacrificed as thank-offerings, were given as entertainments to the poor. (*Deut.*, xii. 5–12, 17–19; xiv. 22–29; xvi. 10, 11; xxvi. 12, 13.)

The *Origin* of the Mosaic legislation is declared in Scripture to be from God, by which we must understand that these laws were sanctioned by God and published by his command. It has already been observed that many of the laws did not originate with Moses, but were ancient observances, which he adopted in his code by the command of God. (See also Iken, *Diss. II. de Institutis et Ceremoniis Legis Mosaicæ ante Mosem;* Reimar, *Cogitationes de Legibus Mosaicis ante Mosem.*) And moreover, when we remember that he was brought up in Egypt, and was "learned in all the wisdom of the Egyptians," (*Acts*, vii. 22), when we compare various parts of his laws with similar institutions which existed in Egypt (for example, the freehold basis of the constitution, the separation of the caste of priests from the rest of the community, the discouragement of commerce, and the measures resorted to for keeping the Israelites distinct from other nations), it becomes highly probable, if not certain, that the Mosaic institutions were largely modeled on those of Egypt. This opinion, which is held by nearly all the best critics who have examined the laws of Moses, has been unaccountably regarded as opposed to the divine character of these laws, as if divine inspiration must necessarily deprive a legislator of the wisdom which he already possesses, and prevent him from adopting, under the sanction of that inspiration, whatever good he may find in the institutions of other nations. On the other hand, there are many points of opposition between the Mosaic and Egyptian laws which it is impossible to overlook. Several of these are adduced by Michaelis, in a paper in the "Comment. Soc. Gotting.;" vol. iv., "De legibus quibusdam a Mose eo fine latis, ut Israelitis Ægypti cupidis Palæstinam caram faceret." The *spirit* of the whole law was, as Moses himself asserts (*Levit.* xviii. 3), diametrically opposed to that of the Egyptian as well as the Canaanitish institutions. For these reasons it is impossible to regard the Hebrew legislation as a mere copy of the Egyptian.

Under the kings, exemption from military service was allowed to the man who had built a house and not yet occupied it, to him who had planted a vineyard or oliveyard and not yet enjoyed its fruit, to him who had betrothed a wife, and to him who had married within a year. (*Deut.*, xx. 5-7.) Cowardice was also a ground of exemption, but attended with disgrace. The spoil taken in war was divided into two parts; that in persons and cattle was collected and distributed among the people, those who went to war and those who remained at home having equal portions, and that in effects was the property of the soldier who seized it. Many regulations are made to promote cleanliness and discipline in the camp, which with this object were declared to be sacred.

Ecclesiastical Police, or the *Ceremonial Law*.—In this part of the Mosaic law, many ceremonies are ordained which appear frivolous and unmeaning, unless we keep in view the fact asserted both in the Psalms and in the New Testament, and fully explained in the Epistle to the Hebrews, that most of the Levitical rites were only types of the blessings to be enjoyed under the Christian dispensation. We do not enlarge on this subject, as we are not here regarding the Mosaic laws in their theological aspect.

Circumcision, which had long before been given by God to Abraham, was adopted in the Mosaic law as the ceremony by which every male was admitted to the civil and religious privileges of the people of Israel. (*Gen.*, xvii. 9-14; *Levit.*, xii. 13.) Every bond-servant among the Israelites were obliged to submit to this rite, and also every stranger who wished to be naturalized among the people and to partake of the Passover.*

---

* *Vide* Salvador, *Histoire des Institutiones de Moise et du Peuple Hebreu;* Pastoret, *Histoire de la Legislation*, tom. iii.; Jahn's *Biblische Archaologie*, th. ii.; Lowman's *Dissertation on the Civil Government of the Hebrews;* Spencer, *De Legibus Hebræorum;* Witsii *Ægyptiaca;* Warburton's *Divine Legation of Moses;* Hale's *Analysis of Chronology*, vol. ii.; Winer's *Biblisches Realworterbuch*, arts. 'Moses,' 'Gesetz,' the Commentaries on the Pentateuch of Vater, Rosenmuller, &c.; Graves *on Pentateuch;* Faber's *Horæ Mosaicæ;* Lane's *Modern Egyptians*, and other works on the Arabians, furnish excellent illustrations of some of the Mosaic Institutions.

BOOKS PUBLISHED

BY

DUANE RULISON,

QUAKER CITY PUBLISHING HOUSE,

33 South Third Street,

PHILADELPHIA.

THE LIFE, SPEECHES, AND MEMORIALS OF DANIEL WEBSTER.—Containing his most Celebrated Orations, a Selection from the Eulogies delivered on the occasion of his Death, and his Life and Times. By Samuel M. Smucker, LL.D. In one large volume of 550 pages, printed on fine paper and bound in beautiful style. Containing excellent Tint Illustrations of his Birthplace and Mansion at Marshfield, and a full-length, lifelike Steel Portrait. The Publisher offers it with confidence to the American Public, and is convinced that it will supply an important want in American Literature. No work was to be obtained heretofore which presented, within a compact and convenient compass, the chief events of the Life of Daniel Webster, his most remarkable intellectual efforts, and the most valuable and interesting eulogies which the great men of the nation uttered in honor of his memory. We present all these treasures in this volume, at a very moderate price.

Cloth, ...$1.75
Handsomely embossed leather...2.00
Same style, gilt edges...2.50
   Do.   full gilt, extra...2.75

MONUMENT TO THE MEMORY OF HENRY CLAY. By A. H. Carrier. In one large volume, over 500 pages, illustrated with appropriate engravings. Bound in handsomely embossed leather, gilt side, and full gilt back...$2.00
Same style..2.50
   Do.   full gilt, (extra)..2.75

THE LAND WE LIVE IN; or, Travels, Sketches, and Adventures in North and South America. With descriptions of their Towns, Cities, States and Territories; their Inhabitants, Manners, Customs, Amusements, Public Works, Institutions, Edifices, etc., together with a great variety of the most Exciting Adventures and Highly Interesting Historical Events of American History. By C. A. Goodrich. One large vol., bound embossed morocco, 879 octavo pages, 130 illustrations..$3.50

A HISTORY OF ALL RELIGIONS: Containing a statement of the Origin, Development, Doctrines and Government of the Religious Denominations in the United States and Europe. With Biographical notices of Eminent Divines. Edited and completed by Samuel M. Smucker, LL.D., 336 pages, 12mo., illustrated. Bound in fine muslin...$1.00
Full gilt sides and edges...1.50

THE BRIDE OF LOVE: or, True Greatness of Female Heroism. By Ruth Vernon. "Thousands of men breathe, move, and live, pass off the stage of life, and are heard of no more. Live for something—do good, and leave behind you a monument of virtue."—*Chalmers*. 320 pages, with beautiful steel plate...$1.00

BOOKS PUBLISHED BY DUANE RULISON.

HISTORICAL AND REVOLUTIONARY INCIDENTS OF the Early Settlers of the United States, with the Life and Adventures of Allen, Kenton, Boone, and other celebrated Pioneers. By C. W. Weber, author of "Hunter Naturalist," "Shot in the Eye," "Old Hicks, the Guide," "Gold Mines of the Gila," etc., etc. 450 pages, tint illustrations......................$1.25

THE MODEL BOOK OF DREAMS, FORTUNE TELLER, and Epitome of Parlor Entertainments. Comprising Interpretation of Dreams, Fortune-telling, Charades, Tableaux Vivants, Parlor Games, Parlor Magic, Scientific Amusements, etc., etc., etc. By Henry Temple and Cordelia M. Ottley. 12mo., bound in fine muslin, 352 pages. Illustrated with nearly one hundred engravings..................$1.00

THE LIFE AND ADVENTURES OF THE CELEBRATED Oriental Traveler, HAJJI BABA, in Persia, Turkey, and Russia. Comprising his Caravan Travels, Encounters with Robbers, his curious performances as *Soldier, Water Carrier, Pipe Seller, Dervish, Courtier, Doctor, Executioner, Lover,* and *Marriage Broker,* and his final elevation to the rank of *Shah's Deputy,* and Secretary to the *Persian Ambassador* to *England,* with numerous *Episodes* and *Incidents,* illustrating Life in *Persia.* Edited by Jas. Morier. 400 pages..................$1.00

HOWARD'S DOMESTIC MEDICINE: Containing an important Family Cyclopedia of Medical Knowledge, pointing out in the most plain and familiar language, the cause and symptoms of the various diseases that human flesh is liable to. Also, the most improved remedies for the Diseases of Men, Women, and Children. Also, an extensive and valuable Treatise on Anatomy, Physiology, and the Laws of Health. The work is illustrated in the most extensive and appropriate manner. The illustrations represent the Anatomy of the Human System, in all its various forms; also, a great variety of Plants, Herbs and Trees, growing on the American Continent, with a minute description of their medicinal properties and uses. Also, rules and suggestions for gathering, preserving and preparing them for use. This important book contains about 1000 octavo pages, with 114 costly illustrations. Bound in beautiful embossed leather, full gilt, with spring back and marbled edges and is supplied to subscribers at the very low price of..................$4.00

ADVENTURES, WANDERINGS, AND SUFFERINGS OF THE MERTON FAMILY; or, Life Scenes among the South American Indians. By Miss Anne Bowen. This is one of the most interesting books of the kind ever written. It contains the adventures of a family who had the misfortune to be cast on the coast of South America, who, after many thrilling, perilous, and amusing incidents, while traveling inland and crossing the Andes, finally settled in a wild and desolate region. It is also very instructive, containing many curious facts from Natural History, Botany, etc. 384 pages, 12mo., 8 fine illustrations on tinted paper..................$1.00

THE MYSTERIES OF THE GREAT DEEP; or, the Physical, Animal, Geological, and Vegetable Wonders of the Ocean. By P. H. Gosse, author of "An Introduction to Geology," "The Canadian Naturalist," etc. This book is full of instructive and entertaining information. One might go to sea for years and not learn as much about the Ocean as he can gather from a few hours perusal of this volume. One volume, 12mo., 378 pages, with 52 illustrations..................$1.00

A HISTORY OF THE MODERN JEWS; or, Annals of the Hebrew Race, from the Destruction of Jerusalem till the Present Time. By Samuel M. Smucker, LL.D. Containing the most memorable and noteworthy events which have occurred in the history of this extraordinary nation during the last 1800 years. To both the Jew and Christian this book will afford a vast amount of valuable information, which cannot be conveniently procured from any other source. It contains the most interesting details respecting the Jewish race, with biographical notices of their most eminent Rabbis, descriptions of their usages and customs, and a learned exposition of their doctrines and belief. 352 pages, printed on fine paper, and bound in rich muslin..................$1.00
Full gilt sides and edges..................1.50

www.ingramcontent.com/pod-product-compliance
Lightning Source LLC
Chambersburg PA
CBHW031847220426
43663CB00006B/522